THE STATE OF FOOD AND AGRICULTURE 1996

FAO Agriculture Series   No. 29

ISSN 0081-4539

THE STATE
OF FOOD
AND
AGRICULTURE
1996

FOOD AND AGRICULTURE ORGANIZATION OF THE UNITED NATIONS

Rome, 1996

The statistical material in this publication has been prepared from the information available to FAO up to July 1996.

The designations employed and the presentation do not imply the expression of any opinion whatsoever on the part of the Food and Agriculture Organization of the United Nations concerning the legal status of any country, territory, city or area, or of its authorities, or concerning the delimitation of its frontiers or boundaries. In some tables, the designations "developed" and "developing" economies are intended for statistical convenience and do not necessarily express a judgement about the stage reached by a particular country or area in the development process.

PER
HD
1401
.S73

David Lubin Memorial Library
Cataloguing in Publication Data

FAO, Rome (Italy)
The state of food and agriculture 1996.
ISBN 92-5-103858-9

(FAO Agriculture Series, no. 29)
ISSN 0081-4539

1. Agriculture.   2. Food production.
3. Food security.   4. Macroeconomic analysis.

I. Title   II. Series

FAO code: 70   AGRIS: E16 E10

Printed in Italy

Foreword

1996 will hopefully be remembered as the year when the achievement of world food security was universally recognized as the most pressing challenge facing humankind. I am confident that the World Food Summit, which will gather this year in Rome representatives of the world's nations at the highest responsible levels, will serve this purpose.

That food insecurity, the oldest of humanity's concerns, remains the greatest contemporary problem would appear unbelievable, were it not for the shocking evidence before us. Yet, the idea of "food security first" still has to gain universal recognition, not only as a moral principle but as a matter of interest to all. Only when societies need not fear for tomorrow's bread can they meaningfully conceive of development and of establishing justice, peace, education or any other basic right.

In proposing the World Food Summit I was guided by the conviction that only the highest political authorities can tackle effectively the multisectoral dimensions of world food security and induce the mobilization of all partners in society towards reaching this objective. Indeed, technical and financial constraints can be overcome through strong and concerted policy commitment at national and international levels.

The earth can produce enough food to satisfy the quantitative and qualitative nutritional needs of every human being, at present and in the future – provided our resources are adequately managed and the benefits shared. As Mahatma Gandhi said: "there is sufficiency in the world for men's need, but not for men's greed". Immediate self-interest has often played a major role in creating or accentuating food insecurity, while also undermining our capacity to ensure sustainable food security for future generations. Yet, in this era of increasingly globalized influences and interests, generosity becomes self-serving in its ultimate effects. There is explosive raw material for chaos, violence and worldwide destabilization in the masses of destitute and food insecure. As John Steinbeck put it: "Must the hunger become anger, and the anger fury, before anything will be done?". On the other hand, there is immeasurable potential for worldwide gain in helping marginalized poor countries and people integrate into world economic and social progress.

Such causes for concern must be underlined in the light of some of the recent trends and developments highlighted in this publication. These include the declining trend in international development assistance, flows of aid to agriculture and food aid availability. Whatever the political, market or financial forces behind such trends, they have deleterious immediate consequences for many poor countries.

Another cause for concern has been the increasing evidence of economic hardship suffered in particular by the poorest segments of the population in many countries committed to macroeconomic stabilization and market-oriented reform. The potential for generalized welfare gain offered by market liberalization is by now universally recognized. However, we have often argued, and must repeat here in the light of the recent experience of many countries, that support to the poor segments of the population must not be allowed to fail, nor must the interests of the poor be neglected, on principles of market logic and economic efficiency. Examples exist to prove that policy emphasis on equity and human development, basic prerequisites for food security, can coexist with pressing financial problems and harsh economic realities. One such example, that of Burkina Faso, is discussed in this publication.

The scale and complexity of the problems underlying world hunger and malnutrition are such that their solution no doubt involves unprecedented effort. Can we do so in a climate of financial stringency and competing priorities? The physicist Kurt Mendelssohn noted the questionable motivations behind some of our most spectacular and costly achievements. He draws a parallel between the enormous efforts and resources devoted to the exploration of outer space and the monstrous sacrifice of sweat and toil made 5 000 years ago to build the Egyptian pyramids. If we are prepared to devote unthinkable effort, cost and commitment to space exploration and military preparedness, what is our justification for not doing the same for the most worthy of all purposes – eradicating hunger?

Turning to recent developments, this publication highlights a number of encouraging trends. The current general features of the world economic environment – steady growth, low inflation, dynamic trade and increasing financial and market integration – are propitious for agricultural production and trade. The vastly improved economic performances in much of Africa, particularly where agriculture is a major driving force, are a most comforting feature of the current economic and agricultural landscape. It is also heartening that several economies in transition have entered a path of positive growth. The resilience shown by the economic and financial systems of Latin America and the Caribbean to the Mexican crisis, the enduring momentum of reform, stabilization and integration and the climate of democratic consolidation and political stability raise expectations for the economic and agricultural prospects of the region. In spite of some deceleration from unprecedented highs, the growth of Asian economies has remained strong, with trade and financial integration proceeding at an astonishing pace. Efforts towards creating a new climate of peace and regional cooperation in the Near East can open new prospects for overcoming many obstacles to agricultural and rural development in that region.

Yet, none of these sources of satisfaction are unmitigated. The surge in commodity prices, which provided much relief to producers in agriculture-based economies, has already subsided for several important products, although expectations are for commodity prices to remain above the depressed levels of the 1980s. The improved economic conditions in many African countries must be seen in the context of a decade and a half of relentless regression that has brought much of the region to intolerable levels of economic and social hardship. Social stress has also mounted in several countries in Latin America and the Caribbean, not least in rural areas affected by disappointing agricultural performances. The rapid economic expansion in Asia has been achieved, in many cases, at heavy environmental cost and the large income gap between urban and rural areas has widened further. Every day the news reminds us of the difficulties of maintaining the political and economic stability needed to pursue and strengthen reforms in the Commonwealth of Independent States and in consolidating peace and cooperation in the Near East region.

Such a mixed picture of positive and negative developments occurs against the background of deteriorating conditions for world food security. World cereal stocks are now at their lowest levels since the global food crisis of the early 1970s. Under the ensuing price increases, the low-income food-deficit countries are currently facing considerably higher food import bills.

Within the wide spectrum of factors affecting food security, those relating to macroeconomic and trade management play a prominent role. These are addressed in the special chapter of this publication, Food security: some macroeconomic dimensions, which discusses the critical role of governments in choosing the appropriate combinations of monetary, fiscal, trade, investment and social policies to create an economic environment that is conducive to the attainment of food security.

It is my hope that this publication, which outlines the major developments and issues that frame the current state of food and agriculture, will contribute to raising the necessary commitment to eradicate hunger along the principles and lines of action defined by the World Food Summit.

Jacques Diouf
DIRECTOR-GENERAL

Contents

PART III
FOOD SECURITY: SOME MACROECONOMIC DIMENSIONS

EXHIBITS

BOXES

TABLES

FIGURES

Acknowledgements

The State of Food and Agriculture 1996 was prepared by a team from the Agriculture and Economic Development Analysis Division led by F.L. Zegarra and comprising G.E. Rossmiller, J.Skoet and S. Teodosijevic. Secretarial support was provided by S. Di Lorenzo and P. Di Santo. Statistical and research support was provided by G. Arena, P.L. Iacoacci and O. Onorascenzo.

Contributions and background papers for the World review were prepared by L. Naiken and P. Narain (External assistance to agriculture), G.V. Everett (Fisheries: catch disposition and trade), M. Chipeta and M. Palmieri (Forestry production and trade), R. Nugent (Urban agriculture: an oxymoron?), B. Huff (Information technology: what it means for agriculture), N. Messer (The threat of desertification) and F. Sandiford (Support services policy for agricultural development). The sections on food shortages and emergencies, the cereal market situation, food aid and international agricultural prices were prepared by the staff of the Commodities and Trade Division units supervised by J. Greenfield, P. Fortucci, W. Lamada, A. Rashid and H. Ryan.

Contributions and background papers for the Regional review were prepared by L. Jacobsen (sub-Saharan Africa), J. Skoet (Burkina Faso), D.H. Brooks (Asia and the Pacific), R. Nugent (Pakistan), J.L. Rhi-Sausi (Latin America and the Caribbean), C.F. Jaramillo (Colombia), M. Ahmad and S. Hafeez (Near East and North Africa and the Palestine Territories), J. Budavari (Central and Eastern Europe), N. Cuffaro (Commonwealth of Independent States), K. Grey (Belorus and Moldova) and C.E. Young (The United States 1996 Farm Act).

The special chapter, Food security: some macroeconomic dimensions, was prepared by F. Sandiford with contributions from D. Culver, K. Farrell and D. Gale Johnson.

The State of Food and Agriculture 1996 was edited by J. Shaw. The graphics were prepared by M. Cappucci and the layout by M. Criscuolo with C. Ciarlantini. The cover and illustrations were produced by Studio Page.

Glossary

ADAS
Agricultural Development and Advisory Service
ADB
Asian Development Bank
ADBP
Agriculture Development Bank of Pakistan
AFTA
ASEAN Free Trade Area
AP
Andean Pact
APEC
Asian Pacific Economic Cooperation Council
ARPs
acreage reduction programmes
ASEAN
Association of Southeast Asian Nations

CAB
Commonwealth Agricultural Bureaux
CAP
Common Agricultural Policy
CBOT
Chigago Board of Trade
CCC
Commodity Credit Cooperation
CCFF
Compensatory and Contingency Financing Facility
CEEC
Central and Eastern European countries
CEFTA
Central European Free Trade Agreement
CGIAR
Consultative Group on International Agricultural Research
CIRDAP
Centre on Integrated Rural Development for Asia and the Pacific
CIS
Commonwealth of Independent States

CPEs
centrally planned economies
CRP
Conservation Reserve Program
CSR
Community of Sovereign Republics

DEIP
Dairy Export Incentive Program

EAP
Emergency Assistance Programme
EBRD
European Bank of Reconstruction and Development
ECLAC
Economic Commission for Latin America and the Caribbean
EEP
Export Enhancement Program
EHDAEs
economies heavily dependent on agricultural exports
ESAF
Enhanced Structural Adjustment Facility
EU
European Union

FAIR
Federal Agriculture Improvement and Reform
FAO
Food and Agriculture Organization of the United Nations
FCI
Food Corporation of India
FDI
foreign direct investment
FY
fiscal year

GATT
General Agreement on Tariffs and Trade
GDP
gross domestic product
GIEWS
Global Information and Early Warning
System
GNP
gross national product
GPS
geographical positioning system
GSP
gross social product
GTZ
German Agency for Technical Cooperation

HIPCs
heavily indebted poor countries

IBRD
International Bank for Reconstruction and
Development
ICAC
International Cotton Advisory Committee
IDA
Internationl Development Association
IDRC
International Development Research
Centre
IEFR
International Emergency Food Reserve
IFAD
International Fund for Agricultural
Development
IFPRI
International Food Policy Research Institute
IIASA
International Institute of Applied Systems
Analysis
ILO
International Labour Organisation
IMF
International Monetary Fund
INCD
International Negotiating Committee on
Desertification

ISA
International Sugar Agreement
ISNAR
International Service for National
Agricultural Research
IT
information technology

LIFDCs
low-income food-deficit countries

MERCOSUR
Southern Common Market

NAFTA
North American Free Trade Area
NGOs
non-governmental organizations
NICs
newly industrialized countries

ODA
official development assistance
OECD
Organisation for Economic Co-operation
and Development
OPEC
Organization of Petroleum Exporting
Countries

PL
Public Law
PRO
Protracted Refugee Operations
PT
Palestinian Territories

SAARC
South Asian Association for Regional
Cooperation
SCF
Save the Children Fund
SDR
special drawing rights
SILICs
severely indebted low-income countries

UEMOA
West African Economic and Monetary Union
UN
United Nations
UNCED
United Nations Conference on Environment
and Development
UNDP
United Nations Development Programme
UNEP
United Nations Environment Programme
UNFPA
United Nations Fund for Population
Activities
UNICEF
United Nations Children's Fund

UNRISD
United Nations Research Institute for Social
Development
USDA
United States Department of Agriculture

VAT
value added tax

WFP
World Food Programme
WTO
World Trade Organization
WWW
World Wide Web

Explanatory note

The following symbols are used in the tables:

-	=	none or negligible
...	=	not available
1994/95	=	a crop, marketing or fiscal year running from one calendar year to the next
1993-95	=	average for three calendar years

Figures in statistical tables may not add up because of rounding. Annual changes and rates of change have been calculated from unrounded figures. Unless otherwise indicated, the metric system is used.

The dollar sign ($) refers to US dollars. "Billion" is equal to 1 000 million.

Production index numbers

FAO index numbers have *1979-81* as the base period. The production data refer to primary commodities (e.g. sugar cane and sugar beet instead of sugar) and national average producer prices are used as weights. The indices for food products exclude tobacco, coffee, tea, inedible oilseeds, animal and vegetable fibres and rubber. They are based on production data presented on a calendar-year basis.[1]

Trade index numbers

The indices of trade in agricultural products also are based on *1979-81*. They include all the commodities and countries shown in the *FAO Trade Yearbook*. Indices of total food products include those edible products generally classified as "food".

All indices represent changes in current values of exports (f.o.b.) and imports (c.i.f.), all expressed in US dollars. When countries report imports valued at f.o.b. (free on board), these are adjusted to approximate c.i.f. (cost, insurance, freight) values. This method of estimation shows a discrepancy whenever the trend of insurance and freight diverges from that of the commodity unit values.

Volumes and unit value indices represent the changes in the price-weighted sum of quantities and of the quantity-weighted unit values of products traded between countries. The weights are, respectively, the price and quantity averages of *1979-81*, which is the base reference period used for all the index number series currently computed by FAO. The Laspeyres formula is

---

[1] For full details, see *FAO Production Yearbook 1994*.

used in the construction of the index numbers.[2]

Regional coverage

Developing countries include sub-Saharan Africa, Latin America and the Caribbean, the Near East and North Africa[3] and Asia and the Pacific.[4]

Developed countries include the industrial countries and economies in transition.[5]

Country and city designations used in this publication are those current during the period in which the data were prepared.

---

[2] For full details, see *FAO Trade Yearbook 1994*.

[3] The Near East and North Africa includes: Afghanistan, Algeria, Bahrain, Cyprus, Egypt, Iran, Iraq, Jordan, Kuwait, Lebanon, Libyan Arab Jamahiriya, Morocco, Oman, Qatar, Saudi Arabia, the Sudan, Syrian Arab Republic, Tunisia, Turkey, United Arab Emirates and Yemen.

[4] Asia and the Pacific also includes the former Asian centrally planned economies: Cambodia, China, Democratic People's Republic of Korea, Mongolia and Viet Nam.

[5] The "industrial countries" include: Australia, Austria, Belgium, Canada, Denmark, Finland, France, Germany, Greece, Iceland, Ireland, Italy, Japan, Luxembourg, the Netherlands, New Zealand, Norway, Portugal, Spain, Sweden, Switzerland, United Kingdom and United States. The "economies in transition" include: Albania, Bosnia and Herzegovina, Bulgaria, Croatia, Czech Republic, the former Yugoslav Republic of Macedonia, Hungary, Poland, Romania, Slovakia, Slovenia, Yugoslavia and the former USSR republics.

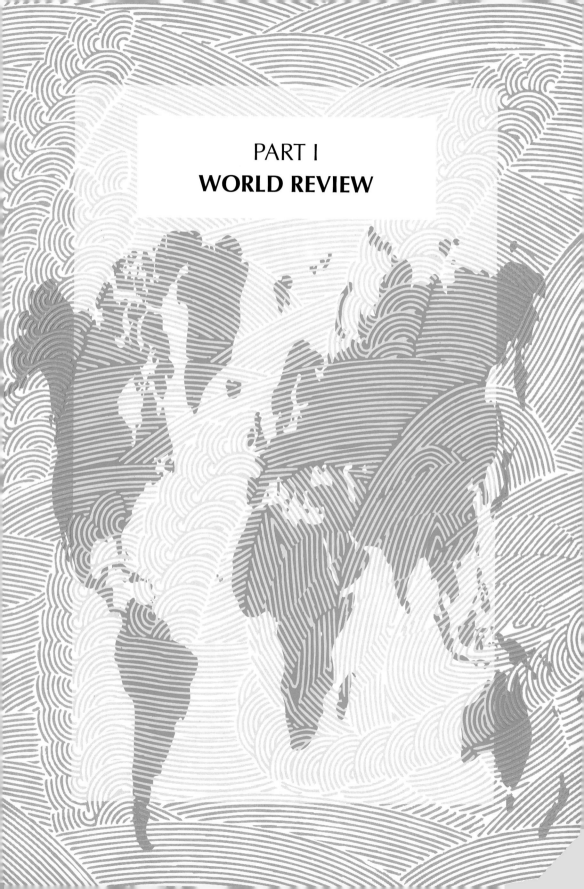

PART I
WORLD REVIEW

WORLD REVIEW
I. Current agricultural situation – facts and figures

1. CROP AND LIVESTOCK PRODUCTION IN 1995

- At the global level 1995 was a year of stagnating agricultural production, as total crop and livestock production expanded at an estimated rate of only 0.2 percent following the increase of 2.8 percent recorded in 1994. Such overall stagnation reflected below-average performances in most developed and developing country regions and virtually unchanged aggregate production levels in the countries in transition.

- The most significant single feature in global agricultural production in 1995 was the 8 percent decline in crop and livestock output in the United States where cereal crops in particular, affected by adverse weather, declined by over 20 percent. As regards other major developed country producers, overall agricultural output in the European Union (EU) continued the declining trend of the last few years, although at a marginal rate (-0.3 percent, compared with -2.3 percent in 1994). On the other hand, Australian production expanded by 12.8 percent, more than offsetting the sharp shortfall of 1994.

- For the countries in transition, 1995 marked the halt of the steady decline in overall agricultural production, which had started at the beginning of their economic reforms, and their total agricultural production remained broadly unchanged at the level of 1994. This outcome was accounted for mainly by expanded harvests in such major producer countries as Poland, which staged a partial recovery from the drought-reduced level of 1994, and Romania. In contrast, production continued to decline in some of the major republics of the former USSR, such as the Russian Federation, Ukraine and Kazakstan.

- All developing country regions, with the exception of sub-Saharan Africa, recorded deteriorating overall agricultural production performances in 1995 relative to 1994. Likewise all developing country regions, except the Far East and the Pacific, registered rates of growth of crop and livestock production below those of population growth.

• While remaining well below regional population growth, the 2.4 percent increase in agricultural production in sub-Saharan Africa in 1995 (up from 2.1 percent the previous year) was the highest among the developing country regions. Such overall modest increase resulted from widely varying country performances. On the one hand, severe drought conditions in southern Africa sharply reduced agricultural production in Botswana (-5.5 percent), Lesotho (-38.8 percent), Namibia (-7.2 percent), Zambia (-5.0 percent) and Zimbabwe (-17.4 percent), as well as in South Africa (-14.4 percent). On the other hand, moderate rates of expansion were achieved in most countries in western, central and eastern Africa. Strong agricultural production increases were recorded for Mozambique (17.2 percent), Burundi (12.8 percent), Angola (9.4 percent), Malawi (6.5 percent) and Uganda (5.7 percent). In Nigeria, agricultural production is estimated to have expanded by only a modest 1.3 percent.

• In the Far East and the Pacific, agricultural production growth slowed significantly in 1995, to 1.8 percent, marginally above the rate of population growth. A major factor behind the slow-down was the sharp deceleration in agricultural production growth in China, to only 1.6 percent (down from 6.2 percent in 1994), the lowest year-to-year expansion since 1989. In India, also, agricultural production expanded at a very modest rate, estimated at 1 percent. Among other major countries, strong agricultural growth was recorded in Bangladesh (7.9 percent), Myanmar (8.8 percent) and Pakistan (6.3 percent), as well as, to a lesser extent, in Malaysia, Nepal and Viet Nam. Major losses in production, on the other hand, were recorded in Cambodia and Laos, which were affected by catastrophic floods.

• Agricultural production growth also slowed down in Latin America and the Caribbean, from 4.0 percent in 1994 to 1.8 percent in 1995. Such a reduced growth rate resulted mainly from a 4 to 5 percent contraction in agricultural production in Mexico, decelerating production growth in Argentina, Brazil, Ecuador, Peru, Venezuela and Chile (although growth did remain vigorous in the latter) and a further decline in agricultural production in Cuba, continuing the sharp downward trend that began in 1992. Most countries in the Central America and Caribbean subregions showed poor or modest production performances, notable exceptions being Nicaragua and Guyana where growth was around 5 to 6 percent. The strongest regional agricultural production performances in 1995 were staged by smaller countries such as Bolivia, Nicaragua and Paraguay.

5

Exhibit 1

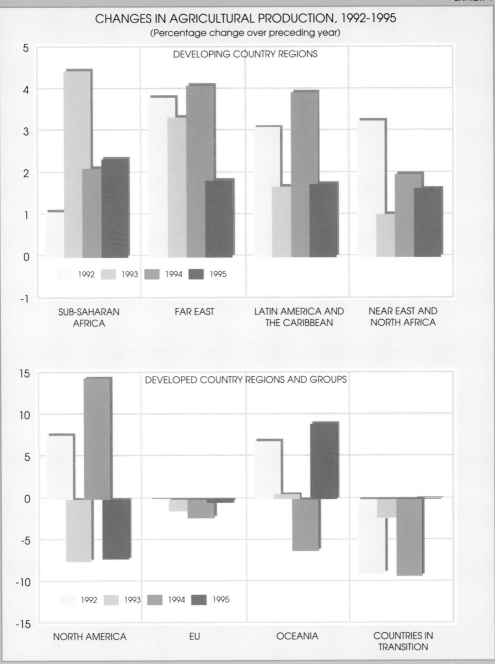

CHANGES IN AGRICULTURAL PRODUCTION, 1992-1995
(Percentage change over preceding year)

Source: FAO

• In the Near East and North Africa, production growth slowed to 1.7 percent, remaining well short of population growth for the third consecutive year. After having recovered in 1994 from severe drought conditions the previous year, Morocco was again hit by drought in 1995, with production declining by an estimated 23 percent. Production also fell in Jordan, by 5 percent, and less pronouncedly in Iraq, the Libyan Arab Jamahiriya, Saudi Arabia and Tunisia. On the positive side, production rose by 7.5 percent in Algeria, thus partially recovering from two consecutive years of decline. A strong (8 percent) expansion of production was also recorded in the Sudan, while Egypt, the Syrian Arab Republic and Turkey showed moderate production increases.

2. FOOD SHORTAGES AND EMERGENCIES

• No fewer than 26 countries worldwide are currently facing acute food shortages requiring exceptional and/or emergency food assistance. More than half of these countries are in Africa.

• Although sub-Saharan Africa's food aid needs fell in 1994/95, a substantial proportion remained unmet. This is largely attributed to tightening world food aid supplies. On current estimates, global food aid shipments in 1995/96 fell to the lowest levels for 20 years. With a major increase in world cereal prices, low-income food-deficit countries (LIFDCs) in the region will face serious difficulties in meeting food deficits through imports.

• In spite of some good harvests, emergency food assistance will continue to be needed in eastern Africa throughout 1996. In *Rwanda*, although there have been favourable weather conditions in recent months, food production remains well below pre-civil war levels and an estimated 1 million people continue to rely on food assistance. In *Burundi,* crop prospects have deteriorated as a result of insecurity and renewed population displacement. Overall, an estimated 2.4 million refugees and displaced people in the Great Lakes region will continue to need emergency assistance throughout 1996. In southern *Sudan,* in spite of an overall improvement in production, food difficulties persist as civil strife and insecurity continue to hamper relief activities. In *Somalia,* as a result of reduced cereal production and persistent insecurity, the food supply situation is expected to deteriorate, especially since May, when stocks were near depletion. Food assistance is also required for vulnerable groups in *Ethiopia* and *Eritrea* – the situation in the latter country was expected to deteriorate from May/June when food stocks would have been depleted.

• In western and central Africa, prospects are slim for recovery in food production in *Liberia,* where renewed civil disturbances continue to disrupt food production and relief efforts. Insecurity and internal conflict also continue to constrain food production in *Sierra Leone*. Elsewhere in the subregion, the food supply situation is generally stable, although localized food supply difficulties persist in several traditional food-deficit areas of *Burkina Faso, Chad, Mali* and *the Niger*.

• In southern Africa, although a bumper harvest is expected in many countries, a large part of production will be needed to replenish diminished stocks following severely reduced harvests last year. In spite of recovery, the food supply situation in *Angola* remains particularly tight as domestic production is expected to cover less than half the country's food needs and there are a large number of internally displaced people. The situation is also tight in *Zambia* where stocks are critically low and commercial imports are constrained by high prices, transport difficulties and the low purchasing power of households. The high cost of commercial imports will also result in food supply difficulties in *Lesotho, Malawi* and *Mozambique*.

• Elsewhere in the world, domestic food production in *Afghanistan* remains constrained by a shortage of inputs, damaged infrastructure and persistent insecurity continuing to displace people, who together with destitutes and returnees still require international assistance in the months ahead. In *Iraq,* the food and nutritional situation has deteriorated further and has reached a critical stage, caused mainly by difficulties encountered by the government in financing imports. Subsidized food rations provide less than half the required energy needs of the population, are of poor quality and lack animal protein and micronutrients. In *Lebanon,* the United Nations has launched an appeal for emergency relief and humanitarian assistance for 20 000 families for three months, following the recent conflict in the south of the country.

• In the *Democratic People's Republic of Korea,* following severe flooding in 1995, low stocks and the inability of the government to import food commercially have resulted in a critical situation and major international assistance will be required if starvation is to be avoided before the next harvest in October. In *Mongolia*, input shortages and economic difficulties continue to constrain food production and commercial imports, resulting in a tight food supply situation, which may be worsened by recent widespread fires. In *Laos,* floods led to a sharply reduced rice harvest in 1995 which resulted in serious food shortages requiring emergency assistance in several provinces.

• In *Haiti,* although the food supply situation is improving, commercial imports remain constrained and international assistance continues to be required to meet domestic requirements.

• In *Bosnia and Herzegovina,* although the food supply situation has eased since the peace agreement in November 1995, which led to an improvement in commercial activities and access to areas where food aid is needed, some 1.9 million refugees and war-affected people still require emergency food assistance in 1996.

• In *Armenia,* the food supply situation continues to improve as a result of increased trade and donor assistance. However, a section of the population seriously lacks resources to purchase food and, together with refugees and internally displaced people, continues to need assistance. In *Azerbaijan* and *Georgia,* although some recovery in food production is anticipated in 1996, the food supply situation remains difficult because of economic problems and reduced imports.

• In *Tajikistan,* the food supply situation is extremely serious, with those populations most at risk being threatened by starvation in the absence of international assistance.

Exhibit 2

FOOD SUPPLY SHORTFALLS* REQUIRING EXCEPTIONAL ASSISTANCE

Source: FAO, Global Information and Early Warning System, June 1996   * In current marketing year

3. CURRENT CEREAL SUPPLY, UTILIZATION AND STOCKS

• World cereal production in 1995 is estimated to be 1 904 million tonnes, about 3 percent lower than in 1994 and well below trend. The decline reflects a sharp drop in coarse grain production, in particular in the United States and the Commonwealth of Independent States (CIS), which more than offset larger wheat and rice crops. World wheat output increased by 4 percent from the reduced crop in the previous year, mostly as a result of the strong recovery in output in Australia after the 1994 drought and larger than normal crops in several countries in Asia and Europe. Rice output also increased by nearly 4 percent in 1995 to a record level.

• Global cereal stocks for crop years ending in 1996 are forecast to decline, for the third consecutive year, to 260 million tonnes, 16 percent less than their opening level and the smallest volume since 1981. At this level, total cereal stocks would be only 14 to 15 percent of the trend utilization in 1996-97, well below the 17 to 18 percent range that the FAO Secretariat considers the minimum safe level for world food security. Most of the decline will be in coarse grains, but wheat and rice carryovers are also anticipated to fall below their already reduced openings.

• Early prospects for 1996 point to a recovery in world cereal production to 2 015 million tonnes. Wheat output is forecast at some 571 million tonnes, 4.4 percent up from 1995 and back on trend after below-trend production in the past two years. Larger wheat crops are expected throughout most regions in response to tight supplies worldwide and strong international wheat prices. World coarse grains output in 1996 is forecast to increase by 10.5 percent, to 883 million tonnes, from last year's much reduced crop. At this level, output would be above the trend, but still somewhat below the record crop of 1994. The bulk of the recovery is expected to come from the developed countries, in particular those in North America, but significantly larger coarse grain crops are also anticipated in Africa and the CIS. As regards rice, assuming growing conditions remain as good as in they were in 1995, paddy output in 1996 could be around 560 million tonnes, almost unchanged from the previous year.

Exhibit 3

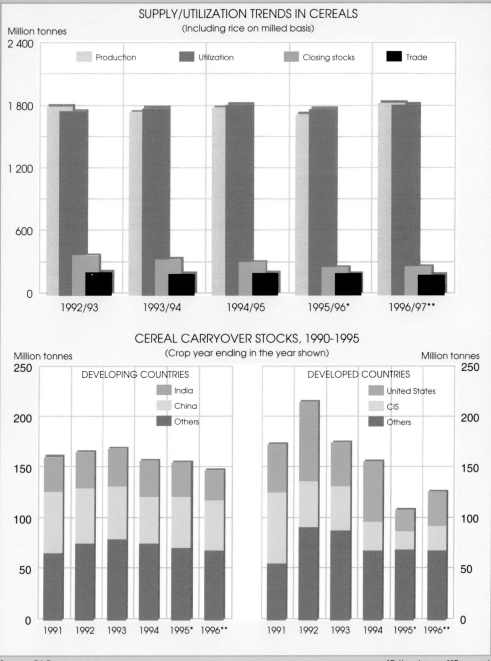

Source: FAO   *Estimate   **Forecast

• If current forecasts materialize, cereal output will be sufficient to meet the expected consumption requirements of 1996-97. However, the supply-demand situation would still remain closely balanced in 1996-97, as the expected increase would allow for only a modest replenishment of cereal reserve stocks after their sharp reduction in the current season. Thus, even assuming a normal growing season, current indications are that global food security will remain precarious, with cereal reserves below minimum safe levels for at least another year.

4. EXTERNAL ASSISTANCE TO AGRICULTURE

• The declining trend in external assistance to agriculture continued in 1994, the latest year for which complete data are available. Total commitments to agriculture, in constant 1990 prices, fell to an estimated US$9 898 million, 11 percent below the previous year's level and no less than 23 percent below the level of $12 881 million recorded in 1990. At the same time the share of external assistance to agriculture in total development financing declined from 13 percent in 1990 to around 10 percent in more recent years.

• The significant decline in commitments to agriculture in 1994 reflected a 30 percent real term contraction in bilateral commitments to only US$3 550 million. This contraction was only partly counterbalanced by a 5 percent real increase in multilateral commitments, which brought them to $6 348 million in 1994. Nevertheless, total multilateral commitments to agriculture in 1994 remained well below the levels recorded prior to 1993.

• While the share of concessional commitments in total commitments to agriculture remained broadly constant at close to 70 percent from 1990 to 1994, the share of grants declined significantly during this period. Indeed, total grants dropped from $5 240 million in 1990 to only $1 675 million estimated for 1994. This negative trend affected both bilateral and multilateral grants.

• Most of the major multilateral donors contributed to the increase in multilateral commitments to agriculture in 1994, with the regional development banks expanding commitments from US$1 409 million in 1993 to $1 771 million in 1994, the International Fund for Agricultural Development (IFAD) from US$234 million to $396 million and the World Bank from US$3 343 million to $3 488 million. The United Nations Development Programme, FAO and the Consultative Group on International Agricultural Research (UNDP/FAO/CGIAR) expanded their combined commitments moderately from US$627 million to $648 million. The Organization of the Petroleum Exporting Countries' (OPEC) multilateral assistance, on the other hand, dropped sharply from US$166 million to $45 million.

• For the regional development banks, the World Bank and UNDP/FAO/ CGIAR, however, the estimated increase in commitments to agriculture in 1994 represents only a partial recovery from the sharp declines recorded over the previous years. For all of these institutions, commitments in 1994 remained below the level of 1993 and well below that of 1990. Only for IFAD did the sharp expansion in commitments in 1994 bring them above the level of 1990.

• As regards the regional distribution of assistance flows, the level of commitments to Asian countries fell more steeply than for other regions during 1990-93. In 1994, for the first time, the republics of the former USSR were recorded as recipients of significant assistance to the agricultural sector at a level of commitments preliminarily estimated at US$110 million.

• Data for 1995 are still incomplete and cover only external assistance commitments to agriculture from multilateral sources. The World Bank Annual Report 1995 reports a 32 percent decline in commitments to agriculture from that institution against a background of an 8 percent increase in its total commitments from the Bank. Likewise, the statement of loans for the Asian Development Bank shows a decline in commitments to agriculture of 19 percent.

Exhibit 4

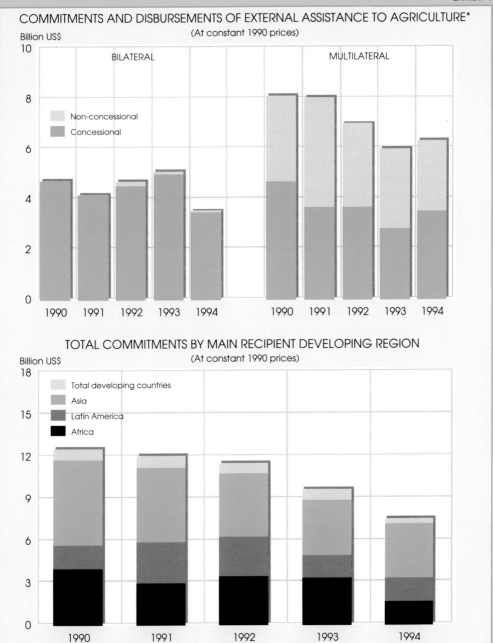

COMMITMENTS AND DISBURSEMENTS OF EXTERNAL ASSISTANCE TO AGRICULTURE*

(At constant 1990 prices)

Billion US$

BILATERAL   MULTILATERAL

Non-concessional
Concessional

TOTAL COMMITMENTS BY MAIN RECIPIENT DEVELOPING REGION

(At constant 1990 prices)

Billion US$

Total developing countries
Asia
Latin America
Africa

Source: FAO and OECD

* Broad definition

5. FOOD AID FLOWS IN 1995/96

• Total food aid shipments in cereals in 1995/96 (July to June) are estimated to be 7.6 million tonnes, compared with 9.2 million tonnes in 1994/95, 12.6 million tonnes in 1993/94 and 15.2 million tonnes in 1992/93.

• The low-income food-deficit countries (LIFDCs) are expected to receive about 6.5 million tonnes, or 85 percent of the total cereal food aid, a similar share to that they received the previous year. At these levels, food aid shipments in the form of cereals to LIFDCs will constitute about 8 percent of the 1995/96 forecast for total cereal imports (including commercial purchases), sharply down from 11 percent in 1994/95 and 13 percent in 1993/94. Within the category of LIFDCs, those in sub-Saharan Africa continue to be the largest recipients of food aid, accounting for more than 30 percent of the total.

• As of March 1996, contributions to the 1995 *International Emergency Food Reserve (IEFR)* had reached 922 000 tonnes of cereals and 245 000 tonnes of non-cereal food commodities, while contributions to the *World Food Programme's (WFP) Protracted Refugee Operations* (PROs) in 1995 amounted to some 504 000 tonnes of cereals and 61 000 tonnes of other food commodities. Total pledges to the 1996 IEFR by nine donors amounted to 280 000 tonnes of food commodities, a volume similar to that which had been pledged at the same time last year. In addition to the IEFR contributions, some 225 000 tonnes of food commodities have also been pledged under the 1996 PROs.

• By March 1996, pledges to the *regular resources of WFP* for the previous 1993-94 biennium amounted to US$1 001 million, representing nearly 67 percent of the target of $1.5 billion. Of the total amount pledged, some $651 million was in the form of commodities and $350 million in cash. For the 1995-96 biennium, total pledges as of December had reached $649 million, representing approximately 43 percent of the target of $1.5 billion. Of the total amount pledged, an estimated $426 was in the form of commodities and $223 million in cash.

Exhibit 5

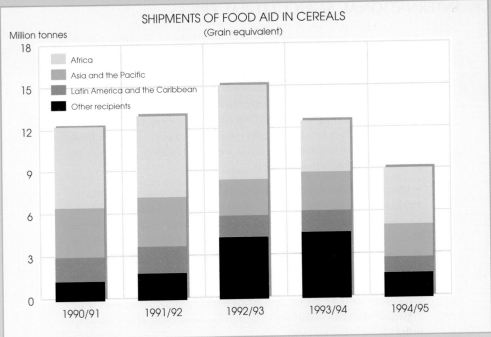

SHIPMENTS OF FOOD AID IN CEREALS
(Grain equivalent)

Million tonnes

Africa
Asia and the Pacific
Latin America and the Caribbean
Other recipients

1990/91 1991/92 1992/93 1993/94 1994/95

Source: FAO

Note: Years refer to the 12-month period July/June

6. INTERNATIONAL AGRICULTURAL PRICES

• Grain prices rose to record levels during the 1995/96 season as a result of production shortfalls, low stock levels and relatively strong export demand. By late May 1996, international *wheat* prices had weakened slightly compared with their record levels in April, yet they were still as much as US$100 per tonne – 60 percent above the corresponding period a year earlier. With major *maize* harvests still months away, continuing strong demand, especially for United States maize, pushed prices to higher levels. By late May, international maize prices were nearly US$95 per tonne – 80 percent above their values last year.

• International *rice* prices were relatively weak in the first five months of 1996 compared with the very high levels reached in the second half of the previous year. The decline in prices was largely a result of reduced demand from Bangladesh, China and Indonesia following a recovery in production in these three countries. Among the different types of rice, the prices of lower qualities fell the most. The prices of higher-quality rice, by contrast, were more resilient, sustained in the first quarter of the year by purchases made specifically for the Chinese spring festival and, later, by the increase in United States rice export prices in anticipation of reduced rice plantings in the United States for 1996.

• The rise in prices for *oils* and *fats*, which started in June 1994, came to a halt during the second half of the 1994/95 season and prices for some oils started falling, with prospects for higher end-of-season stocks and promising 1995/96 crops. During the first half of the 1995/96 season, international prices for most oils and fats moved further downwards, as a result of ample stocks at the beginning of the season and the expectation that total supplies would again exceed total losses. Prices for soybean oil increased, however, during the second half of the season because of lower supplies and sharply rising prices for grains, which compete for land with soybeans. Prices of *oilmeals* over the entire 1994/95 season remained about 6 percent below the average recorded in 1993/94, reflecting a continued abundance of supplies, combined with the continued decline in livestock numbers in the former USSR and Eastern European countries. During the 1995/96 season, prices of soybean, rapeseed and sunflower meals rose sharply, driven by a reduction in overall oilmeal supplies, sustained demand for livestock products and more favourable meal-to-grain price ratios.

• The rise in world *sugar* prices, which began in 1994, reached five-year highs during the first quarter of 1995. The International Sugar Agreement (ISA) daily price peaked at US cents 15.45 per pound (0.45 kg) in January. Forecasts of a large production surplus in 1995/96 caused a sharp drop during August and September. However, prices rose slightly from October until March 1996, mainly supported by the scarce availability of high-quality white sugar from the European Union (EU) and delayed exports from several cane-producing countries. The price has declined substantially since April 1996, reaching a two-year low of US cents 10.50 per pound during the first week of May, as larger quantities of exportable sugar came into the market.

• World *coffee* prices strengthened in 1994 and remained high until May 1995. However, as abundant crop supplies from Colombia, Mexico and Uganda offset Brazilian losses, a downward movement in prices began in June 1995 and lasted throughout the rest of the year. Prices during the first four months of 1996 averaged US$2 336 per tonne which was more than one-third lower than its highest level last April.

• After significant increases in 1995, *cocoa* prices remained at their highest level for six years. The high prices reflected a tight supply situation worldwide which was a result of the steady fall in production in Brazil. Although output increased in Côte d'Ivoire and Ghana in 1995, prices continued to increase, reaching their highest level in April 1996 as demand remained strong and supplies tight.

• World *tea* prices declined further in 1995 as a result of record production in a number of key producing countries and weak import demand. After falling to a historical low in July 1995 (the lowest for 20 years), prices recovered significantly to US$1 745 per tonne for the first four months of 1996. However, world tea prices remain under downward pressure in the short term as a result of weak import demand.

• World *cotton* prices based on the Cotlook A index for March 1996 are some US cents 6.5 per pound lower than the 1995 average price and considerably lower than the price peaks reached during the first quarter of 1995. The International Cotton Advisory Committee (ICAC) estimates world production for 1995/96 to increase by 1.8 percent, to 19 million tonnes. Consumption is expected to increase by about 2 percent. At the end of the 1995/96 season (August/July) global stocks are estimated at 8.11 million tonnes, a 2 percent increase over the previous year. World imports for 1995/96 are expected to decline by almost 0.5 million tonnes from 1994/95 levels, and are expected to decline another 300 000 tonnes in 1996/97. China continues to play a key role in world cotton trade. ICAC projects that on balance production increases are expected to exceed consumption requirements, leading to a rise in stocks, but yield swings, disease and pest problems, combined with the prices of competing crops, particularly cereals, will all influence production over the medium term.

Exhibit 6

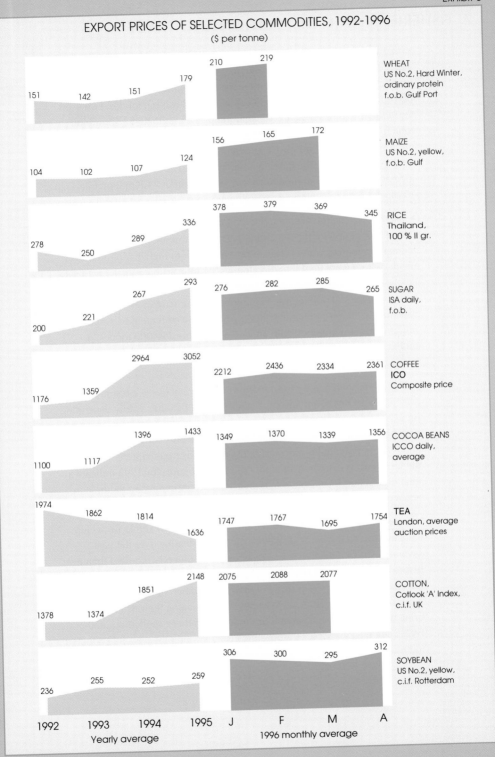

EXPORT PRICES OF SELECTED COMMODITIES, 1992-1996
($ per tonne)

WHEAT
US No.2, Hard Winter, ordinary protein f.o.b. Gulf Port

151 · 142 · 151 · 179 · 210 · 219

MAIZE
US No.2, yellow, f.o.b. Gulf

104 · 102 · 107 · 124 · 156 · 165 · 172

RICE
Thailand, 100 % II gr.

278 · 250 · 289 · 336 · 378 · 379 · 369 · 345

SUGAR
ISA daily, f.o.b.

200 · 221 · 267 · 293 · 276 · 282 · 285 · 265

COFFEE ICO
Composite price

1176 · 1359 · 2964 · 3052 · 2212 · 2436 · 2334 · 2361

COCOA BEANS
ICCO daily, average

1100 · 1117 · 1396 · 1433 · 1349 · 1370 · 1339 · 1356

TEA
London, average auction prices

1974 · 1862 · 1814 · 1636 · 1747 · 1767 · 1695 · 1754

COTTON,
Cotlook 'A' Index, c.i.f. UK

1378 · 1374 · 1851 · 2148 · 2075 · 2088 · 2077

SOYBEAN
US No.2, yellow, c.i.f. Rotterdam

236 · 255 · 252 · 259 · 306 · 300 · 295 · 312

| 1992 | 1993 | 1994 | 1995 | J | F | M | A |

Yearly average · 1996 monthly average

Source: FAO

7. FISHERIES: CATCH DISPOSITION AND TRADE

• In 1994 the *world harvest* of fish and shellfish from capture fisheries and aquaculture reached a record level of 109.6 million tonnes. The 1994 production represents a record increase of 7.3 million tonnes, or about 7.2 percent, compared with the 1993 catch of 102.3 million tonnes. Fish used for reduction to fishmeal and oil amounted to an estimated 33.5 million tonnes in 1994, which is the highest quantity ever used for non-food purposes and represents an 18 percent increase from the 1993 figure of 29.3 million tonnes. The quantity used for human consumption also increased, from 72.9 million tonnes in 1993 to about 74.8 million tonnes in 1994, resulting in a minor increase in per caput supply.

• Marine production accounted for 5.4 million tonnes of the increase and inland production for the remaining 1.9 million tonnes. The production increase in marine waters was almost entirely from higher capture fishery yields, which were up 4.9 million tonnes, mainly attributable to anchoveta catches by Peru and Chile in the southeast Pacific, with mariculture increasing by 450 000 tonnes. In contrast, the increase in inland production was mainly the result of aquaculture, which showed increased output of 1.7 million tonnes, compared with an increase of only 250 000 tonnes for inland capture fisheries. Almost all of the increase in inland water fishery production came from Asia.

• The increase in harvest from *marine capture fisheries* is a result of increased catches of anchoveta, a stock which fluctuates wildly depending on *El Niño* conditions. This increase in no way contradicts FAO's assertion that the majority of species subject to fishing are now fully or overexploited and that the potential for increasing overall yields from capture fisheries in the long term is extremely limited. Preliminary figures for 1995 indicate a total production level similar to that of 1994, representing an increase in aquaculture production and a decrease in capture fishery yields.

• Recent analyses indicate that the proportion of major stocks for which catches are in a declining phase has increased steadily over the past several decades. Effective management is more urgently required than ever before to stabilize biomass and improve economic performance. In order to take the difficult decisions this will require, Member States will have to put in place the infrastructure for assessing and managing their fisheries and bring their management capabilities in line with those spelled out in the FAO Code of Conduct for Responsible Fisheries and other recently adopted international instruments.

• The recent trend of expanding *production* in developing countries and contracting production in developed countries, particularly in the economies in transition which include the republics of the former USSR and Eastern Europe, continued in 1994. Production by low-income food-deficit countries (LIFDCs) continued the pattern of rapid growth which has averaged 6.9 percent per annum since 1988. This figure is deceptive, however, in that growth has taken place mainly in the highest producing LIFDCs such as China (12 percent average for 1988-94), India (6 percent), Indonesia (6 percent), the Philippines (2 percent), Bangladesh (5 percent) and Morocco (5 percent).

• China, since 1989 the highest producing country, reported a record production of 20.7 million tonnes for 1994. Of the 3.2-million-tonne increase, over 1 million tonnes are attributable to aquaculture production of five carp species and the remainder to many cultured species (mainly inland) and some wild species (mainly marine) such as largehead hairtail, scads and, notably, filefishes, which had declined markedly between 1988 and 1993. Production of Japanese anchovy decreased for the first time, reversing the rapid growth trend seen from the start of the fishery in 1990 to its peak of 560 000 tonnes in 1993.

• During the decade 1984-94, total world *aquaculture production* increased at an average rate of 9.4 percent, compared with 2.6 percent for livestock meat production and 1.7 percent for total capture fisheries. Aquaculture production grew at a much faster rate within developing countries than within developed countries between 1984 and 1994; since 1984 total production (in tonnes) has increased by 188.7 percent in developing countries compared with 24.6 percent in developed countries. Developing countries and LIFDCs continued to dominate production in 1994, accounting for 86 percent and 75 percent of total production, respectively.

• In 1994, world aquaculture production totalled 25.5 million tonnes (21.7 percent of total world fisheries landings), valued at US$39.8 billion, compared with 10.4 million tonnes and $13.1 billion in 1984. Production by weight in 1994 consisted of 51.2 percent finfish, 27.1 percent aquatic plants, 17.2 percent molluscs, 4.2 percent crustaceans and 0.3 percent others.

• At present, most of the LIFDCs' finfish aquaculture production is based on the culture of low-value herbivorous/omnivorous freshwater finfish in inland rural communities, within semi-intensive or extensive farming systems that use moderate to low levels of production inputs. These systems produce large quantities of affordable food fish for domestic markets and home consumption. By contrast, about 60 percent of finfish production in developed countries is based on the monoculture of high-value carnivorous species in intensive production systems.

• International *trade in fishery products* increased by about 14 percent between 1993 and 1994 to a total export value of US$47 billion with developing countries accounting for an ever-increasing share which now almost equals that of developed countries. The developing countries' positive trade balance of $15.5 billion in 1994 and the developed countries' negative trade balance of $20.0 billion represented increases from 1993 of 15 and 20 percent, respectively. The overall increase resulted from higher quantities of exports and higher unit values for most food commodities; the latter being a reversal of the downturn in unit values evidenced in 1993.

• For the second year running, Thailand was the world's main fish-exporting country with exports of US$4.2 billion in 1994, a 23 percent increase on 1993. Japan maintained its position as highest importer with imports worth $16.1 billion in 1994, or 31 percent of world imports.

Exhibit 7

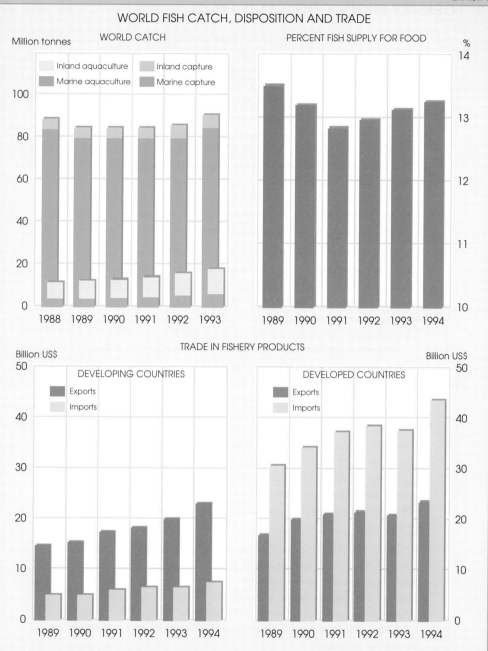

WORLD FISH CATCH, DISPOSITION AND TRADE

Source: FAO

8. FORESTRY PRODUCTION AND TRADE

• The most important feature of 1995 forest products markets was the strong growth of pulp and paper prices in international markets, which reached a peak in October 1995. During that month, Northern Bleached Softwood Kraft (NBSK) pulp, the industry's benchmark product, was quoted at US$1 000 per tonne, 50 percent above the price for the corresponding period in 1994. Thereafter, as paper demand weakened and new pulp capacity grew, prices of wood pulp and less so of paper fell rapidly, to some 30 percent below their peak by February 1996 for pulp, in spite of production cutbacks aimed at reducing supplies. The high prices that prevailed during much of 1995 boosted the value of trade, particularly for the developed countries which dominate exports of these two products. Thus, while the value of total trade in forest products is estimated to have increased by 8 percent, that for pulp and paper rose by some 15 percent.

• World *roundwood* production reached some 3.47 million m³ in 1995, about 1 percent higher than in 1994. Much of this marginal growth was caused by the demand-driven expansion of *fuelwood,* the dominant energy source in many developing countries. World production of *industrial roundwood,* on the other hand, remained at the low level of 1.55 million m³, well below the volume for 1990. This was mainly caused by the continued dislocation of output in the Russian Federation where industrial roundwood removals were estimated to have fallen by a further 15 percent. The decline was also in response to weak construction industry activity in the industrialized countries, the main outlet for mechanical wood products; for example, new housing construction in the United States decreased by 9 percent, with similar declines experienced by Japan and some European countries. Furthermore, the supply of logs continued to be affected by restrictions on harvesting in public forests on the west coast of North America and in key tropical Asian countries, increasingly in response to environmental concerns. In 1995 some African countries, such as Côte d'Ivoire and Gabon, also began to move towards tighter logging and export restrictions.

• Pulpwood and particles were exceptional among roundwood products in that they experienced marked growth in 1995 to serve the buoyant wood pulp industry, which for most of 1995 consumed more pulpwood and particles and at higher prices. Most notable growth was for exports of pulpwood from countries of the former USSR to Scandinavia, for wood chips from Chile (volumes of which grew by 35 percent) and for trade in wood chips in general.

WORLD REVIEW

II. Overall economic environment and agriculture

WORLD ECONOMIC ENVIRONMENT

According to the International Monetary Fund (IMF)[1] world
economic output expanded by 3.5 percent in 1995, down from 3.7
percent the previous year and marginally below the long-term
trend. The growth rate in 1995 resulted from:

- slow output expansion, of 2 percent, in the *industrial countries.*
  All the major industrial countries experienced lower growth
  than in 1994 except Japan, where economic activity began to
  pick up in late 1995, and Italy. Economic performances and
  prospects in Europe deteriorated reflecting eroded consumer
  and business confidence. Fiscal consolidation and the
  reduction of unemployment remain key challenges;
- a robust 5.9 percent growth in the *developing countries.* 1995
  was the fourth consecutive year in which output increased by
  close to 6 percent, led by the dynamic Asian economies in
  particular. Africa and the Near East achieved significantly
  higher growth rates than in 1994, but a marked slow-down was
  recorded in Latin America and the Caribbean (see Developing
  Countries Regional Review);
- further economic momentum in the *transition economies* of
  Central and Eastern Europe (excluding Belarus and Ukraine),
  following the turnaround in 1994. The economies of other
  countries in transition continued to recede, however, although
  output appeared to have bottomed out during 1995 in the
  Russian Federation and a number of Commonwealth of
  Independent States (CIS) republics in Asia.

Expectations for 1996 are for a continuation of slow growth in
the industrial economies, with decelerating rates in the United
States and Europe but a strengthening of recovery in Japan. By
contrast, growth is forecast to accelerate to about 6.3 percent in the
developing countries; this will be the result, in particular, of an

---

[1] Unless otherwise indicated, economic estimates and forecasts in this section
are from IMF. 1996. *World Economic Outlook 1996.* Washington, DC.

economic upsurge in Latin America and the Caribbean and a further strengthening in output growth in Africa. A significant improvement is expected in the Russian Federation, Transcaucasia and central Asia where economic expansion of about 2 percent may be achieved after years of deep recession.

The other main features of the current economic environment are: reduced pressure on already low inflation rates in the industrial countries and considerably reduced price increases in the developing countries; rapid growth of world trade, reflecting progress in market liberalization and dynamic intratrade in developing country regions, particularly Asia and Latin America and the Caribbean; and a general decline in interest rates in the face of weak growth and low inflation in the major industrial countries – although interest rates have remained significantly higher in Europe than in North America and Japan. These features create a generally favourable environment for agricultural production, trade and food security.

Economic outlook and the implications for agriculture

The economic and agricultural outlook of the developing countries will be influenced by the following factors:

- In the years to come, a more stable international economic environment can be expected, with moderate but steady economic growth in the industrial countries, low inflation, increasingly open trade regimes and greater financial integration. These features augur well for the developing countries' prospects for growth and trade.
- Prospects for an extended period of low inflation with continued fiscal consolidation may be expected to contribute to lower interest rates in the industrial countries. This has considerable importance for the developing countries because of the effects it will have on industrial countries' GDP growth, import demand, private capital flows and, most significantly for developing countries, on external debt servicing.
- According to the World Bank, after a dramatic rise between 1990 and 1993, external private capital flows have stabilized in the range of US$160 to 170 billion, despite the Mexican crisis and the rise in interest rates in the United States in 1994. Expectations are for a continuation of moderate growth in private flows, caused by the decline in interest rates mentioned above and the continuing reforms and liberalization of investment regimes in the developing countries.
- External assistance flows have been falling. Official development assistance (ODA), which accounts for two-thirds

of resource flows to low-income countries, declined from 0.35 percent of donors' GDP in 1983 to 0.29 percent in 1994, the lowest for more than 20 years. This unfortunate trend, which, as seen above, also extended to flows to agriculture, is likely to continue for a number of reasons, including fiscal consolidation in donor countries, reduced political rationale for official assistance after the fall of the Berlin wall and changing views on the development role of aid *vis-à-vis private* financing in the current era of economic liberalization.

• A factor of considerable importance for the economic prospects of the developing countries will be the future behaviour of commodity prices. As seen above, the commodity price boom in 1994 lost momentum in 1995 as the essentially transitory forces that had given rise to it subsided. Non-oil commodity prices rose in real terms by 18 percent in 1994 and by 5 percent in 1995 (World Bank estimates). Such relative weakening of prices had a negative impact on the developing countries as it was more pronounced for their main export crops, particularly tropical beverages, while the prices of cereals, a major import item for many developing countries, strengthened. Expectations are for a weakening of non-oil commodity prices in 1996-97, which may erode many of the gains achieved over the previous two years, but for relative stability in the longer term.

Agricultural outlook for the developing countries

Figures 1-5 show mid-term forecasts of economic and agricultural output and trade growth in the developing countries, as forecast by Project LINK. The following main features stand out:

• The mid-term economic outlook for the developing countries as a whole appears somewhat brighter than last year. Economic activity is forecast to stabilize at close to 6 percent growth during 1996-1999. Prospects for agricultural output also appear more favourable than previously forecast. However, agricultural value added, with rates of the order of 4 percent throughout 1996-1999, is forecast to grow at significantly lower rates than total output. This feature would mainly reflect the more dynamic behaviour of the industry and service sectors in the regions of Asia and the Pacific and Latin America and the Caribbean. By contrast, total and agricultural GDP are forecast to grow at approximately the same slow pace in the largely agriculture-based African economies.

• Agricultural value added is forecast to exceed population growth in all the developing country regions except

Figure 1

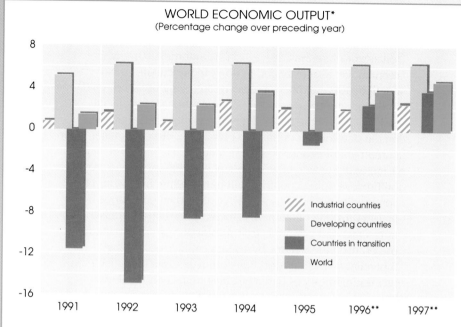

WORLD ECONOMIC OUTPUT*
(Percentage change over preceding year)

///. Industrial countries

Developing countries

Countries in transition

World

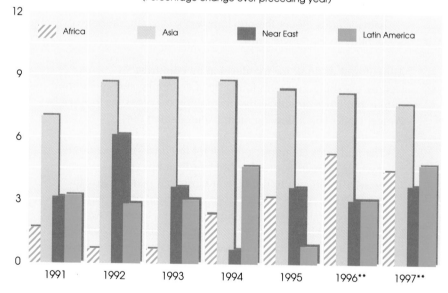

ECONOMIC GROWTH, DEVELOPING COUNTRY REGIONS
(Percentage change over preceding year)

///. Africa   Asia   Near East   Latin America

Source: IMF

* Real GDP or real NMP   ** Projections

sub-Saharan Africa. After a mediocre 1996, Latin America and the Caribbean is expected to accelerate agricultural value added growth to between 4.5 and 4.8 percent. A slight acceleration in agricultural output growth is expected in Asia and the Pacific. By contrast, after buoyant performances in 1996 and 1997, growth in the Near East and North Africa region is forecast to slow down to slightly above 4 percent.

• Prospects for merchandise trade appear particularly bright, with forecast growth rates in value terms approaching 13 percent yearly in Asia and the Pacific, 10 percent in Latin America and the Caribbean and 8 percent in the Near East and North Africa. Although less dynamic, agricultural trade is nevertheless expected to expand at an accelerating pace in all regions.

• In general, the growth of agricultural imports is forecast to exceed that of exports in all developing country regions, implying varying degrees of deterioration of agricultural trade balances. However, while the net trade positions of Latin America and the Caribbean and Asia and the Pacific are not likely to be modified to any significant extent, the trend is expected to have more serious consequences for Africa, where for a long time the tendency has been for agricultural exports to lag behind food imports, resulting in a shrinking of the

Figure 2

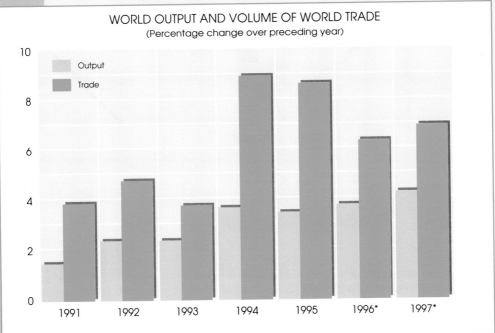

WORLD OUTPUT AND VOLUME OF WORLD TRADE
(Percentage change over preceding year)

Source: IMF

* Projections

Figure 3

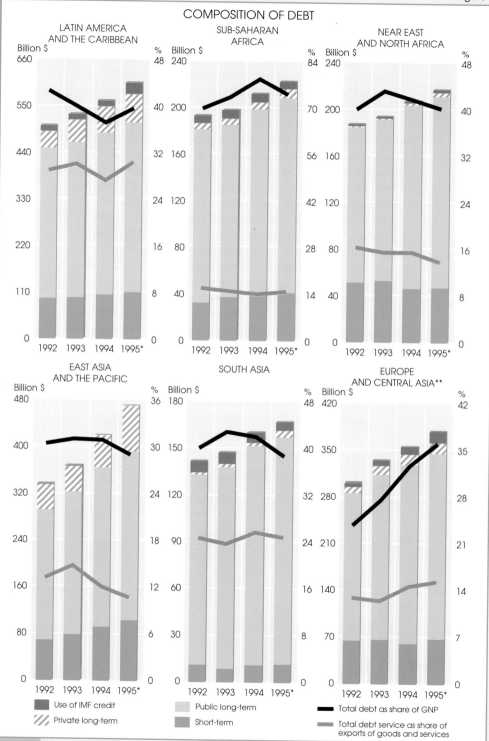

COMPOSITION OF DEBT

LATIN AMERICA AND THE CARIBBEAN

SUB-SAHARAN AFRICA

NEAR EAST AND NORTH AFRICA

EAST ASIA AND THE PACIFIC

SOUTH ASIA

EUROPE AND CENTRAL ASIA**

Use of IMF credit
Private long-term
Public long-term
Short-term
Total debt as share of GNP
Total debt service as share of exports of goods and services

Source: World Bank, *World Debt Tables* 1996

* Projections   **Including former USSR

BOX 2
EXTERNAL DEBT AND FINANCIAL FLOWS
OF DEVELOPING COUNTRIES

The *stock of external debt* of developing countries reached an estimated US$2 068 billion at the end of 1995, a net increase of $147 billion with respect to 1994. The change in external debt was caused by: net debt flows of US$133 billion (long- and short-term debt and IMF credits) against $86 billion in the previous year (the inflow of debt-creating financing includes the exceptional official financing rescue package for Mexico and high levels of new private debt flows to East Asian borrowers); the depreciation of the United States dollar which increased the dollar value of debt denominated in other currencies by US$13 billion; and capitalized interest from debt and debt service reduction programmes accounting for an additional US$9 billion. Voluntary debt reduction in Latin American arrears was offset by growing interest arrears in sub-Saharan Africa.

The estimated *total debt service payments* on all debts reached US$ 224 billion in 1995, a 15 percent increase over 1994, reflecting the fact that many countries have returned to full servicing of their external obligations. As a result of the improved export performance of many developing countries, the *debt-to-export ratio* declined for developing countries as a group, from 163 percent in 1994 to 150 percent in 1995. At the regional level, however, this trend is not uniform. In sub-Saharan Africa the debt-to-export ratio continues to increase and reached an estimated level of 270 percent in 1995. In contrast, for Latin America and the

Caribbean the debt-to-export ratio in 1995 declined slightly from 258 percent in 1994 to 254 percent. The *total debt-service-to-export ratio* also continued to decline reaching just over 16 percent in 1995. For many middle-income countries the debt situation has improved and their economic reforms and stability have attracted strong private capital flows. However, the heavily indebted poor countries, most of them in sub-Saharan Africa, remained strongly dependent on the official resource flows and the debt indicators of these countries continued to deteriorate.

During recent years there has been a rapid rise in bilateral ODA *forgiveness of debt and interest arrears,* which amounted to US$3.3 billion in 1994. Since 1990, some $25 billion have been forgiven to all developing countries, of which $11 billion applied to heavily indebted poor countries.

Aggregate net long-term resource flows, composed of the official development finance and all private flows (comprising debt-related flows and other forms of external financing) to all developing countries increased by 11.5 percent in 1995 reaching a record US$231 billion.

ODA (comprising official grants and official concessional loans), remained almost at the same level in 1995 as during the previous year; US$47 billion, of which $33 billion was in official grants excluding technical cooperation grants. Sub-Saharan Africa, which has limited access to private flows, continued to be the largest recipient of ODA, receiving 36 percent of the concessional flows.

Private capital flows continue to grow and represent an important component of total net flows to developing countries, accounting for 72 percent of total flows in 1995. This was slightly below the peak of 76 percent in 1994, mainly because of the decline in portfolio flows caused by the rise in the United States interest rates and the Mexico crisis.

Net foreign direct investment (FDI) flows to developing countries grew rapidly in the late 1980s and early 1990s. In 1994 they reached an all-time high of US$80 billion, an increase of 17 percent over the previous year (and in 1995 they were estimated to have reached US$90 billion).

Foreign direct investment continued to rise and increase its share in total private capital flows, in 1994 accounting for 50 percent and increasing to 54 percent in 1995. However, private flows remain concentrated mainly in a relatively small number of middle-income countries. In East Asia, China was the largest recipient of FDI, attracting US$38 billion in 1995. In Eastern Europe and Central Asia, FDI increased by almost 50 percent, reaching US$12 billion in 1995. In sub-Saharan Africa, by contrast, this kind of private flow reached only US$2 billion in 1995, against almost $3 billion in the previous year.

Source: World Bank. 1996. *World Debt Tables 1996.* Washington, DC.

WORLD REVIEW
III. Selected issues

URBAN AGRICULTURE: AN OXYMORON?
City farming has a long tradition in many societies, especially in Asia and Europe. Several factors have led to a growing interest in urban agriculture over recent years. These include: increasing urbanization in the developing world; worsening conditions of the urban poor; wars and natural disasters that disrupt food supplies from rural areas; environmental degradation and resource limitations that cause greater food scarcity; the movement for community sustainability; and recognition of non-market values. Few of the above conditions are new, but recurring disasters and worsening trends have led to urban agriculture emerging as a potential solution. Advocates have argued that policy-makers, scientists and the general public should recognize the opportunities provided by urban agriculture and begin to eliminate the obstacles and provide assistance to this valuable activity.

This chapter examines the proposition that urban agriculture offers benefits that rural agriculture does not or cannot provide. It also discusses the policies affecting urban agriculture and what changes should be made in the light of urban agriculture's potential to improve conditions in the world's cities.

What is urban agriculture?
For the purposes of this chapter, urban agriculture is defined as being food production that occurs within the confines of cities. Such production takes place in backyards, on rooftops, in community vegetable and fruit gardens and on unused or public spaces. It includes commercial operations that produce food in greenhouses and on open spaces, but is more often small-scale and scattered around the city.

The narrow definition used here deliberately excludes some of the important aspects of urban agriculture, such as forestry, fisheries and the specific circumstances of peri-urban agriculture, which is frequently a more intensive variety of rural agriculture. While important, such activities have their own distinctive characteristics and an adequate discussion of them is beyond the scope of this chapter.

The products of urban agriculture are as diverse as those of rural agriculture. Urban farming concentrates largely on products that do not require extensive landholdings, can survive with limited inputs and are often perishable. Thus, fruits and vegetables, small livestock, such staples as cassava, maize and beans, fish and the occasional cow can all be seen in cities. Other food products seen in cities include berries, nuts, herbs and spices.

As well as a diversity of products, the demographic make-up of urban farmers varies considerably by region and economic conditions. Most urban farmers are relatively long-term city residents, moderately poor and female. They exist in both developed and developing countries and in all regions of the world, but face a great range of different conditions and opportunities.

Many studies of urban agriculture describe cases in developing countries where the activity is performed by poor city dwellers providing food for their families. While this is not the only important element of urban agriculture, it is the focus of this chapter because of its food security implications and its importance to FAO and other international development organizations.

Developing country urban poor is a difficult group to focus on because of ambiguities in defining urban, differing definitions of what constitutes agriculture and varying levels of data collection in the cities and countries concerned. An even greater hindrance to measuring the effects of urban farming is that much of what is considered urban agriculture is conducted outside normal market channels. In many of the cities where the authorities have noticed urban agriculture, the official reaction is either to turn a blind eye and allow it to continue against land-use regulations or to discourage it.

In spite of these difficulties in quantification, the hidden potential of urban agriculture to alleviate two of the world's most intractable problems – poverty and waste – has been receiving increasing attention over recent years. Even the Brundtland Commission Report (1987) commented on the subject: "Officially sanctioned and promoted urban agriculture could become an important component of urban development and make more food available to the urban poor.... Urban agriculture can also provide fresher and cheaper produce, more green space, the clearing of garbage dumps and recycling of household waste."[2] Both poverty and environmental quality present issues of market failure and the need for government intervention.

---

[2] **World Commission on Environment and Development. 1987.** *Our common future.* **Oxford, UK, Oxford University Press.**

Urban agriculture and the poor

Urban agriculture is cited as a possible solution to several of the trends that are currently causing concern. Foremost among these is the phenomenal growth expected in cities of the developing world over the next few decades. In 1994, 45 percent of the world's population lived in cities and that number will grow to more than 50 percent by the year 2000 and to 65 percent by 2025.[3] The fastest population growth is in the large cities of the developing world, while urbanization has slowed or reversed in some North American and European countries. Within the developing world, Latin America currently has the highest proportion of city dwellers, followed by Asia and Africa. The rate of urban growth is highest in Africa, however, where cities are growing at a rate of 4.4 percent per year, and Asia, where growth is 3.7 percent per year, than elsewhere (Table 1).

Among the direct causes of the urban poor's worsening conditions are civil upheaval, deteriorating or inadequate infrastructure and the burdens on consumers that are imposed by structural adjustment programmes. Such programmes typically include export-oriented market reforms that raise basic commodity prices, currency devaluations that increase import prices and cuts in food subsidies for urban consumers. The short- and medium-term results of conditionality programmes have put an economic squeeze on the poor populations of developing countries, who frequently resort to non-market activities for survival. Additional factors contributing to this phenomenon include a decline in the real wages of urban workers, reduced stability and security in formal sector employment, the lessening of the distinction between formal and informal sectors, the narrowing income gap between rural and urban dwellers and accelerated migration from rural to urban areas.

The contribution of urban agriculture to food security (which is defined as the holding of a certain supply of food to be available and accessible at all times) appears to be substantial in many developing world cities. In addition, a significant, but unknown, share of the food purchased informally (for example, from street vendors) and in local markets is grown in developing world cities. Mougeot claims, and it has been widely repeated, that there are 200 million urban farmers in the world who supply food to 700 million people, or about 12 percent of the world's population.[4]

[3] UN. 1994. *World Urbanization Prospects, 1994.* New York.
[4] L. Mougeot. 1994. *Cities feeding people: an examination of urban agriculture in East Africa.* International Development Research Centre (IDRC). Ottowa, Canada.

TABLE 1

Percentage of the population living in urban areas (by region)			
Region	1970	1995	2025[1]
DEVELOPING	25.1	37.0	57.0
Africa	23.0	34.4	53.8
Asia (excluding Japan)	21.0	34.6	54.0
Latin America	57.4	73.7	84.7
Oceania (excluding Australia and New Zealand)	18.0	24.0	40.0
DEVELOPED	67.5	74.7	84.0
Australia and New Zealand	84.4	84.9	89.1
Europe	64.4	73.3	83.2
Japan	71.2	77.5	84.9
North America	73.8	76.1	84.8

[1] Projections.
Source: UN. World Urbanization Prospects, 1994. New York.

These numbers cannot at present be verified, but they seem to be growing, in part encouraged by an international aid effort to organize local cooperatives and provide information and inputs to urban residents.

The evidence is scattered, but surveys have shown that urban farming provides 30 percent of vegetable consumption in Kathmandu,[5] 45 percent in Hong Kong, 50 percent in Karachi[6] and 85 percent in Shanghai.[7] Overall estimates for Asia are that more than 50 percent of households farm; for North America the estimate is 25 percent.[8] On the other hand, Gutman reported that gardening for home consumption is much higher in North America than in South America.[9] The figures vary widely in African cities (from 25 to 85 percent), which are said to produce from 20 to 80 percent of their household food consumption through urban farming.[10]

---

[5] I. Wade. 1987. Community food production in cities of the developing nations. *Food and Nutrition Bulletin,* 9(2).

[6] Y. Yeung. 1988. Examples of urban agriculture in Asia. *Food and Nutrition Bulletin,* 9(2).

[7] G.W. Skinner. 1981. Vegetable supply and marketing in Chinese cities. *In* Plucknett and Beemer, eds. *Vegetable farming systems in China.* Boulder, Col., USA, Westview Press.

Conditions of urban agriculture among the poor

The poor practitioners of urban agriculture do not fit the stereotypes that might be expected. They tend to be long-term city residents, have full- or part-time jobs, both men and women are involved (depending on the city and crops) and they are not the poorest residents of the city, being marginally better-off. They have lived in the city long enough to have acquired the most important input of all – access to land. The land is rarely their own, but may be granted to them in a formal or informal lease arrangement, or even merely through an understanding with the neighbours, or it may be a public space. This means that urban farmers survive in the city until the conditions are right for them to begin farming. One survey found that migrants to Lusaka, Zambia, waited an average of ten years before investing in urban farming; other studies have found similar patterns. While these characteristics are far from universal, they recur frequently enough in studies of urban agriculture to be regarded as reliable.

The role of women appears to be a critical component in urban food production. Although it is not the case in every city surveyed, women form the bulk of producers in both Africa and Latin America.[11] These women are not employed in the formal sector and typically they add food production to their many other household functions because it is their duty to ensure the family food supply. By tending household or neighbourhood gardens they can either reduce the demands placed on their husbands' wages or supplement those wages with cash. As studies in Kampala found, women may not even let their husbands know the extent to which their gardening is relied on in the household budget.

Urban farmers generally face the growing encroachment of their city surroundings, with all the attendant costs and benefits. The most important crops of urban farmers are perishable fruits and vegetables grown in or near the city by small- or large-scale farmers for home consumption or sale in the urban market. They have a locational advantage of being close to the consumer. They are a relatively high-value crop and can be grown in tight space conditions with some capital. Even medium- to large-scale

[8] IDRC. 1995. *Agriculture technology notes.* Ottawa, Canada.

[9] P. Gutman. 1987. Urban agriculture: the potential and limitations of an urban self-reliance strategy. *Food and Nutrition Bulletin,* 9(2).

[10] See cases in Mougeot, op. cit., footnote 4, p. 45.

[11] J. Smit and A. Ratta. 1995. *Urban agriculture: neglected resource for food, jobs and sustainable cities.* UNDP Urban Agriculture Network. (Unpublished manuscript)

horticultural operations do not have the land requirements that food and feed crops or large livestock operations require, so they can adapt to growth and encroachment from the city.

For the poor, there are many types of fruits and vegetables that need little space to grow, have short growing cycles, provide nutrients not easily obtained from other food sources (thus preventing micronutrient deficiencies), generate their own seeds and shoots, require few tools for cultivation and are familiar components of the diet. The poor are able to supplement their own diets relatively easily with these products, as well as selling any surplus through informal neighbourhood markets or to street vendors. In these ways, many urban poor augment their diet and/or income with fruit and vegetable cultivation.

Livestock production is important in many cities, for traditional and economic reasons. Small livestock can be produced cheaply in restricted spaces, while all forms of livestock are increasingly important sources of protein as rising incomes lead to changing diets. The livestock raised in cities is typically poultry, birds and small animals raised by the less affluent in the dense city centres. People from all social classes in Dar es Salaam reported raising some chickens. Pork and poultry are very common in and around major Asian cities; Singapore is reported to be 100 percent self-sufficient in pork and poultry and Hong Kong produces the majority of its poultry needs within the city. Although in a less systematic and intensive manner, livestock is raised by 17 percent of households in Kenya.

Benefits of urban farming

Urban agriculture provides economic, recreational and ecological benefits to city residents. Foremost among these benefits are the obvious additions to income and household food supply. Precise figures are not known, but urban farming is estimated to provide direct earnings for 100 million people worldwide.[12] A major benefit in many poor countries is that urban farming provides actual or in-kind income through work opportunities, rather than depending on a programme of subsidies from government budgets.

Another positive aspect of urban agriculture is the income flexibility it provides. Urban farming offers city dwellers agricultural income opportunities and in-kind resources which can be produced on a part-time or seasonal basis and which are compatible with child care duties. A survey of 11 Latin American

---

[12] K. Helmore and A. Ratta. 1995. The surprising yields of urban agriculture. *In* UNDP. *Choices.* New York.

countries found that urban agriculture is not efficient enough to be economically advantageous compared with a full-time waged job, but provides partial income support. A survey made in Buenos Aires estimated that between one and one and a half working days a week are required to maintain an urban garden for an average family, saving between 10 and 30 percent of the total food bill. For low-income groups this can represent an in-kind augmentation of income of 5 to 20 percent.[13]

There are other, less visible benefits of urban farming. Shorter distances from producer to consumer mean there is less need for marketing, transportation and packaging than there is for products grown at a distance, providing a cost advantage over rural agriculture. Certain areas in some cities are unsuited for other uses because of environmental sensitivity or undesirability, but are conducive to agricultural uses. Finally, there are the extremely important, but often ignored, ecosystem benefits to hydrologic systems, biological diversity and air quality that can replace some of what the urban systems destroy.

Obstacles to urban farming

Urban agricultural producers face obstacles and hazards that are not common in rural agriculture. Foremost among these is land use. Land used for urban agriculture is more likely to be rented or borrowed than owned. It can be reclaimed at any time and at short notice. This implies a low degree of security for farmers and a disincentive to invest in their farms. Land tenure practices vary widely depending on tradition and enforcement. In some cities, land availability is not the major problem, but access to secure land of reasonable quality is the impediment for poor farmers. A survey of major developing world cities found that an average of 200 to 300 m^2 of unused community land could be made available by city authorities. Instead of established cooperative arrangements, roadsides, rights of way and other unsupervised public areas are often used. These are vulnerable to lead contamination and other pollutants, theft and uneven access for cultivation purposes.

Use of public land presents another problem. The urban bias that still exists in many developing countries extends to the desire to have a city look modern and free of traditional practices associated with the countryside. Thus, city farmers can face severe political and regulatory obstacles, including legal actions and confiscation of their products.

---

[13] **Gutman, op. cit., footnote 9, p. 47.**

Land availability is a particular constraint to the poorest urban dwellers who have recently arrived from the countryside, who do not have jobs and who lack even the meagre resources needed to piece together some farming opportunities. Researchers have found that newcomers to the city, while having some knowledge of farming in many cases, are not sufficiently established within the society to have acquired land or to have found unused land area to be farmed.[14] Non-farmers in urban areas often reply in surveys that they would farm if they had access to land.[15]

Access to other inputs can be very difficult for the poor urban farmer who generally has little or no access to raw materials or equipment and instead substitutes with great amounts of labour. Materials such as seed and fertilizer are often not affordable, chemical fertilizer may pose threats to water supplies, solid waste, which could be used as fertilizer, is not collected or is unsorted and even small implements are not available in the city. Water is often available only at high cost or through illegal means. Credit is unobtainable without secure rights to land, which usually require ownership.

Female urban farmers face the same problems as their rural counterparts – poor access to credit and landownership. Since many urban farmers are women (both heads of households and married), the stability and productivity of urban agriculture is made more tenuous by the traditional prejudices regarding women.

Agriculture in cities is often perceived as wasteful, unsightly or unhealthy. Land-use planners and government officials generally aim to segregate land uses that appear to conflict and have little or no experience in discovering ways to integrate agriculture with other activities. Indeed, agriculture can present competition to existing uses for resources and cause serious problems, such as health and environmental risks. In the most obvious example, livestock farmers face increasing nuisance conflicts the closer they are to the city. They also face losses. Intensive livestock production systems are more vulnerable to environmental degradation and health risks as the waste output from animals becomes concentrated and animal susceptibility to disease increases. As a result, after land-use rights, the largest barrier agriculture faces in cities is official acceptance and provision of essential infrastructure.

As an example of this, the United Republic of Tanzania's National Urban Water Agency expressed strong opposition to urban agriculture's use of water supplies. It estimated that

---

[14] Smit and Ratta, op. cit., footnote 11, p. 47.
[15] IDRC, op. cit., footnote 8, p. 47.

35 percent of the fresh drinking-water supply was lost through leakage and illegal tapping, so a penalty fee is imposed on agricultural uses of water in the city. Substitutes for such practices can be found, but there needs to be a mechanism for bringing authorities and urban farmers together.

Urban agriculture is, thus, not a universal solution to all the most severe problems of food security in cities. Rather, it is a survival technique for the urban poor to use during times of economic stress and to enhance existing food supplies. The addition to food supply is only partial and cannot completely substitute for food subsidies or all wage-earning activities. Some products cannot be grown by urban farmers and the poorest residents have little access to production possibilities. Urban agriculture will do little to change existing income distribution patterns.

Nonetheless, the phenomenon is contributing significantly to feeding poor residents in some cities, both through household production for own-consumption and through increased supply in informal urban sectors. In addition, urban agriculture provides nutrients that may be unavailable to urban residents or unaffordable in the case of import. Crops of fruits and vegetables, pork and poultry may be the most important contributions to urban food security gained from city farming, providing between 10 and 40 percent of the nutritional needs of urban families in developing countries.

Urban agriculture provides a means whereby poor city residents can improve their food security or living standards. Its relatively low productivity and uncertain conditions mean it will not serve well as the exclusive food supply for urban families in most instances. Several factors mean that urban agriculture can never replace or significantly reduce the role of rural agriculture as the source of food for large populations.

First of these factors is the volume of food production occurring in the cities, which is dwarfed by the quantities produced in rural areas. Even with the productivity improvements that could result from broader support, urban agriculture will never have the capacity to produce large volumes of most foodstuffs. It is already constrained and will become more so as city populations grow.

Second, urban farmers are producing for a local market, not for regional, national or global markets. If they have any competitive edge, it is in feeding nearby populations without the typical expenses of packaging, marketing, distribution and transportation.

Policy support for urban agriculture
What, then, can and should be done to improve conditions for urban agriculture? Policy intervention may be called for to assist

urban farmers in locating suitable land and other inputs and in achieving reasonable levels of productivity. There are several possibilities for international development agencies and non-governmental organizations (NGOs) to become involved in such areas as planning, technology transfer, technical assistance and advocacy and assistance in overcoming legal and regulatory obstacles.

Policy-makers must first consider which approaches are appropriate for different regions and whether urban agricultural systems used in various areas are transferable. For instance, in Asia, agriculture has an established tradition in city planning and is relatively institutionalized and commercialized. The high rates of agricultural self-sufficiency in Asian cities cannot be extrapolated to other regions as they are derived from circumstances (tradition of centralized planning, high capital input) that are not easily transferred.

The various policies appropriate to each city are determined by several characteristics: who the farmers are and what their purpose is (subsistence or market-oriented output); how permanent urban farming is; what the farmers' most urgent needs are (basic inputs, knowledge, removal of legal and institutional obstacles, advocacy support); what the relationship is between the city and rural areas; and what the economic and social role of agriculture is within the community. Other issues should be considered according to country and city circumstances. Such preparation for policy-making will take time, a basic conceptual structure for establishing the relevant considerations and further survey work in individual cities.

City planning can, however, begin immediately to accommodate, rather than forbid, the needs of urban farmers. Policies to promote urban agriculture may include encouraging the use of city-owned land for farming, providing community "pea patch" garden spaces where knowledge and resources can be shared and even diverting solid waste and wastewater to city farmers when it can serve fertilization and irrigation needs. Planning should involve collaboration among government entities; in particular, those responsible for energy, water supply, infrastructure, transportation and waste sectors.[16]

Technology transfer could make available hardy and healthy seed varieties, assist in establishing cooperatives for acquiring inputs and marketing products and provide new systems such as

---

[16] E.J. Carter. 1994. *The potential of urban forestry in developing countries: a concept paper.* Rome, FAO Forestry Department.

biological wastewater treatment processes. Among the types of technical assistance already being provided by FAO are workshops on recycling livestock waste and extension education about appropriate crops to diminish health risks and increase productivity. Even small projects that assist families in rainwater collection or provide small tools for indigenous farming methods would be useful. Finally, in dealing with the lack of land-use rights, interested agencies cannot interfere with local government prerogatives but may be able to identify and suggest models where temporary rights and multiple uses have benefited farmers and landowners alike (such as tax incentives for agricultural leasing).

Before a full understanding of the potential and importance of urban agriculture can be reached, some research gaps need to be filled. The first priority is establishing a common definition for researchers performing case-studies. This will begin to allow quantification of the magnitude and growth of urban agriculture. Analysis of the broader costs and benefits of this phenomenon should be performed, taking into account the full range of non-market effects, including the use of waste resources, and health and environmental risks (see Box 3). Finally, the costs of urban production can be compared with those of rural agriculture in order to determine what it costs society to allow or encourage the continuation of urban agriculture in an increasingly urbanized world and whether such policies would be in conflict with improving productivity and the quality of life among rural farmers.

Which characteristics of cities make urban agriculture likely to provide greater benefits than costs and which are most in need of technical assistance and support in establishing such enterprises? The characteristics of cities that are relevant include:

- large and growing poor population;
- excess labour supply and stagnant or declining wages;
- lack of existing waste infrastructure;
- poor rural-urban distribution and marketing systems;
- widespread areas of unused or underused land;
- flexible land-leasing traditions;
- extension or other community-based systems of knowledge dissemination;
- cultural tradition of household agriculture activity.

The phenomenon of urban agriculture exists in most cities. In some it is still relatively invisible and is likely to remain so as the cities expand and the urban farmers adapt to changing circumstances. In other cities urban farming will remain largely a backyard occupation. In yet another group of cities, however,

BOX 3
SUSTAINABILITY OF URBAN AGRICULTURE

Can the development of urban agriculture improve the overall quality of life for a wide array of city dwellers living in different cities? Proponents of urban agriculture claim it can. They say agriculture is one way in which cities can become more sustainable and be better places to live.

The definition of a sustainable city, like that of urban agriculture, is not clear. It is clearly intended to include ecological aspects of a city's existence, but could also take into account social and economic aspects. Elements that could be considered are: reduced dependency on inputs from outside the city; more efficient use of resource flows within the city; and reduction and reuse of waste flows whenever possible.

The following list of the direct and indirect effects of urban agriculture on a city's social, economic and environmental well-being is meant to suggest only the broad benefits and costs of urban agriculture. A more detailed list would need clearer definitions to avoid double-counting. Many of the effects listed are not directly quantifiable in monetary terms, but are real none the less.

Benefits of urban agriculture
• income to producers (market or inkind);
• employment of low-skilled or unemployed residents;
• value of produced output;
• improvement of environment (air quality, hydrology, reduced runoff);
• reduced use of and need for rural-urban infrastructure;

• costs of wastewater treatment avoided;
• costs of solid waste disposal avoided;
• import substitution;
• reduction of urban blight.

Costs of urban agriculture
• use of natural resources (land, water, soil, etc.);
• health risks (drinking-water, lead contamination, sanitation);
• ecological degradation (soil depletion, potential groundwater contamination);
• infrastructure requirements or adaptation of existing systems;
• crime generation from theft;
• social conflicts from mixed use of land.

The list could no doubt be expanded and customized to fit the conditions of each individual city. Certainly the actual benefits and costs to a city of allowing or encouraging urban agriculture depend to a great extent on the social and economic conditions facing the city's people, as well as on the mix of resources available in the city and nearby rural areas. For instance, the benefits of urban agriculture are more likely to outweigh the costs where population density and competition for land are lower. Likewise, a city with a large and growing poor population has more immediate need of using all the resources at hand for survival.

Among the more easily quantified benefits of urban agriculture are the jobs, income and products that result from it. Assuming that the people and resources used in urban farming would otherwise not be employed (often true in developing world cities), the increase in employment and productivity is a clear benefit to society. Other benefits are far more difficult to measure. Examples are the increased value from the care and attention given to otherwise vacant land that becomes an urban farm plot or the contribution to air quality of a city forest. Urban agriculture also creates negative externalities that are difficult to measure, including the smells and sights that people find distasteful when livestock are reared nearby. Externalities avoided by growing food within the city include the pollution created by trucks carrying products into the city from distant rural areas.

An important opportunity for urban agriculture is the use of unused or underused resources. While urbanization leads to competition for land, it also forces residents to respond to worsening conditions. One response is to use free land, water and makeshift tools independently of the uncertain supply lines through the formal market. While of very poor quality, some of the inputs used by poor urban farmers would otherwise be wasted or put through costly treatment processes. In fact, in some African countries, rural land is becoming more degraded while urban land with access to wastewater and fertilizer may become more productive.

Two specific examples of resource reuse for urban agriculture follow.

Livestock waste. FAO found from case-studies that long-term intensive livestock production in peri-urban areas may not be viable without dealing with the waste and attendant environmental and health problems. Care must be taken not to add nutrients in excess of the vegetative absorption capacity or problems such as volatilization (air pollution), leaching (soil and groundwater pollution), surface runoff (surface water pollution) and epidemiological contamination may result. Significant research has already been carried out into how to deal with these environmental and health problems and studies suggest that the nutritional and waste recycling opportunities of livestock rearing may argue for retaining this activity close to the city. For instance, in Dar es Salaam roughly 300 000 kg of cattle and chicken manure are produced every day and most (72 percent) is dumped at roadsides. Transporting this organic matter could be much more expensive than organizing small-scale collection, composting and reuse activities.

Wastewater treatment and irrigation. Aquaculture farms are particularly common near Asian cities and include vegetable and fish crops. Among the earliest examples of city aquaculture are the wetlands east of Calcutta where wastewater-fed treatment ponds produce 8 000 tonnes of fish a year while treating 680 million litres of wastewater per year. Fish are the primary source of protein for Calcutta's residents and it has been estimated that the sewage-fed aquaculture system could double its output from the current provision of 10 percent of the city's daily consumption.

Additional opportunities to develop aquaculture for feed purposes using wastewater treatment ponds have been under investigation by international agencies for several years. The substantial research in this area shows that wastewater is already being used in many arid and semi-arid areas of the world and that this can be done without significant health risks and with greater effectiveness than conventional treatments. Most important for the developing world, the relatively simple technology is inexpensive to construct and maintain. The land required by the ponds used in wastewater treatment (20 ha for every 100 000 persons) is the major requirement.

Researchers have found that virtually all helminths and most bacteria and viruses can be removed by ponding which produces a nutrient-rich and nuisance-free effluent. Wastewater irrigation can supply almost all the nitrogen and most of the phosphorus and potassium required by many crops, as well as important micronutrients. The pond effluent is high in algal biomass content and acts as a slow-release fertilizer. Organic matter in wastewater also contributes to soil tilth and overall long-term fertility of the soil.

The primary cost of establishing such systems is for the collection of wastewater. Many developing world cities currently have no collection systems. However, because of the high priority placed by local and international authorities on controlling disease sources, an opportunity exists to integrate wastewater collection and treatment systems with recycling opportunities, such as urban agricultural uses.

urban farming – and the people it serves – will encounter greater conflicts and obstacles as city life becomes more desperate, demands on urban resources increase and governments become less able to cope with the needs of growing populations.

INFORMATION TECHNOLOGY: WHAT IT MEANS FOR AGRICULTURE
Situation and emerging developments
In many countries, very rapid changes are now occurring in the development and application of information technology (IT).[17] The outcome of these changes will significantly reshape private business and government operations and will affect virtually all aspects of the everyday lives of individuals and businesses in every sector of the economy. Organizations in both the public and private sectors are adopting the new technology as part of a strategy to increase efficiency[18] and competitiveness of the organization or sector, provide better service, introduce new means of training and reduce operating costs. Many governments also see the new technology as a means of creating jobs, in part to offset those lost through its adoption. The rapid change is occurring because of more powerful and less expensive communications and computer hardware (the cost of processing and transmitting information is decreasing by 50 percent every 18 months) combined with an explosion in the development of new software products, the convergence of computer, telecommunications and broadcasting technologies and the phenomenal growth in the use of the Internet.

Opportunities
The new information technology improves the accessibility for clients to information and services. It also enables a better sharing

---

[17] Information technology refers to the advanced information and communications carriers of electronic data, including cable and satellite television, digital and traditional airwave radio, CD- ROMs, broadband, narrow-band and wireless (e.g. cellular) telephone and local-area (LANs) and wide-area (WANs) computer networks, including the Internet.
  Applications of information technology refer to the software and the data, text and audiovisual information provided by the technology.
[18] Increased efficiency or productivity enhancement through information technology come from an increase in availability, quality and timeliness of information combined with enhanced two-way communications that permit organizational changes throughout the business or economic activity and increase the output using the same or fewer resources.

of information among users, enhances the potential for two-way communications between providers and users, greatly expands the availability of specialized information resources and provides broader opportunities to access the global information market in a quick, inexpensive and reliable manner. The new information technology goes beyond the traditional one-way or linear communication. It permits interactive linkages among individuals with similar concerns or interests and this greatly expands the information available to individuals or organizations. Information technology allows organizations' structures to be more flexible, more participatory and less centralized.

In the agricultural sector, new IT applications are becoming increasingly commonplace. Applications include the geographical positioning system (GPS) which allows satellite information to trigger precise micro-level applications of chemicals and fertilizers. Information technology can provide education and skills upgrading such as the provision of management advice and use of on-line distance education techniques. Other applications include access to information, particularly time-sensitive information such as market news and weather. The technology provides search skills for information on research and technology about new products, inputs, markets or farming practices. It provides information about the availability of government programmes or commercial services and may be used to access those programmes or services and it is often used in sharing information through the Internet, electronic bulletin boards and mailing lists.

Beyond the farmgate, IT applications are becoming increasingly critical for the vertical coordination of the food distribution system. Just-in-time delivery, specialized production for niche markets and reduced tolerance for variability in raw material inputs all require increased communication between buyers and sellers at each stage of the production, processing, distribution and retailing processes. Information technology is a pivotal component of that increased coordination among the participants in the food chain. It allows firms to hold smaller inventories, avoid waste, provide a greater variety of products, reduce purchasing costs, assess the impact of promotions and enhance client services. To ensure that quality control standards are met throughout the food chain, some retail products, such as meats, will be traceable from the final point of sale to consumers back to the farm of origin, requiring information technology to collect and maintain the individual product transaction records.

As the global environment becomes more open and trade among countries increases, especially for high value-added products, the need for and value of information in commerce increases.

Information technology is used to market specialized products to niche markets, responding to growing diversity in consumer tastes. It is likely to replace some of the routine brokerage functions of providing basic information on product availability and prices. For example, sellers and buyers may electronically post availability and requirements of commonly traded, relatively standard products with offer and bid prices in a form of electronic auction. In this highly competitive environment, the successful firms will be those with the most innovative IT applications.

Isolation is a major difficulty in maintaining a viable and sustainable rural sector since rural communities do not attract the same level and quality of services found in urban centres. The situation could be improved with the increased ability to access and share information, in spite of the location, through the use of information technology. Remote communities would get new vitality if they could get some of the same services and easy, cheap communication methods as urban centres have. The new information technology improves the comparative advantage of rural and remote areas, as communication costs over long distances decline sharply.

Constraints

While there are many benefits attached to the new information technology, there are also several serious constraints to its increased use. These include: inadequate communications infrastructure; high prices for the purchase of computers, telecommunications equipment and related software combined with high telecommunications operating costs; a deficiency of human capital to provide the skills needed to develop, operate, manage and use the new technology; and lack of a private-sector market to provide the necessary infrastucture, develop the software and promote the applications.

Training and skills development is undoubtedly the most essential element of IT development. Skills development may be the most difficult aspect of the integration of information technology into new applications. As with any new technology, the full benefits are not achieved until the developers, operators and users have the technical skills to take full advantage of it. The rapid developments that are occurring in information technology make it clear that training must be considered a continual process for, among others, system and software developers, operator and maintenance workers and the ultimate users of the information systems. Skills upgrading may range from short courses for casual users to advanced technical training at universities for those involved in the development and maintenance of applications. In many developing countries, high-level technical training university courses are not available and managers lack experience in applications of new information technology for communication and sharing of information. New approaches to management and control are, therefore, required.

The World Bank[19] highlights the disparity among countries concerning telecommunications infrastructure. The inequality in number of telephone lines between the developed and the less developed countries has hardly changed in the past decade and this great gap in infrastructure is expected to remain into the next century. It is estimated that it will take an additional US$30 billion to prevent further deterioration. The reliability of the telecommunications equipment is also much lower in developing countries, partly because of the age of the equipment. Communication infrastructure requires large annual investments and many developing countries have underinvested for a considerable period.

With such a low level of telecommunication subscribers and the poor service environment, developing countries may need to look at a different organizational system and infrastructure for delivering information to clients than are currently found in the developed countries. For example, radio-based cellular phones have low capital costs and the pricing and competition policy in Sri Lanka provides service at one of the lowest costs in the world, but there may be too few subscribers for viable rural applications. Satellite transmission is cost-effective for broadcasting but not for two-way communication (especially in rural areas), as ground transmission is very expensive. In the remote mountainous areas of China, microwave links, instead of cable, are used to connect regions. Governments have traditionally provided the infrastructure (railways, highways, electricity, telecommunications), but budget pressures may force them simply to administer the rules and encourage the private sector in developing the infrastructure for IT applications. This situation is occurring in many developed and developing countries as telecommunications systems are either

[19] The lowest-income countries had, on average, only three telephone lines available per 1 000 residents and even the moderately developed countries had only 45 lines (1990 data). In comparison, the developed countries had 442 lines per 1 000 inhabitants. At the same time, there were five times as many faults reported for each main-line telephone in the lowest-income countries as in the highest-income countries. See World Bank. 1994. Infrastructure for development, Table 32. In World Bank, *World Development Report 1994*. Washington, DC.

privatized or begin to face competition, which tends to promote increased investments and innovation and eventually leads to lower costs across the sector.

With a competitive regulatory environment, there is considerable scope for developing countries to attract foreign investment in communication technology by lowering costs and increasing innovation. This has been the case in a number of countries such as Argentina, Chile, Hungary, Jamaica, Malaysia, Mexico and Venezuela.[20] It is important that developing countries establish an internal capability to produce new IT applications, otherwise they will be net importers of information and information software for a long time and, more significantly, much of the information and software imported may not fit the local situation. It is essential that a local software industry be developed to customize the information requirements for a local market.

There have been a number of successes and considerable new applications occurring in developing countries. It is estimated that Taiwan, Province of China, has more computers per worker than Italy although the per caput income is only half as high. China may have nearly as many telephone lines by 2000 as the United States has today. By the end of 1995, about 14 countries in Africa had permanent real-time Internet connections and, by 1996, most capitals in Africa will have such connections. The United States-based telecommunications company AT&T is proposing to run a fibre-optic cable around the entire coastline of Africa (Africa one). Work is scheduled to start in 1999 and the project will make immense improvements to access within the continent and further afield.

The agricultural sector in developing countries (and even in some developed countries) is confronted with considerable difficulties in its efforts to use the new technology. These are the results of rural areas not being well served by telecommunications infrastructure; the low number of current users, which limits the market for specialized software development; and the low educational level and limited skills of many producers, which restrict current and potential applications. The agricultural sectors in the lowest-income, developing countries experience the most severe form of these problems and, in spite of the social and technological developments that are occurring in the urban centres of developing countries, new IT applications, such as multimedia, appear to be an impossible dream in the foreseeable future throughout much of the developing world.

---

[20] World Bank. 1994. *World Development Report 1994.* p. 63. Washington, DC.

BOX 4
UNITED STATES: COOPERATIVE EXTENSION SERVICE

The United States Cooperative Extension Service was one of the early users of the Internet to provide information to its clients. By 1995, most of the state Cooperative Extension Services had established their own World Wide Web (WWW) site. These sites are a communication and marketing device for the extension service and, typically, they announce the programmes and services available, but occasionally a WWW site provides current information on markets. It is not clear how widely the Internet is used as a source of information to provide service to clients. Many existing staff are not skilled in the use of information technology as an information source and it appears that no widespread training programmes have been used.

One example of the use of the Internet is a project called "Ask an Expert" which is a software package developed by the United States Department of Agriculture (USDA) for use by the Cooperative Extension Service to allow it to communicate effectively with clients using a variety of tools such as WWW or electronic mail. As well as the communication aspect, the software provides a searchable database of frequently asked questions and expert answers that is designed to be information of first resort to which users who are trying to obtain answers to agricultural questions using the Internet can refer first.

The program involves three phases. First the question arrives at a special gateway program that enters it into a database of unanswered questions and makes it available to a group of experts. Second, one or more of the experts may choose to respond to the question, but if no one responds the system automatically assigns the question to the next available expert. Finally, the set of questions and answers may be browsed or searched by anyone with access to the Internet. This allows experts to focus on new questions rather than repeating answers frequently.

The software package was used during two farm shows in Indiana in September 1995. Extension specialists from USDA and seven states were available to provide responses to questions raised by clients at the farm shows with a time lag of about one hour. While the experiment was considered very successful, there are questions as to whether or not extension specialists would be willing to commit themselves to the effort required and how they could get credit for these activities in their own organizations.

BOX 5
CANADA: PROJECT BARLEY

The Agriculture, Food and Rural Development (AFRD) Department of the Canadian Province of Alberta established a Project Barley team to provide electronic delivery of information to 76 farmers and to farm suppliers in 13 farm districts in the province. The information for the project is on such topics as crop production and management, farm equipment and dealers, soil fertility, irrigation, harvesting and storage, marketing, market outlook, markets and costs of production. It represents a significant portion of the AFRD department's information and services. The project also provides guided access to other Internet information that is of interest and value, a discussion forum for users of the pilot and electronic mail access to both clients and project staff.

The project provides about 600 pages (4 megabytes) of information, electronically on barley production and marketing in Alberta. In addition, electronic links are identified and made to 165 other sites around the world providing access to nearly 5 000 documents.

Throughout Alberta 14 office sites (kiosks) were selected where the clients could be exposed to the Internet. Approximately 450 farmers and agribusinesses used the kiosks and at least that many more attempted to do so but could not get on-line. During a three-month period, the site had about 4 800 visits – about 2 425 were from Alberta (including from the kiosks), 575 were from staff and the rest (1 800) were from elsewhere in the world.

Over 90 percent of the pilot users continued on the Internet after the pilot although they had to start paying for the service. They saw it as a way to communicate with specialists and to make specialists more accessible to them. Users adapted quickly to the Internet as an alternative to the "office" approach to the provision of specialist services.

AFRD gained a great deal of status with both producers and staff for taking on such a new initiative. Producers (the pilot users) were very enthusiastic and supportive of the initiative, despite a great deal of technical frustration, often poor service-provider support and the fact that the pilot operated during planting time. Producers were keen to experiment with the Internet. Front-line information providers however felt that they were not prepared to launch the project. The specialists who developed the information were extremely pleased about their team effort and the rapid progress made, but were frustrated by a lack of technology support and training.

The project identified several critical factors for future success, including: providing adequate training and technology support for staff; getting department staff, especially specialists and scientists, connected to the system and using it to communicate among themselves and with producers; creating a major cultural shift in the department with respect to the technology, thus preventing people from operating in the old way with the new technology; establishing a dedicated core group of people responsible for the implementation of electronic delivery of information and services; formalizing staffing arrangements and organizational structure with respect to the project; maintaining the status and profile of the project among departmental staff so that they want to be involved and can see the benefits to themselves of being involved; keeping the content alive through discussion groups and daily contributions from specialists, while not allowing the system to become a "dump site" for data; and developing partnerships with other groups to expand the breadth and depth of the system and to increase recognition and credibility of the site.

Source: Information obtained from the Alberta Agriculture Food and Rural Development Department report on Project Barley which incorporates information from a Price Waterhouse Evaluation Report.

BOX 6

MEXICO: SUPPORT SERVICES
FOR AGRICULTURAL MARKETING

The Mexican marketing agency, Apoyos y Servicios a la Commercialización Agropecuaria (ASCERCA), uses the national television system to provide agricultural marketing information throughout the country. Users of specially manufactured television sets can find economic and commodity market information on one of ASCERCA's television channels in any location in the country. The system, called *teletexto*, is widely known among the rural residents of Mexico and a recent survey of agricultural producers showed a high level of recognition of the system (70 percent). The benefits of this approach in the application of information technology are that it uses a relatively simple existing technology, which does not require wired communication infrastructure, for clients to access. As well as agricultural information, there is other economic information provided through this service so that the cost of providing it is distributed across several sectors. There has, however, been limited use because of the requirement for the special television sets and the lack of promotion by the television manufacturers.

Policy issues

Closing the gap between the "haves" and the "have nots". Many agricultural and food sector businesses in the more developed economies are adopting new information technology and are benefiting from improved productivity. At the same time, agricultural and food sector businesses in the less developed economies without access to the required communication equipment, software or the necessary information technology skills, risk falling further behind in the technology race. With the increased globalization of markets, lack of access to productivity enhancing tools reduces their competitive position. It is critical that agricultural ministries in developing economies recognize the need to ensure universal access to new technology, at reasonable cost, as a means of narrowing the technology gap and that they initiate steps to implement a development plan for the agricultural and rural sectors.

Overcoming infrastructural constraints. One of the main constraints facing the agricultural and agrifood sectors in all countries is the lack of communication infrastructure in the rural and remote sectors of the country. Much private-sector investment is focused on the urban centres where distances are limited and the payback from infrastructural investments more likely. Low-income, less developed countries have on average only about three telephone lines per 1 000 inhabitants, whereas the developed countries have over 400. It is critical that producers in the agricultural and rural sectors of developing countries press governments to reduce communication costs as much as possible and to encourage investment in expanding and modernizing the telecommunications sector.

Developing countries may have to apply different approaches to adopting information technology than those followed in developed countries, especially in areas where there are very few telecommunication lines. For example, creating information centres that producers and agrifood industry clients can access easily may be more appropriate than structuring the technology around the use of computers in every business.

Effective training and skills development. The most important constraint in the adoption and effective use of new information technology may be the development of adequate human capital. Skills development requires a variety of approaches for different applications. Training and skills development can be a very costly process and can be wasteful if the users cannot readily apply the new skill or if the training is not suitable to the application. The use of private-sector or educational institution providers may be the most cost-effective solution.

Defining the government role. It is important that governments develop clearly defined objectives and outline their strategy for information technology for the agricultural sector. Governments can provide critical leadership and act as a role model with respect to the adoption of information technology in the sector. For example, because the government is a major user of information technology it can strongly influence national IT development and use through its purchases of hardware and software. The government can provide an example to the sector in supplying access to its own services, information and programs. It can also encourage the development and use of technology through assistance programmes and by encouraging the sharing of information on new developments.

In many countries, large budget deficits or strong competing priorities for investment funds require that decisions made be based on carefully defined government priorities. It is essential, in all cases, that the approach used be based on client-driven priorities.

Ensuring appropriate information content. The purposes of information technology are to provide information and services in a more accessible and efficient way and to improve communications. There is a critical need to ensure that the information content is client-driven and up to date and that the application provides a more effective way of delivering services. If the information content becomes dated or is insufficient to interest users, they will be discouraged from accessing that application and the experiment will fail.

Equally unsatisfactory for users is a surfeit of information, irrelevant to their needs for decision-making purposes. More focus needs to be put on the development of information technology applications to filter the flow so as to provide clients with the right information at the right time for decision-making. Information specialists may also play this role.

Developing partnerships. Governments cannot afford to be the sole organization in electronically providing information and information services to the agricultural sector. There must be partnerships among government departments and agencies, with the private sector and with university and other educational institutions. This approach can provide clients with "single-window" access, at a cheaper cost and with higher-quality information and service. Agriculture needs to graft on to the infrastructure and applications used in other sectors, such as health, as a means of accelerating developments and minimizing the costs of establishing and operating systems.

User paying. Information and information services should be viewed as a commodity for which there can be a functioning market. Such a market would allow private-sector participants to develop the infrastructure, software and new services that decision-makers and individual clients wish to have. Information and information service providers should be considered in a similar way to those providing legal, financial or accounting services. Governments may consider some form of user paying system for information and information services which would allow them to expand certain services while getting market signals on those services which users consider to be the most important.

The role of government and international organizations in promoting the use of information technology

Develop a strategy. Governments need to develop a national strategy for the use of information technology that would enhance productivity and communications in the rural, agricultural and food sectors and permit governments to provide better service to clients at lower costs. A well-defined strategy for such applications needs an explicit timetable, additional resources and a commitment to make it work. Agricultural ministries must recognize the opportunities from the new information technology and take action themselves to realize these benefits. Such action includes ensuring appropriate access to the technology at reasonable costs for the agricultural and food sectors. This may require promoting, within government, the need for regulatory reforms and competitive pricing for the benefit of the rural sector.

Promote the upgrading of skills and capital investment. Governments can play an important role in promoting and implementing programmes for the development of skills and the investment of capital in the application of the new information technology. For skills upgrading, governments may develop partnerships with educational institutions and private-sector providers. Skills upgrading needs to include a focus on young people. Governments must also encourage locally developed information technology applications, in either government or the private sector, to avoid import dependency. To promote new developments, governments can establish a clearing-house of new IT applications and illustrations of the best practices used in the sector. Governments can also promote common standards so that systems are compatible, information is easily shared and users are not confronted with a myriad of systems.

Do things differently. Governments need to take a comprehensive approach in the introduction of new information technology. More complicated solutions will be required than simply transplanting systems from a paper to an electronic environment. It will be essential to examine the whole process and understand how users adapt to the new service. Only by changing the whole process can all of the benefits of the technology be obtained, although it may be best that governments start on a small scale, such as with a pilot project to gain experience in operating the system and get effective feedback from clients. It is important that progress be displayed concretely and the use of pilots may allow a total systems development that is more effective and easily accepted by users.

Encourage private commercial services. Governments can help indirectly in the introduction of private commercial services (such as banking, insurance, legal, accounting and information) for the agricultural and rural sectors of the economy through making their own information, information services and programs available electronically to clients. Government and commercial services, when introduced in rural areas, will reinforce each other and encourage the adoption of information technology which offsets the impact of distances. They may also create additional employment in rural areas. Equally important may be for governments to ensure a suitable telecommunications environment, with such features as low rates and adequate infrastructure, to encourage commercial IT services. Adoption rates are severely affected when modems cost four times as much in India as in the United States and Internet access in Thailand costs 12 times as much.

International lenders must recognize the financial and other benefits. The financing of investments in new technology requires that international lenders recognize the payoffs from these investments. More analysis is required to demonstrate that the adoption of new information technology will have a high return to both the sector and the economy. It is important that international agencies and donor countries work together to create awareness, to develop investment and skills and to provide an introduction to improvements in information technology. There needs to be a representative for the rural sector to ensure that there is adequate and competitively priced infrastructure available to allow the rural sector to use the new information technology. It is important that there be a solid business plan established for economic applications which would ease the financing of information technology projects and programmes.

Create an awareness of the benefits. The role of international organizations such as FAO includes creating an awareness of the benefits of adopting new information technology. For example, FAO can provide a demonstration by the use of technology and by providing electronic access to its information and services, such as disseminating all data and reports electronically, video conferencing and interactive fora for providing technical information. International agencies can also help in the analysis of the benefits of information technology, especially for those areas where there is limited experience in conducting such analysis and where the use of information technology is at an early stage of development. They could also play an important role in developing an international clearing-house of electronic information sources and applications, assisting in coordination among governments and aid agencies and in skills development.

THE THREAT OF DESERTIFICATION

The term desertification[21] does not refer to the moving forward of existing deserts but to the formation, expansion or intensification of degraded patches of soil and vegetation cover, especially around densely populated rural areas and urban centres, poorly managed farms and water points. Desertification can occur under any type of climate, but the most affected areas are in the arid, semi-arid and dry subhumid regions, collectively referred to as the drylands (approximately 30 percent of the global land surface). A significant part of the dryland regions has suffered for a long time from the degradation of its human and natural resources during long periods of drought, to the point that the degradation may become irreversible. This has caused a complex set of economic, ecological and social problems, collectively referred to as desertification and very different from the functioning of established desert ecosystems.

---

[21] The term was first used by A. Aubreville in A. Aubreville. 1949. *Climats, forêts et désertification de l'Afrique tropicale.* Paris, Société d'Editions Géographiques, Maritimes et Coloniales. Generally the term does not refer to the movement of mobile sand bodies, which does occur but is estimated to be no more than 10 percent of the entire process. The southern limit of the Sahara, for example, has been expanding or contracting depending on annual variations in rainfall; longer time-series of data are necessary to determine the tendency.

BOX 7

FAO'S GLOBAL INFORMATION AND EARLY WARNING SYSTEM

An important example of the way information technology can be applied to address agricultural and food security problems is FAOs Global Information and Early Warning System (GIEWS). GIEWS is the only comprehensive international source of data and analysis of current and prospective food supply and demand situations in all countries of the world. It was established in 1975 at the request of the 1973 FAO Conference and the 1974 World Food Conference.

GIEWS' main objectives are continuously to monitor prevailing food supply and demand conditions, including production, consumption, stocks and imports and exports, based on the most up-to-date and accurate information, and to identify countries facing imminent food shortages and their emergency requirements. It provides warnings not only about food shortages but also about exceptional food surpluses. It also makes early forecasts of production, consumption, stocks, imports and exports, food aid requirements and availability, emergency needs, donor commitments and shipments. All the elements likely to affect food supply and demand are considered, including factors such as weather, animal and plant diseases and pests, range- and cropland conditions, transportation and storage problems and government policies affecting production, consumption, prices and trade in basic food, as well as ocean freight rates.

GIEWS is operated by the Global Information and Early Warning Service in the Commodities and Trade Division at FAO headquarters. The system maintains regular contact with most of FAO's technical units for information sharing and acts as a focal point for the Organization's emergency coordination activities. Since 1975 institutional links and information-sharing agreements have been forged with 110 governments, three regional organizations and over 60 non-governmental organizations (NGOs), which act as both providers and users of information. Numerous international research institutes, news services and private-sector organizations also collaborate, providing information on a voluntary basis. Donors of food assistance are the main users of GIEWS, but also fulfil an important role in the provision of information as well as support for the development of the system itself. Bilateral donors are committed to informing GIEWS of all pledges and deliveries of food aid.

Drawing on 20 years of time-series statistics, GIEWS country monitors continuously update and analyse data on food production, trade, food aid, stocks, consumption and sub-national food security. GIEWS monitors the condition of food crops in all regions and countries of the world. Information is gathered on all the factors that might influence planted area and yields. A purpose-built computer workstation facilitates a wide range of data processing ranging from interpreting satellite images to estimating food import requirements. For drought-prone areas of Africa where there is a lack of continuous and reliable information on agrometeorological and crop conditions,

GIEWS relies on monitoring and interpretation of satellite images. The cold cloud duration (CCD) estimates the likelihood that significant rainfall has fallen while the normalized difference vegetation index (NDVI) traces plant growth through an entire season to spot the occurrence of drought.

GIEWS also monitors world food markets. It estimates global food supply and demand by aggregating country-level information and monitors world market export prices and trading on the main international grain exchanges. The system reports on major events in markets and on underlying trends in the key variables, warning if there is a risk of major food price rises. Although global in scope, country monitoring is concentrated on the group of 82 particularly vulnerable, low-income food-deficit countries (LIFDCs). The main focus of the analysis is on cereals as information on other types of food is often extremely weak, but the system is expanding its coverage of non-cereal staple foods, particularly in countries where non-cereals constitute a large part of the national diet. In some of the world's most food insecure countries, where accurate food information is often lacking, GIEWS relies on rapid assessment missions.

Recently GIEWS has sharpened its focus on sub-national food security. For this purpose a computer tool, designed to interpret complex interactions of local food economies, has been developed side-by-side with the preparation of country-specific risk maps for the famine-prone regions.

Rapid and effective communications are a key component of the system and computer technology has enabled GIEWS to speed up the production and dissemination of reports. The regular publications of GIEWS are *Food Outlook, Foodcrops and Shortages, Food Situation and Crop Prospects in Sub-Saharan Africa* and the *Sahel Report*. In addition, about 30 special alerts and special reports are published annually. GIEWS publications are freely available to all institutions and individuals. The system also responds to specific information requests.

GIEWS has invested in electronic communication to broaden its audience and to speed up the information dissemination process. The system's output, including all the latest publications, is now available on FAO's main Internet web server. GIEWS information has been made available in francophone countries on a Minitel server and by electronic mail distribution through the *Réseau Intertropical d'Ordinateurs* network in Africa. The search for innovative measures continues towards strengthening the collection, processing and analysis of vital food security data.

The United Nations Conference on Environment and Development (UNCED) which was held in Rio de Janeiro, Brazil, in June 1992, negotiated the following definition: "Desertification is land degradation in arid, semi-arid and dry subhumid areas resulting from various factors, including climatic variations and human activities."[22]

The diverse processes of land degradation are not all active at the same time and place. Relationships among climate, desertification and society are locality-specific. The various stages leading to desertification are evolutionary in character and are not always visible on a local scale, i.e. to farmers and pastoralists. Their timescale is consequently rather different from that of other phenomena such as drought and, moreover, their effect is continuous. Unlike the visible effects of drought, desertification processes cannot be detected comprehensively at an early stage but entail a progressive breakdown of the fragile ecological balance that has allowed vegetation, human and animal life to evolve in the arid, semi-arid and dry subhumid regions.

The characteristic features of drylands are low and highly variable rainfall, giving rise to large fluctuations in biomass production and therefore fluctuations in the ability of the land to produce food, fodder and biofuels. Drylands ecosystems have demonstrated great resilience and will nearly always recover after dry spells – provided it has not been grossly mismanaged during the dry phase, even mismanaged land can be restored. Traditional land-use practices in drylands are often opportunistic; traditional dryland farmers try to maximize removal during good periods and minimize losses during dry periods. A complex set of production systems, often characterized by mixed cropping, livestock and agroforestry land uses, allows such practices. With the exception of irrigated agriculture, new and more productive systems for the drylands have not had significant success so far.

Much of the world's carbon is stored in the soils and vegetation of the drylands. Desertification affects exchange in the carbon cycle and carbon depletion contributes to the "greenhouse effect". The impact of human activity on rainfall patterns remains the topic of much debate, but future effects are likely to include considerable alterations in amounts and regularity of rainfall, which will have

---

[22] In 1990, a UN-hosted ad hoc consultative meeting of experts concluded that there is no point in distinguishing desertification from land degradation in the dryland regions, since to do so only confuses the whole problem. In this chapter the two terms are used interchangeably; UNCED's denotation is used as a working definition.

repercussions on all processes of land degradation. In the absence of any large increases in rainfall a predicted global increase in temperature will magnify evapotranspiration and ultimately lead to further desertification in the arid, semi-arid and dry subhumid regions of the world.

The type of soil plays an important role in vulnerability to desertification processes, especially through human (anthropogenic) activities. Like all other elements in the chain of the ecosystem, humans affect desertification processes and are also affected by them in several ways. Human practices have sometimes triggered and accelerated these processes, and/or exacerbated their impact. On the whole, the causes and consequences of land degradation are most acute among the poorest segments of the populations of developing countries, whose actions are often driven by the need to respond to emergencies through short-term survival strategies rather than by taking a longer-term view.

Extent and causes of desertification

In the arid, semi-arid and dry subhumid regions, the processes of desertification are influenced by interaction among the density of population, economic conditions and locality-specific factors. Climatic variation plays a less significant role, at least in the dry subhumid zones where land degradation is mainly the consequence of inappropriate resource management. Human-induced land degradation is by no means a recently observed phenomenon; references to the human element in desertification date back to the 1930s.[23] Land-carrying capacities decrease as desertification causes the sustained decline of the biological productivity of the land. In many countries this combination of factors constitutes a serious threat to food security. Pressure on the natural resource base and its prospective overexploitation imply that the livelihood systems (and ultimately the survival) of some human communities are at risk and that a massive loss of biological diversity is likely to occur.

On a global scale, nearly 2 billion ha of land are affected by land degradation to various degrees. Figure 6 on p. 76 indicates that, in absolute terms of surface area, the semi-arid and dry subhumid zones of Asia are most at risk, followed by the arid zones of Asia and Africa. The latter account for over 70 million ha that can be classified as strongly degraded and for the highest extent of

---

[23] See the work of E.P. Stebbing, for example, E.P. Stebbing. 1938. The man-made desert in Africa. *Journal of the Royal African Society*, 36.

extreme soil degradation (3.5 million ha). Thus, about 70 percent of the world's drylands – over 20 percent of the global land surface – is already degraded to some degree.

There are marked regional differences in the main causes of desertification in dryland areas (Figure 6). Activities directly related to agriculture represent a significant factor in land degradation in all regions except Australia, and in North America they account for no less than 52 percent of the degraded arid areas. The worst-affected areas are northern Mexico and the Great Plains of the United States and Canada. To varying degrees, farming activities also contribute to land degradation in the developing country regions in several ways. In sub-Saharan Africa, but also in other regions, increased crop production and diminishing fallow periods have often resulted in net export of soil nutrients and considerable loss of soil fertility in the longer term. During the 1980s, the accelerated development of cash crops (often prompted by the need to restore external imbalances under structural adjustment programmes), led in many cases to a reduction of fallow periods and dryland degradation and it has sometimes destroyed the structure of soils where mechanization has involved agricultural machinery that has proved to be unsustainable on fragile soils. In recent years, cutbacks in fertilizer credit and subsidies, related to the accelerated process of market liberalization, have in some cases reduced farmers' ability to improve agricultural productivity and contributed to further expansion on to marginal lands.

Overexploitation of forests, other woodland areas and trees and shrubs is another major factor of land degradation. Asia, followed by Latin America and the Caribbean, has the highest figures for land degraded by deforestation, which is the second-most significant cause of desertification, after overgrazing, in these areas (Figure 6). Clearing of woody vegetation is generally done in order to extend agricultural and pasture areas, while overexploitation results mostly from harvesting fuelwood beyond the regenerative capacity of the stands and trees, overgrazing and repeated bushfires. The tree canopy and vegetation cover are the most important source of protection from solar radiation. The albedo (the reflectivity of the earth's surface), surface temperature and levels of evaporation will change if they are completely or partially damaged or removed. Depending on the intensity of use, the specific degree of soil vulnerability and the resilience of the ecosystem (the ability to return to its former state following disturbance), such changes, in turn, can lead to land degradation.

Desertification is also caused by the overgrazing of grasses, shrubs and herbs. Figure 6 shows overgrazing to account for 678.7 million ha, over one-third of the total of degraded drylands.

Figure 6

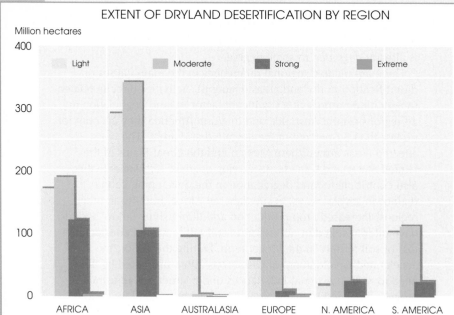

EXTENT OF DRYLAND DESERTIFICATION BY REGION

Million hectares

Light   Moderate   Strong   Extreme

AFRICA   ASIA   AUSTRALASIA   EUROPE   N. AMERICA   S. AMERICA

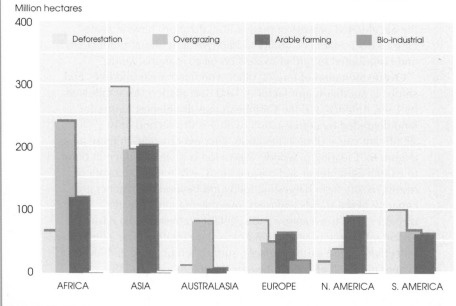

MAIN CAUSES OF DRYLAND SOIL DEGRADATION BY REGION

Million hectares

Deforestation   Overgrazing   Arable farming   Bio-industrial

AFRICA   ASIA   AUSTRALASIA   EUROPE   N. AMERICA   S. AMERICA

Source: FAO/UNEP

Especially in eastern Africa and the Sahel the high rate of overstocking of cattle, which has led to severe land degradation, is partly caused by tree felling in rangelands (leading to a lower fodder content) and a lack of herd management when improved veterinary care has led to lower mortality.

Underlying the above causes of land degradation have been the general process of demographic expansion confronting finite land resources, combined with technical and institutional issues relating to land use and ownership. Population pressure has led to the overexploitation of wood resources and the fuelwood crisis of rural sub-Saharan Africa. Pressure on the local resource base implies that some traditional agricultural practices, such as shifting cultivation, progressively lose viability in certain parts of the world. Nomad sedentarization and transmigration plans proposed by countries with a highly unequal population distribution have not always paid sufficient attention to these factors. Migration (especially seasonal and annual migration) can contribute to the unsustainable harvesting of trees, which need longer periods of time for regeneration, a natural process that becomes seriously impaired if migrant settlers lack the necessary experience and environmental information on their new surroundings. The problem has been exacerbated over the last decade by increasing numbers of environmental and political refugees. Land-leasing systems can also influence the processes of land degradation, if farmers who lease or rent land are forced to exploit it to the maximum during their contractual term. Farmers may be not very interested in long-term investments on such lands, and landowners may be absent most of the time.

Annual rainfall and rainfall-to-evaporation ratios are the most important microclimatic variables affecting the lowering of the water-table, which is associated with intensive agricultural, urban and bio-industrial land use. Soil texture, hydrology and physiographic relief play a crucial role in wind and water erosion. Water erosion affects nearly half of the total degraded land area in the arid regions. In Africa it has caused severe degradation of over 50 million ha of drylands; it is also important in southern Asia. The salinization, sodication and alkalinization of soils are problems that may be aggravated by badly managed or ill-conceived irrigation schemes. FAO studies have found that more than 35 percent of African soils north of the equator are affected by either salinization or erosion. Irrigated farmland deterioration is sometimes caused by waterlogging (the rising of the water-table), mainly as a result of inefficient drainage and/or excessive irrigation.

Increased population pressures and excessive human expansion into drylands during long wet periods increasingly leave people stranded during dry periods. The removal of critical production elements for alternative uses (e.g. dry-season grazing lands) through introduction of irrigated and non-irrigated crops and the industrial and urban uses of water at the expense of rural agricultural producers break links in traditional production chains – where these are not compensated they lead to a breakdown in the whole production system. At the same time, the loss of social cohesion (e.g. community and tribal authority) and collective practices (such as transhumance and nomadism) has aggravated the vulnerability of dryland populations to climatic variations.

Policies to prevent and combat desertification

The fight against desertification is political, social and technological. As laid out by the International Convention to Combat Desertification, policy implications vary according to specific geographical and agroclimatic settings. In many circumstances, however, an effective way of reducing pressure on land is to support income diversification in rural areas. Non-farm income can "buy time" for farm households to try out and learn new activities, allow perennials (which help soil rehabilitation) to reach full maturity and reduce pressure to extend agriculture on to marginal lands by providing cash for food purchases. Thus, it facilitates land-use intensification by encouraging the adoption of new technology, which becomes a less risky investment even in unstable agroclimatic settings.

Intensification of agriculture will remain a necessary strategy since, unless investment in productive resources can be realized, growing population densities will in the long term lead to impoverished soils and a low level of equilibrium. Income diversification would take pressure off currently overgrazed pastures; notably in areas where there is a strong tendency to provide "self-insurance" by building up livestock against drought and cropping shortfalls. In many areas where there is a relatively low potential for agricultural development, however, livestock husbandry is a comparative advantage and should be encouraged as a complement to cropping, in terms of both income and production, as long as soils are not too fragile.

Diversification of non-farm sources of income should be accompanied by measures to diversify agricultural activities and value added to the greatest possible extent. Where possible, fisheries and aquaculture should be promoted and developed. Apiculture and non-timber forest product processing should be considered in zones with sufficient marketing infrastructure and development potential. Innovative technologies may have important additional effects if, by reducing the time and energy

BOX 8
THE CONVENTION TO COMBAT DESERTIFICATION

The international Convention to Combat Desertification was drafted by the Intergovernmental Negotiating Committee on Desertification (INCD) at the urgent request of the African representation at UNCED. It was adopted in June 1994 and by the end of January 1996 it had been signed by 115 countries, 25 of which have already ratified it. The June 1994 INCD session marked the establishment of two working groups and the plenary. These met again in August 1995 and started preparations for the first Conference of the Parties (scheduled for late 1997). It is expected that by September 1996 multilateral funding mechanisms should be resolved and the Convention be ratified in most signatory countries. The Convention recognizes in particular:

• an integrated approach to the issue;
• the combination of local and modern technologies;
• the participation of local target communities in the development of national action programmes.

The challenge for the interim phase of the Convention has been to implement the resolution on urgent action for Africa, without at the same time neglecting action in other affected countries.

Mali was among the countries that reacted most quickly and implemented a national component of the urgent action for Africa at the ratification of the Convention to Combat Desertification. In October 1994, the Government of Mali merged the planning processes for the establishment of a National Environmental Action Plan and the drafting of the National Action Plan to Combat Desertification; established an institutional body regarding environment and desertification that includes an interministerial committee at the political level, a Consultative Committee to monitor progress technically and focus technical work and a Permanent Secretariat to coordinate the formulation of the National Action Programme on Environment and Desertification; and approached the Government of Germany and FAO to assist in the preparation of the programme.

Through the assistance of the latter, the contribution of the United Nations Development Programme (UNDP) and the involvement of national expertise, the Malian action plan was put into practice in January 1995. It included a first phase of information and awareness building on environmental issues (especially natural resource degradation), keeping track of many factors through the organization of a dialogue process involving the local population and a reporting mechanism of national consultants. This two-way mechanism of information gathering and awareness building culminated with the organization of a National Forum on the National Action Programme in February/March 1996. The Forum discusses and makes specific proposals on major problems of, and elements for action on, the conservation and rehabilitation of natural resources; the problems caused by urbanization, industrial development and pollution; the institutional problems and need to engage in sustainable environmental protection and desertification control; and the planning process within the framework of the Convention, particularly regarding the nature of national participation, democratization, decentralization, development at the local level and the total engagement of national human resources at all levels.

With support from the German Agency for Technical Cooperation (GTZ), FAO, UNDP and other donors, Mali has been engaged in the second phase of its programming exercise since March 1996.

This is expected to include an integrated national programme including strategic approach, objectives and content of national initiatives, a detailed set of specific national programmes and a number of local area development programmes that will help implementation at the decentralized (village) level, led by local forces and institutions. The programme will include necessary legal measures, regulations and funding arrangements, particularly those geared to mobilizing local resources and to detecting adequate funding mechanisms at the local level.

required for food production and other daily tasks, they enable the increasing participation of rural households in measures of environmental conservation.

Combating desertification requires close interaction among the various public and private agents involved in land use and management. Collaborative institutional and administrative approaches require decentralized decision-making and should provide for extensive feedback mechanisms. More authority needs to be delegated to members of rural communities, particularly women, who are left out of these procedures in most of the affected areas (except in regions with a history of high male emigration). Local commitment is favoured by improved social conditions, which are in turn influenced by a positive national and international policy environment. At the community level, people should be able and encouraged to participate in programme preparation, implementation and monitoring. Land-management strategies should be based on the formation of resource-user community groups, such as water user groups or irrigation rotation systems, as already happens in South Asia. At the same time, agricultural researchers should find ways of articulating rural people's knowledge systems with their own investigations. Problems can thus be identified, discussed and prioritized, and this should lead ultimately to locality-specific policy strategies and measures.

The green revolution has made fundamental contributions to global food security, but some "second-generation" problems linked to intensive farming technology need to be addressed. A variety of technical propositions, not necessarily costly or sophisticated, can be envisaged to this end. Integrated agrarian systems can be developed through the introduction of wood crops that allow the application of agroforestry practices. Fencing and relay grazing systems allow for ecologically sound cattle-range management. Special revegetation and cultivating equipment can rehabilitate the soil and crops can be planted without triggering desertification processes; polycultures rather than monocultures are more effective for this type of soil treatment. Where the revegetation of degraded land is feasible, adequate equipment should be used to plant trees, shrubs and grass strips for sustainable soil conservation and watershed management. This does not need to be capital-intensive. Barriers of vegetation strips sometimes provide better solutions to the problems of desertification than high-technology engineering projects. Bunds, terraces, culverts and windbreaks contribute to sustainable land improvements, particularly for households that lack access to credit, especially for conservation-related activities.

The legal aspects of land use should be examined, since behaviour tends to vary according to access to and rights on land. Communities that feel more secure welcome longer-term planning incentives and, to promote integrated natural resource management, guaranteed medium-term use of land is desirable. Although land legislation is a notoriously complex issue in many countries, in many cases the importance of land preservation alone would justify priority attention from national authorities.

An integrated programme for dryland development and to fight desertification including the above action elements requires substantial financial resources. However, the magnitude of the economic, social and environmental costs of desertification defies quantification. Leaving aside non-economic factors, the long-term economic loss involved in land degradation (in terms of income foregone per year) has been calculated at US$250 per hectare of irrigated land, $38 per hectare of rainfed cropland and $7 per hectare of rangeland; the total annual loss thus amounts to $42.3 billion.[24] The maintenance of soil quality is of paramount importance, not only because of the direct implications in respect to land productivity, but also because if soils become degraded, so will the dryland ecosytems and, even where fertility loss is not irreversible, soils can sometimes be rehabilitated only at a very high cost. The costs of not protecting soils must also be taken into account. For a society to accept the costs involved in desertification prevention and control it must be fully aware of what is at stake. Such awareness must be raised both among the directly affected population, for whom the enabling conditions for active participation need to be created, and among the development aid community. Steps in this direction have included the publication of a number of easily readable guides to the International Convention to Combat Desertification.

Mention should also be made of the many UN projects and activities dealing with the subject, particularly the studies undertaken by FAO in collaboration with the United Nations Fund for Population Activities (UNFPA) and the International Institute of Applied Systems Analysis (IIASA), on estimating potential population-carrying capacities of lands in developing countries.

---

[24] At 1990 prices, see H. Dregne, M. Kassas and B. Rozanov. 1991. A new assessment of the world status of desertification. *Desertification Control Bulletin*, 20: 6-18; UNCED (1992) estimated the cost of a worldwide programme from 1993 to 2000 at a total of US$8 730 million per year (excluding the national development programmes, of which it should really form a part).

Determining critical thresholds of population density and reducing the risks of, and vulnerability to, climatic hazards and other disasters are necessary to ensure future food security. Changes in soil quality over time are difficult to monitor and this restricts the ability of researchers to analyse the negative environmental externalities of technologies and policies. Agricultural research institutes should develop a set of soil quality indicators, ensuring international uniformity and financial sustainability of the data collection methodology. Remote sensing data should be made available through databases such as FAO's GIEWS. Some countries (e.g. Ethiopia) have a national early warning system for drought and famine.

Finally, given the often very high cost of rehabilitating already degraded land, policy-makers should emphasize measures and regulations that prevent such degradation to occur in the first place.

SUPPORT SERVICES POLICY FOR AGRICULTURAL DEVELOPMENT
Agricultural support services in development
Farms that produce for the market need three types of support services:

- backward linkages that support on-farm production;
- forward linkages that support the producer to consumer transformation of agricultural output;
- downward linkages that support the farm as a business unit.

Backward linkages include input services such as aerial sowing of pasture seeds, land clearance, lime and fertilizer spreading, spray management and technical information. The forward linkages include output services such as grading and packing of produce, cool storage, transport and marketing information. Examples of downward linkages are accounting and legal services, farm business management advice and planning and training.

As the agricultural system becomes more developed, the support services it requres become increasingly varied in their scope and specialized in their nature. Highly productive agriculture depends on the availability of a wide range of specialized support services, many of which may be bought in under contract rather than provided by the farm itself. This is especially true where the technology used by the service is subject to economies of size of operation – aerial sowing and spraying are obvious examples – or relies on sophisticated information and skills, such as tax planning and compliance with legislation. Such specialized services are increasingly provided by the private sector, with government services assuming less and less importance or even being totally absent. In fact, the sorts of agricultural support services that are associated with more developed agriculture are characterized by an ever-greater requirement for specialized information. "Information is data endowed with relevance and purpose. Converting data into information thus requires knowledge. And knowledge, by definition, is specialized".[25] Information of a general nature becomes decreasingly important as farming becomes a more highly developed business. Relevant and useful information is farm-specific and, in the face of ever-increasing quantities of raw and semi-processed data, farmers are willing to pay to have these data converted into information that can be used to improve the running of their farm business.

At low levels of development, few support services are available and those that are tend to be far less specialized and more likely to be provided by the public sector. The information component, however, may be of more general application, but it remains just as important. For example, fertilizer and pesticide sales need to be accompanied by impartial information about the profitable and safe use of the product – safe for the user and safe for the environment and the consumer. The adoption of more productive agricultural technologies that improve agricultural profitability and reduce food prices is a key element in economic growth. Yet agricultural development is constrained by the lack and poor quality of service provision, while good-quality, reliable, private-sector support services cannot easily develop where agriculture is of low productivity and profitability. Thus agricultural development and the development of the rural economy as a whole are both hindered. Research, extension and training in support services are therefore needed. Accurate and timely information about input availability and prices and output marketing opportunities and prices is critical for the development and smooth functioning of competitive markets and the commercialization of smallholder agriculture.

An FAO study of the organization and management of agricultural services for small-scale farmers in Asia found that: "...a considerable proportion of agricultural holdings are operated by small farmers, who are dependent, to a great extent, on the state policies and state support services.... The support service system and input delivery mechanism are managed and administered by various government departments, statutory bodies, boards and corporations as well as NGOs."[26] The major conclusions of the

---

[25] P.F. Drucker. 1990. *The new realities.* London, Mandarin.

study were that inadequacies in service provision, such as input supply and produce buying, were the major constraints to increased production. A similar situation is found in much of sub-Saharan Africa where, despite structural adjustment programmes that have given some prominence to the private-sector provision of farm services, there have been many cases of late delivery of fertilizer, loans promised but never disbursed, key tractor parts that are unavailable, delays in payment for produce procured and many other similar problems.

There are compelling causes for concern about government delivery of agricultural support services.[27] First, public employees often have little incentive to deliver services effectively and efficiently, especially as regards timeliness. Second, incentives to further private interests are often strong, leading to favouritism and, at worst, corruption. Third, the public provision of services that could be provided by the private sector can stifle private-sector development. Finally, public-service provision has an inherent tendency to be ineffective because it is supply- and not demand-driven. Even where the first three problems are not encountered, the last may be, as has happened in several cases of the introduction of charges for services. For example, during the process of commercializing the United Kingdom's Agricultural Development and Advisory Service (ADAS): "at the outset of charging, ADAS made the classic marketing mistake of developing products and then attempting to sell them, rather than first finding out the needs of the market and then developing products to fulfil these needs".[28] It should, however, also be noted that some public-sector entities are delivering services in a highly satisfactory manner; Roberts[29] cites the Bank of Agriculture and Agricultural Cooperatives in Thailand as one such example.

The issue of government delivery of agricultural support services concerns policy implementation, and what the government's role is in implementing its own policies.

[26] A. Salehuddin and R. Shafiqur. 1991. *Organization and management of agricultural services for small farmers in Asia.* Rome, FAO and Dhaka, Centre on Integrated Rural Development for Asia and the Pacific (CIRDAP).
[27] R.A.J. Roberts. 1995. *Agricultural services: their role in development.* Paper presented at the Agricultural Economics Society Conference, University of Cambridge, United Kingdom, March 1995.
[28] R.J. Dancey. 1993. The evolution of agricultural extension in England and Wales. *Journal of Agricultural Economics*, 44(3), 375-393.
[29] Roberts, op. cit., footnote 27.

The development of agricultural support services

Public versus private-sector delivery of support services. The economic case for continuing government provision of agricultural support services that could be provided by the private sector (e.g. fertilizer delivery, output marketing and credit) is based on the fact that in many liberalizing economies the private sector remains underdeveloped in key areas. Governments are, therefore, sometimes reluctant to withdraw the public sector from involvement in activities of an essentially commercial nature, even where its involvement has been singularly ineffective. Both policy and commercial risks affect the private sector's willingness to enter the arena, which probably explains why the private sector is far more active in output marketing than in fertilizer supply in a number of African countries. The problem is exacerbated by a high proportion of low productivity, semi-subsistence farmers, low population densities and poor infrastructure.

One approach taken in Andhra Pradesh, India, was to establish planned rural service centres with a mixture of public and private provision, initially to increase agricultural productivity and then to expand their services to meet the demands for consumer goods that resulted from increased incomes. An investigation of one such centre [30] showed that over time the private sector expanded to provide services in the areas of health, transport and distribution of fertilizers, pesticides and agricultural machinery that competed with those provided by government agencies. This type of approach may be helpful in creating the demand for services that can eventually be supplied by the private sector. Great care must be taken, however, to ensure that the government has no monopoly of supply or hidden subsidies in any of its relevant commercial operations, otherwise the private sector will not be able to compete.

Where there is no private-sector involvement or interest, another approach may be to set up a private-sector operation on a project basis, i.e. with funding assistance for the first few years until the market is sufficiently developed for the assistance to cease. There are obvious dangers here, the main one being that such an operation could become yet another inefficient state-run monopoly, and so the project phase has to be very carefully designed to ensure the application of commercial principles and practices from the outset. One notable case where such an approach succeeded is

---

[30] S. Wanmali. 1993. *Service provision and rural development in India: a study of Miryalguda Taluka.* International Food Policy Research Institute (IFPRI) Research Report No. 37. Washington, DC, IFPRI.

the Grameen Bank in Bangladesh.[31] In this regard, a point for consideration by governments where the private-sector institutions are very weak or non-existent is whether, in the face of increasing budgetary constraints, the limited funds should be used to support agriculture directly or to support the overall development of the rural economy, which would also benefit farmers. Investment in rural institutions as "soft" infrastructure may be as important as investment in "hard" infrastructure, such as rural roads.

The case for government provision of certain other types of support service, most notably extension but also research and training, rests on a number of beliefs: that the social benefits of those services outweigh the private benefits and so private provision will be lower than is socially optimal; that information in the public domain is a public good, with the characteristics of non-rivalry in consumption and non-excludability in provision, such that its costs of provision cannot be recouped and, therefore, the private sector cannot supply it at all (this issue is addressed in more detail below); that to have certain types of information in the public domain is in the public good; and that it is in some sense wrong to expect farmers, even rich ones but especially poor ones, to pay for something of such basic importance for agricultural development and national food security.

Whatever the validity of these beliefs, a distinction needs to be made between who pays for the provision of the service and who delivers it; thus, although there may be a strong economic justification for saying that some services will be underprovided or not provided at all by the private sector, this is quite different from saying that such services cannot be provided at least in part through the private sector. The distinction is becoming much more obvious as the traditional role of government departments as both policy advisers and policy implementers is being questioned. In many countries, attempts have been, and are being, made to overcome the perceived problems of public-sector service provision by instituting markets and market disciplines for the provision of government-produced goods and services or by taking

---

[31] **The bank originated as an action-research project in 1976 to provide credit to the rural poor. It is now a financial institution established by government order, with an excellent loan recovery rate and a clear focus on the poorest groups in society. An explanation of its special approach and philosophy is given in M. Hossain. 1988.** *Credit for alleviation of rural poverty: the Grameen Bank in Bangladesh.* **IFPRI Research Report No. 65. IFPRI and the Bangladesh Institute of Development Studies; P.S. Jain. 1996. Managing credit for the rural poor: lessons from the Grameen Bank.** *World Development,* **24(1): 79-89.**

the public sector out of services provision altogether.[32] In the United Kingdom, for example, the delivery of agricultural advisory services has been fully commercialized and the old Agricultural Training Board privatized; in New Zealand, the agricultural ministry's science functions have been transferred to nine new crown research institutes and the extension service has been sold off to a private-sector company; China has created agricultural technical services companies and introduced an agricultural technology responsibility scheme that links the remuneration of extension staff to the effectiveness of the extension services they provide;[33] Chile discontinued government extension provision to medium- and large-scale farmers and introduced two new services subcontracted to the private sector for different parts of the smallholder sector, with some cost-sharing between government and farmers;[34] in Mexico, extension services are subcontracted to private consultants by the government and the proportion paid by farmers is related to their ability to pay;[35] in some countries, government extension agents augment their low salaries by selling their skills to even the poorest farmers (e.g. in Sierra Leone), by entering into sharecropping arrangements (e.g. in Ecuador) or by acting as sales staff or demonstrators for private input supply companies (e.g. in Southeast Asia);[36] and partial cost recovery through fees for service is increasingly widespread. Assessing the extent to which these initiatives have been successful depends critically on the performance standard chosen and what success criteria are used in the assessment. For example, in many cases budgetary costs may have been reduced, but so has the size of the target group. It would be useful to evaluate the changed policy delivery system in terms of effectiveness, efficiency, equity and enforceability against the stated objectives of the policy.[37]

The first policy decision that a government needs to make concerns the funding and coverage of public provision of

[32] F. Sandiford and G.E. Rossmiller. 1996. *Many a slip: studying policy delivery systems.* Paper presented at the Agricultural Economics Society Conference, University of Newcastle-upon-Tyne, United Kingdom, 27 to 30 March 1996.
[33] D.L. Umali and L. Schwartz. 1994. *Public and private agricultural extension: beyond traditional frontiers.* World Bank Discussion Paper No. 236. Washington, DC, World Bank.
[34] Ibid.
[35] Ibid.
[36] Ibid.
[37] A framework for such a performance evaluation of policy delivery systems is given in Sandiford and Rossmiller, op. cit., footnote 32.

agricultural support services. What are the policy objectives of the support service provision? What agricultural support services does the government want to fund? Does it want to fund them in their entirety, recover some part of the overall cost or charge in full for specific services? Does it want to discriminate between different income levels of farmers in terms of coverage and charging? Does government funding have to be channelled to the service provider directly or can farmers be issued with, for example, an "extension stamp" that enables them to purchase extension services up to a predetermined value from whomsoever they choose? An important point to consider in any discussion about charging is whether the Treasury is willing to allow the Ministry of Agriculture to develop separate cost centres with self-accounting status; if not, any revenues generated from cost recovery of service provision will go to the general revenue fund rather than to the Ministry of Agriculture, which will therefore have no incentive to embark on such a scheme.

The second policy decision concerns how the service in question should be delivered. Should it be delivered by a government department, a university or research institute, an autonomous government agency, private-sector agents, international agencies, NGOs or a combination of different bodies? Should a different pattern of provision be used over the life of the strategy? How can the private sector be enabled to develop the skills and capacity to take over the provision of certain specified services, thus freeing public-sector resources? How should the relevant government departments be staffed and organized so as to provide support services effectively, efficiently and when needed? What are the advantages and disadvantages of the alternative service providers? What are the requirements that need to be met in the overall policy environment for successful policy implementation?

The issue of service provision is not simply a matter of public versus private sector, but rather of assigning appropriate roles to each in the given circumstances.

Information: some special problems. One aspect of agricultural support service provision that seems to pose particular problems is that of information. The case has often been made that, in economists' parlance, information is a public good – economists define a pure public good as one that is "non-rival in consumption", which means that one person's consumption does not reduce the amount available to everybody else, and "non-excludability in provision", which means that nobody can be denied access to the good once it has been provided. Examples of pure public goods are clean air and defence. The characteristics of a pure public good are such that the quantity of it provided by the market will be less than is socially optimal because its non-excludability precludes the possibility of recouping the full costs of provision. Information is clearly non-rival in consumption, but it is not necessarily non-excludable in provision. Certainly as the information embodied in an agricultural support service becomes more time- and location-specific, it also becomes a private good that the private sector is willing to supply, as the increasing sophistication of agricultural support services demonstrates. Developments in information technology have, in some cases, made it easier to exclude non-payers from receiving information (e.g. cable and satellite television), but in other cases they have made widespread dissemination cheaper and easier (e.g. Internet).

The problem for governments is, therefore, not so much one of information as a public good, but one of ensuring that information considered to be in the public good is actually in the public domain. This has implications on the way in which research is carried out as an agricultural support service. Research has a vital role in agricultural development and long-term food security, which is why governments need to have a long-term policy and strategy for the funding and provision of agriculture-related research. If governments wish to ensure that the results of research are and remain in the public domain, they should consider very carefully how any privatization or commercialization of research institutes and activities is carried out.

The quality of research work depends in part on the independence of the researchers in terms of their scientific methodology and judgements. Independence is also required to ensure the reliability of the data on which research results depend. It can be argued that the preservation of the independence of the data collecting organization is particularly necessary with regard to financial data, such as farm accountancy data. There should therefore be no interference in these strictly scientific areas from the government, governmental organizations or any other party with an interest (including commercial) in the results. For example, individual politicians may be tempted to influence the reporting of scientific research so that the findings support their own particular policy lines, but governments need to ensure that society's needs and priorities are reflected in any state-supported research programme.

This does not imply that agricultural research institutes should be fully dependent on the Ministry of Agriculture for financing and programming their research. Nor that there is no role for the private sector and other institutions. The government does, however, have to ensure that the research necessary for underpinning policy preparation, implementation and evaluation can be and is carried out, and that research-generated information that is in the public good reaches those who can benefit from it. Alternatives to the full government funding of research institutes could include guaranteeing the core funding necessary to ensure the continued existence of a particular institute, together with an annual lump sum for the provision of ad hoc policy advice and for carrying out regular work such as the preparation of annual reports. Short-term projects and longer-term research projects could then be implemented on a contract basis, for which the government could, in some cases, seek cofinancing. The resources of the research institutes can be complemented by those of other institutions, such as the universities, and the International Service for National Agricultural Research (ISNAR) is working on a project to strengthen the role of universities in national agricultural research systems.[38] The international research insitutions of the Consultative Group on International Agricultural Research (CGIAR) network also have a role. Private-sector organizations may also be suitable for carrying out certain types of research.

The information transfer is not a one-way process. Information needs to flow back from farmers to and through such service providers as agricultural advisory and extension agents and thence to researchers if the suppliers of the services are to be in a position to tailor their products to what is wanted and needed. The government also needs information so that support service policy decisions – and agricultural policy-making is or should be a dynamic process – are based on a good understanding of what is happening at the farm level. Whatever combination of public- and private-sector bodies is chosen for policy implementation, these information flows need to be safeguarded.

Ideally, governments should think in terms of a well-defined, long-term policy for the whole agricultural information system, to be realized through a medium-term strategy for the provision of all related agricultural support services including basic and adaptive research; advisory services – technical (agricultural and environmental), economic (prices and marketing) and farm business management; and agricultural and related training and education, including training to facilitate the private-sector provision of support services.

---

[38] ISNAR. 1995. *A framework to strengthen the role of universities in national agricultural research systems.* ISNAR Briefing Paper No. 24. The Hague, ISNAR.

Sequencing changes in agricultural support service delivery. In addition to the question of what are the appropriate roles of the public and private sectors in a given set of circumstances, there is the question about how to handle major changes in those roles. The sequencing of changes as the public sector withdraws from service provision or commercializes its own service provision is now recognized to be of great importance and needs to be supported by the actions of donor agencies and NGOs. For example, it is not helpful to the development of private-sector fertilizer suppliers if donors deliver fertilizer as aid to government marketing agencies who then supply it to farmers at less than the economic cost.

Although the sequencing issue has been particularly emphasized in the context of countries undergoing structural adjustment programmes, it is of just as much relevance in countries in transition from centrally planned to market economies. This transition process involves changes in the way in which support services are provided. For instance, large state or collective farms were able to employ technical specialists to give animal and crop husbandry advice, while small family farms cannot. Once the structural transformation of agriculture has been accomplished, the next stage in the sequence of reforms is the provision of technical advice to the new small-scale farmers. Transition may also require the provision of entirely new services to facilitate the development of markets, for example, farm business management advice and the establishment of market price and location information. In these cases, there is no pre-existing demand because the services were not previously needed, and the new support services can be introduced only after key markets have been liberalized. In sequencing policy reforms for the agricultural sector, both types of agricultural support service need to be planned for and their provision organized.

A good example of sequencing policy reforms is the establishment of a market information system in Albania. As a result of tight fiscal policies, the government had to withdraw rapidly from the public domain, particularly the agricultural sector, at a time when the market economy was still very underdeveloped. However, agriculture had been privatized and agricultural marketing liberalized so it was possible to sequence policy measures that would support market development at little cost to the government:

> What was absent in Albania was a public reporting service of
> agricultural retail prices from the markets in the country. This was the
> reason for establishing a market reporting service primarily aimed at
> the agricultural industry, particularly farmers, enabling the market

participants to make decisions concerning the production, distribution and marketing of produce.... Other functions that the market information service can facilitate are:

- price signals signifying profit opportunities that in turn indicate production incentives for farmers;
- information can improve the bargaining position of weaker participants in the marketing system who are usually the smaller farmers;
- information reduces supply and demand imbalances by shifting production to meet market requirements; and
- market information can facilitate more effective policy formulation as a result of greater awareness of price trends.[39]

Data collection and dissemination are carried out on a timely basis and the whole system has been geared to the needs of the users. The response has been good and new users with specialized needs are starting to approach the marketing office of the Ministry of Agriculture and Food. There is an increasing awareness in the agricultural sector of how to use market price information, which is the foundation of an agricultural market economy.[40]

Sequencing of policy changes is also of relevance in the developed economies. Reference has already been made to the commercialization of advisory services in the United Kingdom. This was a carefully planned and phased process that took place over a ten-year period, with repeated reassessments of how the process was progressing. Some of the lessons learned in the early days of charging have a much wider applicability as more countries attempt some degree of service charging. Initially, cost targets were introduced in the form of revenue targets:

Faced with revenue targets alone, there was an initial tendency for staff to go after, and to take on, any job, however small. This meant that the Service quickly built up a large customer base each paying small amounts for work which was costly to service. At the same time, because of the long tradition of extension work, and the desire to be of service to the farmer or grower, insufficient attention was given to matching the time spent on delivering the service to the fee negotiated.

[39] C. Grace. 1996. *The Establishment of the Albanian market information service.* Paper prepared for the Network for Agricultural Policy Research and Development Meeting, sponsored by FAO, Bucharest, 25 to 28 April 1996.
[40] An interesting approach to the provision of market information to illiterate or semi-literate farmers in countries where there is high inflation or as part of the sequence of policy reforms for structural adjustment programmes is based on the Braudel measure of small-scale entrepreneur purchasing power. A summary is given in the *World Bank Social Dimensions of Adjustment Newsletter,* 1(2), Summer 1991.

This led to considerable over-delivery of services. [Because of the revenue targets] too little attention was given to the costing of individual jobs. Nor, indeed, were the systems in place to allow such costings to be made.... The change to targets couched in terms of cost recovery rather than revenue alone was significant. It resulted in a major rethink of the way in which ADAS planned its operations; costs came under closer scrutiny and the service became much more discerning about the type of work undertaken.[41]

Conclusions

In the final analysis, each country needs to plan for (rather than to plan as such) the provision of the agricultural support services needed for agricultural development. To do this adequately it needs information about: what services are already being provided and whether they provide what farmers need rather than what the providers want to supply; the capabilities of the public and private sectors to deliver services effectively, efficiently and equitably; the willingness and ability of farmers to pay for different types of services; and the essential services the provision of which the state must ensure in its long-term interests. Obtaining this amount of information (some of which must be culled from an analysis of masses of raw data) is a resource-intensive procedure and one for which the international agencies might be well placed to assist.

---

[41] Dancey, op. cit., footnote 28, p. 85.

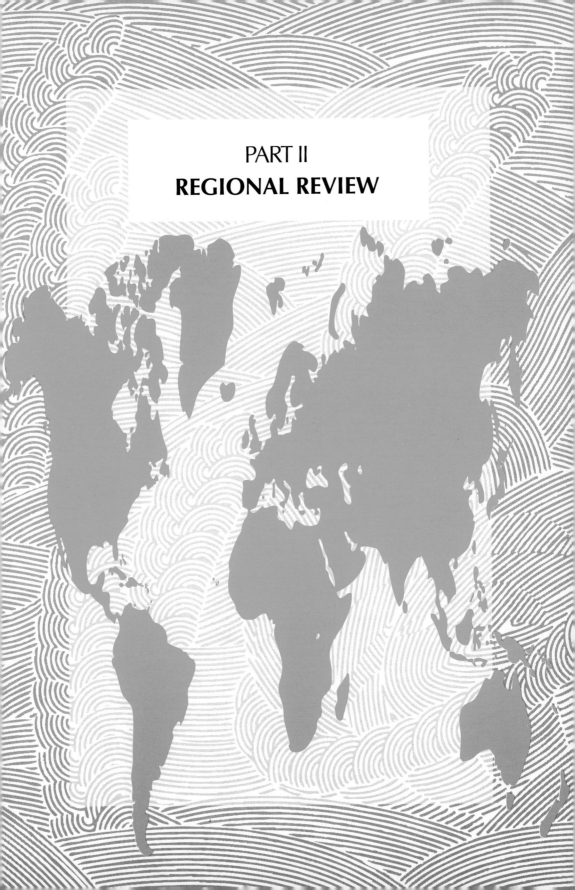

PART II
REGIONAL REVIEW

REGIONAL REVIEW

I. Developing country regions

SUB-SAHARAN AFRICA

REGIONAL OVERVIEW

For more than two decades sub-Saharan Africa, with its deep-rooted development constraints, has been experiencing a deteriorating socio-economic performance. Life expectancy is 51 years, more than ten years lower than the world's average, and sub-Saharan Africa lags behind other regions on all other main indicators of socio-economic development. Over the past two decades, in all but a few years, the region's economic expansion remained well below the population growth rate. Indeed, sub-Saharan Africa's real per caput GDP declined from US$630 in the early 1980s to about US$500 in 1994.

Against this background, the vastly improved economic performances in much of Africa in 1995 were the main positive feature of the current world economic landscape. The economic growth rate for that year in sub-Saharan Africa is estimated at about 3.8 percent, up from 2 percent in 1994 and 0.5 percent in 1993. In fact, it is the first time during the 1990s that the economic expansion for sub-Saharan Africa has exceeded the level of the yearly population growth rate of 3 percent. GDP growth rates of 5 percent or more were recorded in about one-quarter (12) of the countries in sub-Saharan Africa.

Underlying the region's improved economic performance was the dynamic behaviour of the export sector. The region's exports were boosted by higher export prices for non-oil primary commodities; the economic upturn, however modest, in developed countries (especially in western Europe to which two-thirds of the region's exports were directed); and, in the case of countries in the CFA franc zone, the devaluation of the CFA franc combined with remarkable success in containing inflationary pressure in the countries

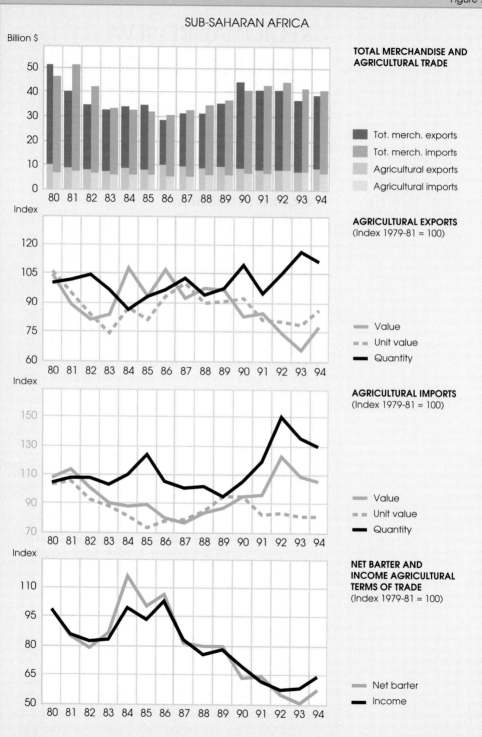

SUB-SAHARAN AFRICA

Billion $

TOTAL MERCHANDISE AND AGRICULTURAL TRADE

- Tot. merch. exports
- Tot. merch. imports
- Agricultural exports
- Agricultural imports

Index

AGRICULTURAL EXPORTS
(Index 1979-81 = 100)

- Value
- Unit value
- Quantity

Index

AGRICULTURAL IMPORTS
(Index 1979-81 = 100)

- Value
- Unit value
- Quantity

Index

NET BARTER AND INCOME AGRICULTURAL TERMS OF TRADE
(Index 1979-81 = 100)

- Net barter
- Income

Source: FAO

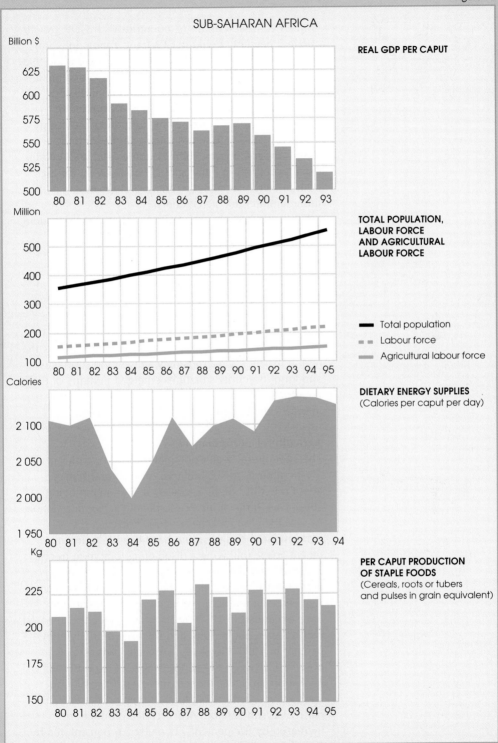

SUB-SAHARAN AFRICA

Billion $

REAL GDP PER CAPUT

625
600
575
550
525
500

80 81 82 83 84 85 86 87 88 89 90 91 92 93

Million

TOTAL POPULATION, LABOUR FORCE AND AGRICULTURAL LABOUR FORCE

500
400
300
200
100

80 81 82 83 84 85 86 87 88 89 90 91 92 93 94 95

━━━ Total population
╍╍╍ Labour force
━━━ Agricultural labour force

Calories

DIETARY ENERGY SUPPLIES
(Calories per caput per day)

2 100
2 050
2 000
1 950

80 81 82 83 84 85 86 87 88 89 90 91 92 93 94

Kg

PER CAPUT PRODUCTION OF STAPLE FOODS
(Cereals, roots or tubers and pulses in grain equivalent)

225
200
175
150

80 81 82 83 84 85 86 87 88 89 90 91 92 93 94 95

Source: FAO

concerned (seven of the 12 countries with GDP growth above 5 percent are in the CFA franc zone – inflation rates for the zone as a whole were -0.5 percent in 1993, 33.0 percent in 1994, 11.8 percent in 1995 and are a projected 3.5 percent in 1996). Other contributory factors to the economic improvement were much-improved weather conditions in vast areas previously affected by drought, further progress in economic reform programmes in some countries and, to a certain extent, progress in intraregional cooperation (through both bilateral ties and the renewed emphasis on intraregional trade agreements).

While civil unrest and armed conflicts eased in some countries, particularly in southern Africa, new ones emerged or worsened in others. In Sierra Leone rebel attacks severely disrupted economic and agricultural activities. Civil strife and political crises also affected Burundi, Liberia, Somalia, the Sudan and Zaire. Coups and coup attempts in the Comoros, the Niger, Sierra Leone and Sao Tome and Principe also highlighted the fragile political situations prevailing in large parts of the region in 1995. Unsurprisingly, grave food shortages and food insecurity situations emerged in many of these countries, requiring emergency assistance from the international community (see World Review).

Agricultural performances
The agricultural sector dominates the economies of most countries in sub-Saharan Africa, contributing about one-third of the region's GDP and employing about two-thirds of the economically active population. As was the case for other sectors, however, the performances of agriculture have been faltering in recent years, following a disquieting long-term trend.

Preliminary data for 1995 suggest a less dynamic performance of agriculture than other economic sectors. Aggregate agricultural production was estimated to have expanded in 1995 by about 2.3 percent compared with 2.1 percent in 1994 and the exceptionally high 4.5 percent in 1993. However, a marked contrast was observed between the performances of export crops *vis-à-vis* food products. Indeed, the overall production increase accrued mainly to cash crop production. In particular, sub-Saharan Africa coffee production increased by 9.7 percent, cocoa by 7.6 percent, tea by 6.8 percent and cotton by 3.8 percent compared with

101

SUB-SAHARAN AFRICA

1994. Improved market and price conditions accounted primarily for the good performance of export crops. The 1994 devaluation of the CFA franc was also an important influence, as farmers in the CFA franc zone responded favourably to higher local prices paid for export commodities. The devaluation also contributed to an increasingly dynamic intrazone trade. In particular, Côte d'Ivoire and Cameroon benefited greatly from the expanded trade in 1995 with other CFA franc zone members. In addition, Senegal imported rice from Mali in 1995 rather than from Thailand, which had previously been its main supplier.

As regards food products, preliminary estimates indicate that production in 1995 virtually stagnated at the 1994 level, as the net result of an 11 percent fall in cereal production and expanded output of other food products. The cereal shortfall stemmed from a sharp (16 percent) decline in coarse grain production offset by increases in rice (7 percent) and wheat (9 percent).

Cereal production performances in 1995 varied substantially among subregions. While cereal production in western Africa declined slightly from 1994 levels, it increased by 15 percent in central Africa. In eastern Africa cereal production increased by 2 percent, with above-normal harvests in both Kenya and the United Republic of Tanzania, reduced increases in Uganda and Ethiopia and reduced crops in other countries. In southern Africa cereal production decreased overall by some 38 percent, although Botswana and Mozambique recorded cereal production levels close to those of 1994 and in Madagascar production actually increased. The coarse grain harvests were affected by the severe drought conditions in southern Africa which were prevalent until late 1995. The production of maize, the staple food, was sharply reduced – by more than 60 percent in South Africa and by over one-half in Zimbabwe – compared with 1994. In Zimbabwe 1995 was the fourth consecutive year of drought.

Crop expectations for 1996 are much improved in southern Africa, thanks to abundant rainfall in late 1995 which continued into 1996. In fact, a favourable crop season is expected throughout the continent, except for in those countries affected by civil strife. Agricultural recovery should contribute to a significant revival of the region's economy as a whole, expectations being for

GDP growth in 1996 once again to exceed population growth by a significant margin.

Policy developments

In 1995, policy reforms continued in most countries. Various degrees of progress in liberalizing trade, price, foreign exchange and investment regimes in the context of structural adjustment were recorded in particular in Ethiopia, Ghana, Kenya, Tanzania, Uganda, Zambia and Zimbabwe. Reform, however, especially in the public sector, has been generally slow for technical and socio-political reasons: in Zimbabwe relations with the International Monetary Fund (IMF) became strained because of pressures for reform; in the Congo, Ghana and Djibouti there was social unrest; and in Benin, the parliament voted against a structural adjustment loan of US$98 million because of opposition to a programme of national marketing restructuring. These events underlined the difficult task of pursuing necessary but painful measures of reform in a region where the past record of achievements in this area remains at best inconclusive, margins for fiscal restraint are slim and large segments of the population are unemployed and/or close to subsistence levels. Indeed, only a few countries can be credited with clear progress in achieving stabilization and adjustment (Kenya, Mauritius, Uganda, Zambia and Ghana), while others still have a long way to go towards restoring macroeconomic equilibrium (notably Nigeria, Zaire, Tanzania and the Niger).

One difficult area of reform, with major implications for agriculture, has been the privatization of public enterprises. Such privatization has been an important precondition for obtaining structural adjustment lending from international financing institutions, since the dominant role of public enterprises in many sub-Saharan countries is seen as a significant factor behind poor economic performances. Indeed, a large proportion of lending from these institutions has been earmarked for privatization purposes. Most countries are still in the early stages of their privatization programmes, however. A major concern limiting progress in this area has been over the implications on employment, given the fact that the state is the main employer in many countries. It is generally assumed that, in the long term, better-managed and more

SUB-SAHARAN AFRICA

profitable private companies may actually create jobs. The short-term problems are, however, how to re-employ or otherwise compensate public enterprise employees who initially lose their jobs as a result of privatization. As regards the latter, policies and procedures differ substantially from country to country – at one extreme Togo applies no compensation at all, while at the other extreme Guinea has an elaborate scheme in place.

Mozambique has the lead in sub-Saharan Africa regarding the total number of privatizations. Since 1992, more than 550 public companies, of which 45 are large ones, have been privatized. The privatization in Mozambique extended to agricultural enterprises such as those dealing in tea and copra. The rate at which firms have been sold off has increased recently and is expected to accelerate further in the near future. Companies up for sale in the second half of 1995 included large tea plantations of the state company Emocha, citrus groves, the Boror Copra plantations and processing plants. Finally, a new land policy approved by the government makes it possible to transfer land titles between citizens or from a foreigner to a national. While the principle that land is state-owned still prevails, the new policy is seen as a significant move towards privatizing land.

Other significant examples of privatization moves in 1995 include that of *Côte d'Ivoire,* where measures to liberalize the coffee-cocoa network were confirmed in August 1995. This represented a radical departure from the previous system instituted after independence, through which the marketing of these crops had been managed entirely by the state. The World Bank, France and Germany will provide financial assistance for this purpose and the government will no longer intervene in producer prices, which will instead be negotiated in the market.

In *Uganda* the government is turning to the private sector to revive its cotton and garment industry. Nine state industries operating in this area were put on sale and measures to liberalize cotton marketing were introduced. These are to be achieved with financial assistance, particularly from the International Fund for Agricultural Development (IFAD) and the World Bank.

In *Mauritania* the remarkable progress achieved by the agricultural sector in recent years has been largely

SUB-SAHARAN AFRICA

attributed to a strong entry of the private sector and the privatization of agricultural credit. These have encouraged national authorities to aim for the difficult objective of achieving self-sufficiency in food by 2000. Major investment programmes are under way in irrigated agriculture, agricultural credit and environment projects with assistance from international financial institutions.

In *Rwanda*, after a period of paralysis following the civil war, market liberalization and privatization returned to the policy agenda and a national privatization commission has been created to deal with what is considered to be a particularly delicate issue. Supported by the European Union (EU) and international financing institutions, the state has significantly liberalized the coffee sector and authorized private-sector collection, transportation, processing, financing and exportation of the crop.

The Government of *the Congo* decided to privatize the fisheries sector, a decision that will entail the dissolution of the National Department for Continental Fisheries and SAGAP, a state management and vessel company, both agencies having encountered major financial difficulties for several years. It is hoped that the move will reduce the fish import needs of the country, currently in the region of 50 000 tonnes per year.

Finally, *Senegal's* national groundnut company, SONACOS, which after a particularly large turnover in 1994 had become the country's largest enterprise, is being put up for sale.

Along with the above important moves towards market liberalization and privatization, examples also abound of serious problems faced by governments, which have often forced them to backtrack on previous policy decisions in that direction. In many cases the process has been hindered by deteriorating economies and social protest at the rising cost of living. For instance, in Gabon price controls on essential food products (bread, rice, flour, sugar, milk, tinned sardines) were enforced in order to counter the effects of inflation and the imposition of value added tax (VAT), which led to huge price rises especially of rice. Similarly, Zimbabwe's consumer council pressed for the reintroduction of food subsidies and price controls, in the face of sharply rising prices of maize.

SUB-SAHARAN AFRICA

In other cases, the process of privatization was hindered by conflicting views on its effects. An example was the announcement in late 1995 that a large number of farmers in Kenya had dropped the state-owned Coffee Board, the only agency mandated to market Kenyan coffee, and turned to private marketing agents, raising a debate over the risks involved in dismantling the system. A strong body of opinion, chiefly among small farmers and cooperatives, believes that private traders, who may initially offer better purchasing conditions, would be free to manipulate prices once they have a firm grip on the market. Similarly, the ongoing debate over the privatization of the Cameroon state agencies SODECOM (cotton), HEVECAM (natural rubber) and SOCAPALM (palm oil) centres to a large extent on the implications of losing control over markets (as in the case of cotton already plagued by large illegal exportation) and the risks for farmers of losing employment and social services provided by those agencies.

BOX 9
ENVIRONMENTAL CONCERN

Growing awareness of the long-term consequences of environmental degradation in Africa has prompted intense debate and a proliferation of new national and international initiatives to counter the problem. The ravages caused by recurrent droughts in recent years have created a new sense of urgency over the problems of desertification. Evidence of massive areas of forest land disappearing, and with them thousands of species of fauna and flora, have also induced national authorities to reinforce legislation to conserve the forests, limit timber cutting and exporting and encourage alternative uses for forests, such as wildlife tourism.

Recent international action to address these problems has included that under the International Convention to Combat Desertification, drawn out on urgent request of the African representation at the United Nations Conference on Environment and Development (UNCED) (see section The threat of desertification on p. 70). Another important intraregional move in this direction has been the Desert Margins Initiative, initially involving Botswana, Burkina Faso, Kenya, Mali, Namibia and the Niger. More countries are to be included at a later stage. Led by six research centres with the participation of the Consultative Group on International Agricultural Research (CGIAR), the United Nations Environment Programme (UNEP) and other organizations including FAO, the project is intended to cover 1.3 billion ha and benefit 400 million people threatened by environmental degradation. Research is to be carried out in each of the countries concerned on various aspects of the problem and this will constitute the basis for coordinated policy action.

At the national level, recent measures to prevent resource degradation included the adoption by Côte d'Ivoire of an environmental action plan for the period 1996-2010. The first phase (1996-2000) aims at finding solutions to the rapid disappearance of forests. The government is also considering issuing an environmental code to update current inappropriate and incoherent legislation. In Burkina Faso, under the reforestation programme initiated in 1994 with the objective of planting 15 million trees in five years, three-quarters of the 6 million trees planted so far have taken root. An additional million trees are being planted as part of the programme to combat desertification, with the participation of young volunteers from France and western Africa.

The implementation of initiatives to preserve the environment has encountered considerable difficulties, however. These derive from both financial constraints and administrative weaknesses in the public sector and from the fact that, in a region beset by pressing economic problems, short-term profitability objectives tend to prevail over long-term conservation concerns. For instance, for years the Congolese Government has had a national forestation programme which has enabled 50 000 ha of savannah to be replanted, but the programme has been beset by enormous financial difficulties and has been able to limit to only a small extent the acute problem of deforestation, which is estimated to affect between 20 000 and 30 000 ha yearly of a total forest area of 20 million ha. Another example illustrating the dilemma that often faces governments in the region is the project to develop a large-scale titanium dioxide mine in Madagascar. On the one hand, the project would involve an investment of US$350 million, would create 500 direct and 1 500 indirect jobs and would yield up to $20 million a year to the government's treasury when fully operational. On the other hand, the project would mean considerable forest destruction and, according to the Minister of Environment, the likely disappearance of 23 species of fauna and 30 species of flora, several of them unique to that section of the forest. This would occur against a background of a past record of forest exploitation that has already resulted in the disappearance of 85 percent of the forest that once grew on the island.

BURKINA FASO
General characteristics

Burkina Faso is a landlocked country with a total land area of 274 000 km^2. The topography of the country is characterized by its relative flatness with altitudes ranging from 125 to 749 m above sea level. The main characteristic of the climate is the scarce and irregular rainfall. The total population in 1995 amounted to 10.3 million, according to UN estimates, and had been growing at a rate of 2.8 percent over the preceding decade. Since colonial times labour migration, particularly to other countries of western Africa, has been a constant characteristic of the country so that today nearly half of Burkina Faso's nationals live abroad, making expatriate remittances a major source of foreign exchange.

With GNP per caput in 1993 estimated at US$300,[1] Burkina Faso is one of the poorest countries in the world. The poverty of the country is also reflected in the low level of social indicators. In 1992 Burkina Faso ranked as number 169 out of a total of 174 countries in the United Nations Development Programme's (UNDP) human development index. Average life expectancy, infant mortality, adult literacy and school enrolment rates compare unfavourably with those of the least-developed countries and sub-Saharan Africa as a whole.[2] The country faces major constraints to development with a poor resource base, unfavourable climatic conditions and low levels of human development.

Within sub-Saharan Africa the development experience of Burkina Faso presents a number of points of particular interest. The agricultural population still represents a larger portion (at more than 80 percent) of the total population than it does in the majority of African countries. Burkina Faso is also a country with a long tradition of relatively prudent macroeconomic management through which it has managed to avoid macroeconomic imbalances of the magnitude experienced by many other developing countries. It has achieved steady rates of economic growth, above those of Africa as a whole, even though it started at an extremely low level of development at independence in 1960.

The government, with the assistance of the international lending organizations, is currently

[1] World Bank. 1995. *World Development Report, 1995.* Washington, DC.
[2] Ibid.

involved in a series of major policy reforms aimed at creating improved conditions for growth and development. The framework for current economic policies is provided by the structural adjustment programmes negotiated with the World Bank, together with sectoral adjustment programmes for the agricultural sector, the transportation sector, public sector management and the environment.

The role of the agricultural sector in the economy
Few countries are as dependent as Burkina Faso on agriculture. The contribution of agriculture and livestock to GDP was estimated at 27 percent in 1992, while a further 6 percent was accounted for by forestry, fisheries and hunting.[3] At the same time, the food, beverages and tobacco industry represented 9 percent of GDP. Some 86 percent of the economically active population have agriculture as their main occupation; livestock production is the main occupation of a further 3 percent of the active population.

No less important is the role of the agricultural sector in the external accounts. In recent years the share of agricultural products in total merchandise exports has oscillated around 50 percent (Table 2). The main export crop, cotton, has in recent years accounted for around 70 percent of agricultural export revenues, with livestock products (mainly live animals and hides and skins) accounting for the bulk of the rest. The main exception to this pattern was observable in 1994, the year in which devaluation of the currency, the CFA franc, provided an immediate boost to livestock exports while cotton exports were slower to react.

On the side of imports, in recent years foodstuffs have accounted for a share of around 20 percent of total merchandise imports with cereals alone representing from 5 to 10 percent, depending on the year (Table 3). In years of adequate rainfall Burkina Faso is largely self-sufficient in cereals, the only major exception being rice, which is consumed mostly in the urban areas and for which approximately three-quarters of domestic food needs are met from imports. Cereal imports in the period 1990-94 have corresponded in volume terms to roughly 6 to 8 percent of domestic production and between 5 and 11 percent, depending on the year, of food needs.[4] Imports of rice alone, however, represent between one-half (in years of high cereal import levels)

[3] Institut National de la Statistique. 1994. *Annuaire Statistique du Burkina Faso.* Ouagadougou.
[4] Calculated on data from the Ministry of the Economy, Finance and Planning.

TABLE 2

Merchandise exports (billions of CFA francs)

	1990	1991[1]	1992[1]	1993[1]	1994[1]
Total merchandise exports	96.4	75.9	62.2	74.3	125.4
Of which:					
Cotton	23.4	29.3	25.0	22.2	32.8
Livestock products	9.5	8.2	8.7	8.2	32.9
Other agricultural products	1.7	1.1	2.7	2.5	5.2

[1] Estimates.
Source: Ministry of the Economy, Finance and Planning.

TABLE 3

Merchandise imports (billions of CFA francs)

	1990	1991[1]	1992[1]	1993[1]	1994[1]
Total merchandise imports	141.8	138.4	131.1	133.4	202.7
Of which:					
Cereals	9.4	13.4	12.2	9.9	14.7
Other food products	17.1	11.5	10.8	18.2	31.0

[1] Estimates.
Source: Ministry of the Economy, Finance and Planning.

and three-quarters (in years of lower aggregate import levels) of total cereal imports in quantum terms and between 65 and 85 percent in value terms.

Characteristics of the agricultural sector
Agriculture is essentially rain-fed and dependent on limited rainfall which in addition is highly irregular in both time and volume. Average annual rainfall ranges from a minimum level of approximately 400 mm in the northernmost part of the Sahelian zone to about 1 200 mm in the southeast. About one-third of the total land area is cultivable. The potential for irrigation is estimated at 165 000 ha, of which only one-tenth is currently utilized.

Agriculture in Burkina Faso is to a large extent a subsistence agriculture and is centred on cereal production for domestic consumption. Indeed, out of a total cultivated area of 3 431 000 ha, 3 014 000 ha

SUB-SAHARAN AFRICA

(88 percent) are planted to cereals as the main crop.[5] The most important cereals produced are millet, which occupies some 43 percent of the total area planted to cereals, followed by white sorghum, occupying 38 percent of cereal area, red sorghum (10 percent) and maize (6 percent). Rice covers less than 1 percent of the area planted to cereals. After cereals, the largest portion (347 000 ha) of remaining cultivated area is occupied by cash crops. Some 120 000 ha are planted to cotton, but because of climatic constraints these areas are concentrated in the western part of the country. Groundnuts, which cover 217 000 ha, are produced across the country and are commercialized mostly within the country itself. Other, less important, cash crops are sesame and soybean, while smaller areas are occupied by fruit, vegetables and root crops. The above distribution of cultivated area is, however, simplified from a somewhat more complex reality, which is that of mixed cropping.

Livestock production is practised across the entire country and comprises cattle, sheep, goats, donkeys, pigs and poultry. Livestock numbers are not known with precision but were estimated in 1995 to be about 4.4 million head of cattle, 5.8 million sheep, 7.2 million goats, 500 000 to 600 000 pigs and 400 000 to 500 000 donkeys. Cattle raising is to a large extent transhumant, particularly in the Sahelian zones of the country.

As well as unfavourable climatic and environmental conditions, agricultural and livestock production are seriously constrained by archaic and low-technology methods of production and the low education levels of producers. Agriculture is based on small-scale family farming. Some 72 percent of agricultural households are composed of more than six persons and households of 20 or more members represent 7 percent of the total.[6] No less than 87 percent of agricultural household heads are illiterate and only some 36 percent of household heads have links with extension services (the percentage is even lower for female family heads). Landholdings are extremely fragmented; each household farms an average of 9.6 plots of land, the average size of which is approximately 0.4 ha. Farm equipment is very limited; less than 30 percent of households own a plough (the total number of tractors in use in the country was estimated at 135 in 1993) and

[5] Estimates of cultivated area come from the Division of Agropastoral Statistics of the Ministry of Agriculture and Animal Resources. 1995. *Enquête Nationale de Statistique Agricole, Rapport Général.* Ouagadougou.

[6] This and the following data are from the Department of Agropastoral Statistics of the Ministry of Agriculture and Animal Resources. 1995. *Enquête Nationale de Statistique Agricole, Rapport Général.* Ouagadougou.

BOX 10
ENVIRONMENTAL CONSTRAINTS
TO AGRICULTURAL PRODUCTION

The natural resource base for agriculture in Burkina Faso is facing increasing pressures. Two major problems are water scarcity and population pressure on the land, phenomena which present themselves in different degrees and with somewhat different implications in the various regions of the country. Since the early 1970s and the period of prolonged drought 1970-73 a decrease in rainfall levels has been observed. Among the consequences of this are a diminishing potential for agricultural production and smaller quantities of surface water leading to a reduction in the recharging of groundwater and a consequent decline in the water table to the order of 20 m since 1970. In addition, the reduction in vegetative cover has led to overgrazing in the traditional Sahelian livestock area to the north of the country and to the movement of grazing to areas further south.

Population pressures have reduced per caput availability of land, causing land to be worked beyond its capacity. This is the case especially for the central areas of the country which have particularly high population densities. Among the consequences are a reduction (or elimination) in fallow time and the underutilization of production factors that enhance soil fertility. Other effects are massive land clearing and conversion of pasturelands to crop production as well as emigration to the less densely populated southwestern areas of the country. In these areas the natural environment has been profoundly modified by the introduction of cash crops, human settlements and increasing livestock herds in ways that do not adequately consider the need for conservation of productive resources and, in the longer term, threaten the productive potential of the area.

The rate of deforestation has been rapid. Over the last 15 years (from 1980 to 1995) Burkina Faso has lost more than 50 percent of its forest cover. The government estimates the forest area cleared for agricultural purposes at more than 50 000 ha a year, while shortages of fuelwood are increasing.

Concern for the environment led to the adoption in 1991 of the first National Plan of Action for the Environment, which was subsequently revised in 1993 following UNCED held in Rio de Janeiro in 1992. Recently the government has taken steps to strengthen its capacity for devising and implementing environmental policies with the institution of a new Ministry for the Environment and Water. In late 1995 the new ministry was in the process of preparing a global strategy paper for the environment and water, some of the main elements of which would concern the implementation of the International Convention on Desertification Control, reforestation and forest management and water management, with the priority to be given to the rehabilitation and maintenance of existing infrastructures.

70 percent of families own no traction animals (oxen or donkeys). Likewise, fertilizer use is restricted. Nitrogen, potassium and phosphate fertilizers (NPK) and urea are applied. Total NPK use is estimated at about 26 000 tonnes, corresponding to 7.5 kg per hectare of total cultivated area. Use is concentrated on cash crops (mainly cotton), however, and total NPK application corresponds to 74 kg per hectare sown to cash crops.

Historic performance of the economy and the agricultural sector

Although still at very low levels by international comparisons, in terms of incomes and social indicators, Burkina Faso has nevertheless achieved steady but slow economic progress since independence in 1960. GDP growth has been consistently higher than the average for sub-Saharan Africa, although subject to quite significant annual fluctuations caused by the dependence of the most important economic sector, agriculture, on erratic weather conditions. Thus, GDP increased in real terms by an average annual rate of 4.4 percent over the period 1970 to 1980 and 3.7 percent from 1980 to 1993, compared with rates for the two periods of 3.8 and 1.6 percent respectively for the whole of sub-Saharan Africa.[7] This means that, in spite of a certain slow-down of growth in the 1980s relative to the preceding decade, Burkina Faso, unlike the subcontinent as a whole, maintained positive rates of per caput GDP growth. This was achieved in a context of moderate inflation, with an average annual rate for the 1970-1980 period of 8.6 percent compared with a weighted rate of 13.8 percent for the whole of sub-Saharan Africa. Over the period 1980 to 1993 Burkina Faso saw the average rate of inflation decline to 3.3 percent, while the weighted average for the whole of the sub-Saharan region increased to 16.1 percent. The merchandise trade performance of Burkina Faso has also been consistently superior to that of the subcontinent as a whole, with merchandise exports increasing at an average annual rate of 7.2 percent (compared with 1.0 percent for sub-Saharan Africa) over the period 1970-1980 and 4.1 percent (compared with 2.5 percent) from 1980 to 1993.

The relatively high rates of per caput growth are also reflected in improvements in a number of social indicators, which nevertheless tend still to compare

[7] **World Bank, op. cit., footnote 1, p. 108.**

SUB-SAHARAN AFRICA

unfavourably with the averages for sub-Saharan Africa. Thus, for example, life expectancy at birth increased from 36 years in 1960 to 47 in 1992, compared with an increase from 39 to 51 for the whole of sub-Saharan Africa, while the infant mortality rate per 1 000 live births fell from 205 in 1960 to 130 in 1992 (from 165 to 97 for the whole subcontinent).[8] Over the period from 1970 to 1992 the adult literacy rate doubled from 8 percent to the still modest rate of 17 percent, while the improvement made by the whole of the subcontinent over the same period was a doubling from 27 to 54 percent.[9] Quite a significant improvement has, however, been achieved particularly in the primary education enrolment rate, which from an extremely low level of 13 percent of the age group in 1970 was brought up to 31 percent in 1992, while the whole of the subcontinent managed an increase from 50 to 67 percent. At the secondary level, education enrolment rates over the same period were brought from 1 to 8 percent, compared with an increase from 7 to 18 percent for the whole of sub-Saharan Africa.[10]

The contribution of the agricultural sector to overall economic growth has not been uniform throughout the postindependence history of Burkina Faso. Amid major annual fluctuations, imputable primarily to uncertain climatic conditions, agricultural production rose only 1.2 percent during 1961-1984, well below population growth. Agricultural production growth accelerated from 1984 to 1994 to an average annual rate of 4.8 percent, with a particularly strong expansion in 1985, but with a certain slow-down after 1992. Per caput food production over the same period increased annually by an average 2.1 percent. The major factor behind the accelerated growth was cereal production, which increased from 1984 to 1994 by an annual rate of no less than 6.9 percent, following the mere 1.3 percent per annum recorded from 1961 to 1984. This rapid rise in production was the result of increases both in harvested areas (3.8 percent annual expansion compared with 0.3 percent annually from 1961 to 1984) and in yields (2.9 percent per annum compared with 0.9 percent during 1961-1984). In particular maize production expanded very significantly over the decade 1984-1994 with an annual growth rate of 14.0 percent (8.7 percent in yields and 4.8 percent in area harvested), although this cereal still covers only 10 to

[8] UNDP. 1995. *Human Development Report 1995.* New York.
[9] Ibid.
[10] World Bank, op. cit., footnote 1, p. 108.

15 percent (according to the year) of total cereal production in tonnes. Other coarse grains, millet and sorghum, however, contributed the bulk of the total increase by expanding by 5.8 and 6.4 percent per annum respectively. Among cereals a much more limited expansion of 3.9 percent per annum was recorded for rice, as area expansion was restricted to an annual rate of only 1.6 percent.

Agricultural production growth from 1984 to 1994 has not been restricted to cereals however. At the same time, production of the most important cash crops expanded, with cotton production increasing by an annual rate of 3.7 percent, although it peaked in 1990, and groundnut production expanding at a rate of 6.0 percent.

The accelerated agricultural and food production growth from the mid-1980s translated into a significant increase in per caput dietary energy supplies, which through a particularly strong improvement in 1985 and 1986 shifted from an average level (although with significant annual fluctuations) of 1 600 to 1 700 calories per caput per day during the decade 1975-1984 to 2 100 to 2 200 calories in the period 1986-92.

The marked acceleration in agricultural production growth since the mid-1980s was largely the result of new development policies based on a strong participatory grassroots approach, embodied initially in the new Programme Populaire de Développement for 1983-84. These policies granted absolute priority to agricultural and rural development with 44 percent of the investments foreseen by the programme allocated to agriculture and water development.[11] The focus on agriculture was continued with the Plan Quinquennal de Développement Populaire 1986-90, under which approximately 42 percent of the investments executed went to rural areas.[12] The heavy investment focus on agriculture translated, *inter alia,* into the construction of a large number of small- and medium-scale water reservoirs. The investment efforts in the agricultural sector were accompanied by other policy measures in support of the sector in fields such as dissemination of production techniques, strengthening of farmers' organizations and improved producer prices.

Current economic policies: structural adjustment
As in many other developing countries, current economic policies in Burkina Faso are conducted

[11] See P. Zagré. 1994. *Les politiques économiques du Burkina Faso, une tradition d'ajustement structurel.* Paris.
[12] Ibid.

SUB-SAHARAN AFRICA

within the framework of structural adjustment programmes agreed with the Bretton Woods lending institutions. Compared with most other African countries, however, Burkina Faso came relatively late to "orthodox" structural adjustment. Preparations for a World Bank-supported structural adjustment programme began in 1988, with actual negotiations with the Bank starting in 1989 within a context of a far lower degree of economic emergency than was the case in the majority of other countries.

Since 1984 macroeconomic policies had been characterized by attempts at self-imposed economic adjustment without external assistance, aimed at restoring fiscal discipline and reducing the budget deficit while at the same time promoting the productive sectors of the economy (in particular agriculture) and improving social services and education.[13] Overall performance of the economy during the period 1984-1988 had not been unsatisfactory, with favourable GDP growth rates accompanied by low rates of inflation and, in particular, significant increases in agricultural production. Nevertheless, in spite of an initial significant improvement in 1985, the budget deficit in the following years remained persistent, while payments arrears accumulated. From the point of view of the external accounts, although the current account (excluding grants) gradually worsened during the second half of the 1980s, external indebtedness remained moderate. Indeed, in 1989 the total external debt stock corresponded to 33 percent of GNP and total debt service to 9.6 percent of exports of goods and services.[14]

Structural adjustment in Burkina Faso differs from that of most other countries not only in the overall less critical macroeconomic situation in which it was implemented, but also in the modalities and timing of its preparation. Indeed, the absence of a real economic emergency situation, in spite of the worsening internal and external imbalances, allowed a careful preparation of the programme, in particular at the political level. For this purpose, the government took the time to submit the proposed structural adjustment programme deliberately to open debate by the civil society and to provide careful information to the public prior to the programme's finalization in order to ensure widespread support. Thus, with initial contacts with the World Bank

[13] From January 1985 to July 1988 no new loan to Burkina Faso was approved by the World Bank, see P. Zagré, p. 164, op. cit., footnote 11.
[14] World Bank. 1995. *World Debt Tables 1994-95.* Washington, DC.

SUB-SAHARAN AFRICA

dating from early 1988, the government drew up its own proposed adjustment programme in September 1989 and a final agreement with the World Bank was reached in March 1991.

The first structural adjustment programme covered the period 1991-93 with the quantitative goals of an annual GDP growth rate of about 5 percent throughout the period, a current account deficit (excluding transfers) not exceeding 12 percent of GDP (compared with the 10-11 percent prevailing at the beginning of the programme)[15] and a rate of inflation to be kept within 3 percent (a rate of some 3.2 percent was recorded in 1991). At the same time the budget deficit was to be reduced to 1 percent of GDP by 1997 from the 2.4 percent estimated in 1991. Other objectives were the elimination of national and foreign debts and an attack on some of the major constraints to sustainable economic growth, such as the high rate of demographic growth, the poor development of human resources and environmental degradation. The strategy envisaged for reaching these objectives was centred on improved management of public finances, increased agricultural production, stronger incentives for investments and private enterprise, the promotion of human resources through better education and health services and enhanced management capacity in the public sector. The first structural adjustment programme for 1991-93 was followed by a subsequent one for the period 1994-96.

Within the context of structural adjustment a number of reforms have been undertaken or are envisaged in various sectors and fields of economic management. These include budget reforms – affecting, on the one hand, revenue collection through reforms of taxation and customs tariffs and, on the other hand, improved expenditure control and management – restructuring of the banking system and restructuring and privatization of public enterprises. Another important area of reform, where significant steps have been taken, concerns liberalization of external trade and prices which, together with a revised investment code and new (enacted or under preparation) commercial and labour codes as well as legislation on land security, aim at stimulating private investment and enterprise. Within structural adjustment, particular emphasis has also been put on the development of human resources with the

---

[15] Data from the Ministry of the Economy, Finance and Planning.

reallocation of budgetary expenditures in favour of education and health. The structural adjustment programme has been accompanied by a series of sectoral adjustment programmes, most notably a sectoral adjustment programme for agriculture, a national plan of action for the environment, a sectoral adjustment programme for transport and a programme for promotion of the private sector.

In the middle of the structural adjustment process the devaluation of the CFA franc in January 1994, with a change in parity with the French franc from 50 CFA francs to 1 French franc to 100 CFA francs to 1 French franc, introduced a new element into the macroeconomic context and enabled Burkina Faso's economy to improve its international competitiveness significantly while contributing to restoring external balance. Among the expected benefits were increased production and exports of cash crops such as cotton, fruit and vegetables, groundnuts and other oil crops as well as of livestock products. This should be accompanied by reduced imports of foodstuffs, especially rice, together with a stimulus to domestic production and a shift in consumption towards locally produced cereals. Other expected effects were a shift in import composition towards intermediate goods and inputs and an overall improvement in the trade balance and the balance of payments.

Current economic policies, as spelled out in the government's Policy Framework Paper for 1995-97 endorsed by the IMF, are in the direction of further efforts towards reducing financial imbalances and a deepening of economic and structural reforms to improve the economic competitiveness of the country, liberalize the economy and improve public-sector management. Among the quantitative policy objectives for the period are an annual real GDP growth rate of 5 percent, a consumer price inflation rate of 3 percent and a current account deficit not in excess of 12 percent of GDP. The deepening of the structural reforms and of economic liberalization is hoped to lead to a consolidation of the gains in competitiveness resulting from the CFA franc devaluation and accelerated growth in exporting and import substituting sectors. The main objecitves of the continued reform efforts are planned to be in the improvement of government efficiency and financial management, further deregulation of the

economy, the development of health services and education and the strengthening of basic infrastructures.

Recently the Government of Burkina Faso, recognizing the insufficient progress in improving the living conditions of the population, has put added emphasis on policies for human development. The new emphasis is expressed by the Letter of Intent on a Policy for Sustainable Human Development 1995-2005, presented to the donor community at the third round table conference of Burkina Faso with its aid donors, held in October 1995. The Letter states the government's main objectives and strategies for human development, while indicating that additional studies will be needed to lay out the strategic guidelines and formulate specific programmes and projects. It emphasizes an appropriate macroeconomic setting as a precondition for reducing poverty and stresses the need for continuing current macroeconomic and structural reforms. The fairly ambitious main objectives laid out for the year 2005 are to increase per caput GDP by at least 3 percent per annum, to double the literacy rate from 20 to 40 percent of the population and to add about ten years to life expectancy. The Letter spells out the main elements for the development of human resources on the basis of sustainable economic growth: a strategy for containing population growth; policies for job creation and income generation; an enhanced role for women; and improved access to education (with the objective of increasing the school enrolment to 60 percent by 2005), health services and drinking-water. The government estimates the financial resource requirements to meet the objectives at 68 billion CFA francs per annum from 1996 to 2000 and 102 billion CFA francs from then to 2005.

Agricultural policies: sectoral adjustment

Reforms in the agricultural sector and in agricultural policies are an integral and essential component of the ongoing economic policy and structural reforms. Preparatory work on a sectoral adjustment programme for the agricultural sector began in 1989 leading to the formulation of a programme, endorsed by the World Bank in 1992, containing a series of measures to be implemented over a three-year period.

The three main objectives for the 1992-95 agricultural sector adjustment programme were:

SUB-SAHARAN AFRICA

modernization and diversification of production; strengthening of food security; and improved management of natural resources. To achieve these objectives the programme laid out five main lines of policy action: intensification of production and natural resource management; liberalization of trade and prices for agricultural products and inputs; restructuring of the institutional environment; improved efficiency in public finances; and consolidation of a food security policy. These were translated into a series of specific actions, to be undertaken in the course of the programme, affecting the main agricultural subsectors. Almost all of the proposed actions had been implemented by late 1995.

In the context of the sectoral adjustment programme for the agricultural sector a series of important reforms have already been carried through. For the purpose of improved resource management, new framework legislation and regulations on agrarian organization and community land management have been introduced, although large-scale implementation and application of such legislation must necessarily be a longer-term proposition and traditional systems for land-use rights and land management remain the rule. Major liberalization has taken place in trade and price setting. The measures adopted include the elimination of all export monopolies on agricultural products except cotton and of all import monopolies except for rice (although in late 1995 a partial opening of rice imports to private traders was agreed), wheat and sugar. In addition, the state fixing of producer prices and approval of retail prices were eliminated and trade in agricultural inputs was liberalized. Administrative obstacles to exports have been lifted and export taxes on livestock and meat abolished.

Other measures include the putting in place of regulations governing private supply of veterinary and pharmaceutical products as well as the introduction of market prices on behalf of the parastatal Office National d'Approvisionnement et de Distribution des Intrants Zootechniques et Vétérinaires (ONAVET). At the same time, work, partly preparatory, is being carried out to reorganize the institutional environment for the agricultural sector, with the disengagement of government and the reformulation of its activities, focusing on research, extension and advisory services,

agricultural training, land-use and natural resource management and the creation of infrastructure. The majority of other government interventions are to be transferred to producers' associations and private operators. This has been accompanied by efforts to improve public financial management in the sector. In addition to the sectoral programme for agriculture as such, important activities for the sector are being implemented within the context of the sectoral programme for the transport sector, with an increase in budgetary allocations for road maintenance and construction.

Of particular importance, given the crucial role of the sector, are reforms undertaken in the cereal sector. Until recently the government had an interventionist role in the sector, attempting to control or influence prices. The national cereal agency, Office National des Céréales (OFNACER), was responsible for distributing food aid, managing national food security cereal stocks, guaranteeing prices to producers and stabilizing prices. The interventions of OFNACER on the domestic market were, however, generally of limited effect, as purchases were effected at fixed official prices but with funds that were too scarce to allow any appreciable market impact. In June 1994 OFNACER was liquidated within the context of a complete restructuring of the cereal market.

The cornerstones of the new cereal market policies are the liberalization of prices and trade in cereals and an enhanced role for the private sector in marketing and stocking (both at the village level and commercially). Up to now, the main exception to the liberalization of trade and prices has been rice, which occupies a special situation in the food balance of the country being the only major cereal the majority of which is imported. Rice occupies a significant place in the consumption pattern in urban areas, and the increasing levels of consumption, together with the consequent increasing import bill, have given rise to concern. Hence the caution in liberalizing this subsector, alongside special efforts now being devoted to expanding domestic production favoured also by the improved competitive position of domestically produced rice, following the CFA franc devaluation in 1994. Thus, in 1995, domestic prices for rice continued to be controlled and imports to be subject to monopoly.

Nevertheless, late in the year a partial opening of imports to private traders was decided as the first step in a gradual liberalization of imports.

Together with the liberalization of the cereals market, a new institutional framework has been established for conducting and monitoring cereal and food security policies in close coordination with the donor community and the private sector. A committee, with a permanent secretariat, for consultation and monitoring of such policies, Comité de Réflexion et de Suivi de la Politique Céréalière et de Sécurité Alimentaire (CRSPC), has therefore been instituted with the participation of the government, external donors and representatives of national private agents and non-governmental organizations (NGOs) intervening in the cereals subsector. A newly created company, Société Nationale de Gestion du Stock de Sécurité Alimentaire (SONAGESS), has been charged with managing national food security cereal stocks of 35 000 tonnes and financial resources allowing the purchase of a further 25 000 tonnes. Emergency and rehabilitation interventions for food security are to be conducted by a national committee for emergency aid and rehabilitation, Comité National de Secours d'Urgence et de Réhabilitation (CONASUR), which in case of emergency takes charge of cereals from the stocks managed by SONAGESS. Types of intervention envisaged, depending on circumstances, are free distribution and sales at subsidized or market prices. A coordination committee for information on food security, Comité de Coordination de l'Information pour la Sécurité Alimentaire (CCI), is responsible for an integrated information system. It manages and coordinates the generation of information necessary for the management of food security policies. In this context the statistical department of the Ministry of Agriculture and Animal Resources prepares a monthly bulletin on the food situation and has been working to improve its early warning system through a diagnostic model developed by the department with the assistance of the World Bank.

Cereal and food security policies are supported by a cereal development fund, Fonds de Développement Céréalier (FODEC), which is constituted from national budgetary allocations, counterpart funds from food aid and financial assistance from donors and is managed by

SUB-SAHARAN AFRICA

a committee with equal representation of the
government and donors. FODEC funds are used to
finance emergency food distribution and the national
food security stock managed by SONAGESS, as well as
to finance activities for the promotion of the cereal
sector. The latter include the opening of credit lines to
support the production, transformation and distribution
of cereals, as well as contributions to the financing of
projects for cereal development.

With implementation of the first sectoral adjustment
programme for agriculture largely carried through, work
has been under way for the preparation of a second
adjustment programme, to take effect in 1996. The
main lines of policy action will remain unchanged,
while the reforms commenced under the first sectoral
adjustment programme will be continued and
deepened. Among the areas to be emphasized in the
new programme are the restructuring of agricultural
services – comprising both central structures within the
Ministry of Agriculture and Animal Resources and
technical support services to producers – and the
development of a rural credit system, for which studies
are currently under way and which should lead to the
formulation of concrete policy proposals. At the same
time the process of privatization of parastatals and
publicly owned companies in the sector will be
continued. Other areas subject to preparatory studies
with a view to policy formulation are the distribution of
inputs and technical equipment, the enhancement of
professional capacities in the rural areas and the levels
of tariff protection to be applied to imported food
products (rice, wheat, sugar) and agricultural inputs
subsequent to liberalization of the import regimes.

Following the CFA franc devaluation, particular
importance is assumed by the strengthening of the
export sectors, which have seen their potential
enhanced. This applies to the traditional main export
sectors, livestock and cotton, but also to fruits and
vegetables, for all of which measures of promotion and
strengthening are envisaged in the context of the new
agricultural adjustment programme. In addition, it is
proposed to undertake a study on support to the
oilseeds sector (groundnuts, sheanuts, sesame). These
have a potential as cash crops, largely complementary
to food crops and not as geographically limited as
cotton, that is largely underexploited as a result of

underdeveloped production techniques and support and distribution services.

Impact of policy reforms

Overall, the impact so far of policy reforms and the devaluation in terms of reducing macroeconomic imbalances has been positive if somewhat short of expectations. In particular, a reduction has been recorded in the external trade deficit since the beginning of the decade, while the current account deficit has been kept within the set limits of 12 percent of GDP.[16] The major danger arising from the devaluation, that of a fuelling of inflation, appears to have been controlled as the inflation rate was reduced in 1995 after an initial, expected, rise in consumer prices in 1994 of 25 percent. The budget deficit, on the other hand, has been more persistent than planned and actually increased between 1990 and 1994.

The economic reform efforts have been slower than hoped for in providing a sustained stimulus to economic growth. Indeed, the real GDP growth rate was only 1.2 percent over the period 1992-94 following a jump of close to 10 percent in 1991.[17] An acceleration in GDP growth occurred in 1995 with the rate of expansion for the year projected at 4.3 percent,[18] lower however than the average of 5.5 percent estimated by IMF for the entire West African Economic and Monetary Union (UEMOA).[19] This expansion in 1995, however, occurred in spite of a 1.6 percent drop in cereal production, as production of other crops, particularly cotton and groundnuts, increased significantly and contributed to a 6 percent expansion of the primary sector.

As regards the devaluation, an FAO study on its impact conducted in 1995 concluded that some 18 months later an increase had taken place in the area planted to export crops (cotton) and import competing crops (rice). An increase was also detected in exports of cotton, livestock, hides and skins, oil crops and fruit and vegetables, as well as a reduction in imports of rice and dairy products, which would probably have been bigger had the government not prevented the increased import prices from feeding fully through into consumer prices. At the same time, agricultural input prices also recorded increases. For local cereals, on the other hand, no effect on prices or production was yet

[16] According to data from the Ministry of the Economy, Finance and Planning.
[17] Ibid.
[18] Projection by the Ministry of the Economy, Finance and Planning.
[19] UEMOA comprises Benin, Burkina Faso, Côte d'Ivoire, Mali, the Niger, Senegal and Togo.

discernible, largely the result of the existence of significant stocks from previous crop years and of the only partial transmission of price increases for imported cereals on to consumers. On the consumption side, in urban areas a decrease had taken place in consumption of meat and imported foodstuffs, while consumption of local cereals had increased. Low-income urban households had been forced to reduce overall food consumption, however, following the increase in the overall consumer price index.

Although there are signs of a recent acceleration in economic growth following economic reforms and the currency devaluation, it must be emphasized that economic performance and the adjustments in the economy over the period following the devaluation are the combined results of many other factors. It should be borne in mind, *inter alia,* that the devaluation coincided with a strengthening of international commodity prices affecting, among other products, cotton, and that this provided an additional stimulus to the export sector. With cotton prices having peaked in the second quarter of 1995 this additional favourable price effect for Burkina Faso's major export commodity is fading.

In any case, it would still be too early to make any conclusive judgement on the medium- to long-term effects of either the devaluation or the structural reform efforts. Such sharp changes in relative prices in the economy as those introduced by the devaluation implies the need for major adjustments in production and consumption patterns in the economy. These adjustments necessarily require time. The same would apply to the impact of the structural reforms undertaken across the economy as a whole and within the agricultural sector. Particularly in the agricultural sector, where sectoral adjustment has been under way for a shorter period and is still being pursued, it is still too early to expect a significant impact. In the medium term, however, the structural adjustment efforts and the currency devaluation should have a mutually strengthening impact. Indeed, if inflationary pressures can be kept under control, Burkina Faso seems well placed to consolidate the competitive gains deriving from the devaluation.

The Government of Burkina Faso is itself optimistic as far as future growth prospects are concerned. This is expressed by the GDP growth objective for 1995-97 of

5 percent per annum that was spelled out in the Policy Framework Paper for 1995-97 and even more by the objective expressed in the Letter of Intent on Sustainable Human Development of increasing per caput income from the current US$300 to $500 by 2005 through a further gradual acceleration in GDP growth to reach 8 percent per annum from the year 2000 onwards. Although GDP growth objectives spelled out in the past structural adjustment programmes have until now not been met, the 5 percent per annum medium-term growth objective does not seem unrealistic if the process of determined policy reforms is carried forward. Such a growth rate is after all not far from rates historically achieved, such as the average annual rate of about 4.5 percent recorded from 1982 to 1987 and during the 1970s. Although the higher growth objectives of the government for the following years may seem excessively optimistic, the possibility for Burkina Faso of ensuring consistent gains in per caput income in the medium term does seem within reach.

Conclusions

Burkina Faso has been making extremely determined efforts at reforming its economy and laying the foundations for sustained long-term economic growth. Given the country's high degree of dependence on agriculture, reforms in this sector are a crucial element of the adjustment efforts, just as there can be no doubt that for many years agriculture will continue to have to provide the main contribution to economic growth and to the livelihood of the population.

In spite of its extreme poverty and its poor resource base, Burkina Faso has a number of political and social assets that provide reasons for optimism for the years to come. As mentioned above, the country has a tradition of serious and credible economic management which, among other things, has prevented it from running into persistent macroeconomic imbalances of the magnitude experienced by many other developing countries in Africa. Aspects of this are the recognized integrity in the management of public affairs and the fact that corruption, a pervasive phenomenon elsewhere, is recognized as being marginal in Burkina Faso. This tradition should only be further enhanced by the establishment of democratic institutions in 1991. The

SUB-SAHARAN AFRICA

country likewise has a tradition of participatory development based on community participation from which a strong associative movement has emerged. This is accompanied by a strong commitment to social objectives in development efforts and the similarly strong attention traditionally paid to environmental protection.

The long-term development of the country will continue to depend critically on the overcoming of some serious constraints. Notable among these are the environmental constraints and the still very poor degree of human development in terms of levels of general education and access to adequate health services. The latter, in particular, appears as a critical factor for development, the progress already made since independence notwithstanding. Continuous determined efforts in economic reform and human development, with particular emphasis on agricultural and rural development, will hold the key to sustained economic growth in the long term. In pursuing these efforts, Burkina Faso needs and deserves the full support of the international community.

ASIA AND THE PACIFIC

REGIONAL OVERVIEW
Economic developments

In 1995, the developing countries in Asia and the Pacific again outperformed all other regions with an economic growth of 7.9 percent, down slightly from 8.2 percent in 1994. Economic expansion in the People's Republic of China slowed to a still-high 10.2 percent, and in India declined slightly to 6.2 percent. The newly industrializing countries, Hong Kong, the Republic of Korea, Singapore and Taiwan Province of China, continued to restructure their economies and upgrade industrial technologies in the face of rising labour costs and as a group achieved slightly better growth than in 1994. All countries in Southeast Asia registered accelerated output expansion with the subregional average rising from 7.8 percent in 1994 to 7.9 percent in 1995, largely on the strength of economic activity in Malaysia, Viet Nam and Thailand. Overall growth in South Asia remained steady, slowing down in Bangladesh, India and Sri Lanka but accelerating in Pakistan. Regional growth is expected to continue to be strong but to slow to 7.1 percent in 1996 and then rising to 7.3 percent in 1997.[20]

The Asian developing countries have experienced a rapid expansion in exports since about the mid-1970s. Their export and income growth rates have consistently exceeded global rates and those of other developing regions. As a group, Asian developing countries have almost tripled their share of world exports. Since 1979, intra-Asian trade, excluding that with Japan, has increased more than eightfold and risen from 21 percent of developing Asia's exports to more than 35 percent. When Japan is included, almost half of Asia's exports are intraregional.

Greater market integration and trade liberalization facilitate technology transfer, specialization based on comparative advantage and improved resource pricing and management. Liberalization of foreign investment regimes has contributed to large increases in foreign direct investment flows, particularly to East Asia. Together with domestic investment, these liberalization efforts and the resulting foreign investment inflows continued to support sturdy export-led growth. The

---

[20] The economic growth rates and projections are based on Asian Development Bank. 1996. *Asian Development Outlook 1996 and 1997.*

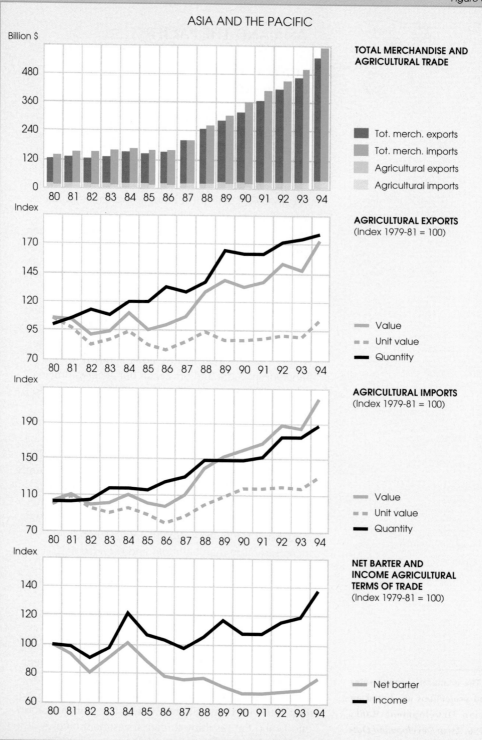

Figure 8A

ASIA AND THE PACIFIC

Billion $

TOTAL MERCHANDISE AND
AGRICULTURAL TRADE

- Tot. merch. exports
- Tot. merch. imports
- Agricultural exports
- Agricultural imports

Index

AGRICULTURAL EXPORTS
(Index 1979-81 = 100)

- Value
- Unit value
- Quantity

Index

AGRICULTURAL IMPORTS
(Index 1979-81 = 100)

- Value
- Unit value
- Quantity

Index

NET BARTER AND
INCOME AGRICULTURAL
TERMS OF TRADE
(Index 1979-81 = 100)

- Net barter
- Income

Source: FAO

Figure 8B

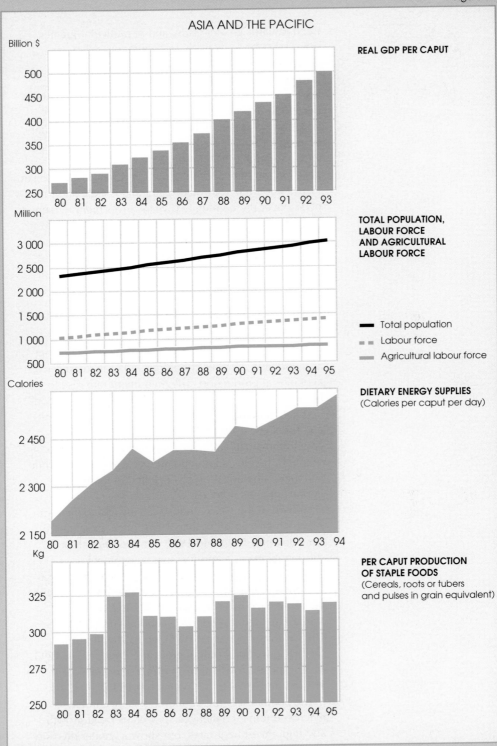

ASIA AND THE PACIFIC

REAL GDP PER CAPUT

TOTAL POPULATION, LABOUR FORCE AND AGRICULTURAL LABOUR FORCE

— Total population
- - Labour force
— Agricultural labour force

DIETARY ENERGY SUPPLIES
(Calories per caput per day)

PER CAPUT PRODUCTION OF STAPLE FOODS
(Cereals, roots or tubers and pulses in grain equivalent)

Source: FAO

trend towards greater trade, and in particular greater intra-Asian trade, is likely to continue to drive economic growth in the region.

Over the past 15 years the economy of *China* has been booming, with average annual GDP growth of 9.4 percent and a declining incidence of poverty. The economy has opened up and attracted a large amount of foreign direct investment. Merchandise exports have grown rapidly as a share of GDP. The gradual deceleration of economic growth in China which began in 1994 continued through 1995 and is expected to persist over the coming two years. Investment remained high, at 39.5 percent of GDP in 1995, merchandise exports grew by 23 percent and inflation declined significantly but, at 14.8 percent, remains the highest among the major economies of the region. Reform of the state-owned enterprise sector remains a crucial priority.

In *India,* economic liberalization has been much more recent and performance more modest. However, in 1995 growth continued at a substantial 6.2 percent as favourable weather conditions led to increased agricultural production. The investment rate rose to 24 percent of GDP, reflecting both optimistic expectations and the continuation of the liberalization programme, and fiscal consolidation continued as well. Export growth remained strong at 21 percent, led by agrobased products, textiles, clothing and electronic goods, while economic liberalization has resulted in increasing imports of capital goods.

Growth in the newly industrializing economies was slightly higher in 1995 than 1994, but is expected to slow down in 1996 and 1997. On the strength of substantial exports and massive government expenditure on infrastructure, *Hong Kong* grew at 4.6 percent in 1995 and is expected to continue at roughly the same pace in 1996 and 1997. *The Republic of Korea* extended its economic rebound from 1994 to 1995 with 9.2 percent growth led by the industrial sector. Agricultural output grew at 6.1 percent in 1995. In *Singapore,* growth slowed from the double-digit rates of 1993 and 1994 to 8.9 percent in 1995.

The Southeast Asian economies share similar macroeconomic challenges, as well as rapid growth and high investment rates, but show a greater diversity in living standards and levels of development.

ASIA AND THE PACIFIC

Economic growth in *Indonesia* increased marginally to 7.6 percent in 1995, based on rapid growth in the industrial and services sectors and strong private investment growth supported by continued substantial foreign direct investments. The range of Indonesian exports has widened considerably in recent years and the share of manufactured exports in total exports has risen from 14.8 percent in 1980 to 78.3 percent in 1995, as the shares for agriculture and oil and gas declined. The economy of *Malaysia* grew at 9.3 percent with improved agricultural performance and strong industrial growth. The recovery of *the Philippines* economy, which began in 1992, continued in 1995 with 4.8 percent growth, as political stability, prudent macroeconomic management, the easing of some infrastructural constraints (especially power) and structural reforms helped to improve private-sector confidence and investment. *Thailand* grew by 8.6 percent in 1995, only slightly less than in 1994. In *Viet Nam*, GDP growth reached 9.5 percent in 1995, following growth of 8.8 percent in 1994, which was led by the industrial sector.

The countries of South Asia continue to rely on the primary sector for economic activity and export generation, and share relatively lower per caput income growth. In spite of stagnation in agriculture, strong industrial sector growth in *Bangladesh* kept the overall economy growing by 4.1 percent in 1995 and the strong performance of small-scale private enterprises is expected to continue to be the main engine of growth. Real GDP growth in *Pakistan* remained at 4.7 percent, primarily the result of the poor cotton crop. GDP growth in *Sri Lanka* remained constant in 1995 at 5.6 percent, but wide-ranging reforms in the trade and industrial policy environment should provide continued scope for exports and expansion of the industrial sector and supporting services. The principal issues facing South Asia are whether recent accomplishments in macroeconomic stabilization and structural reform can be sustained and improved upon and whether further liberalization efforts and transport infrastructure improvements will be undertaken.

Agricultural performance and issues
In *China*, the 1994 decline in agricultural output was reversed to 4 percent growth in 1995 and output is

ASIA AND THE PACIFIC

expected to rise by 4.5 percent in 1996, primarily the result of greater incentives provided by the government. Even so, cereal prices continued to rise in the first half of 1995. Grain coupons were reintroduced by some large and medium-sized cities to ensure that low-income groups would have access to foodstuffs. In general, the lagging agricultural sector needs further stimulation, not only to meet rising food requirements but also to address the widening income gap between rural and urban areas. The Ninth Five-Year Plan has again highlighted the need for agricultural land conservation, greater capital investment in agriculture and greater use of modern techniques for generating higher yields.

Departing from the recent trend, the Government of *India* raised the 1994-95 minimum support prices for wheat and barley by 3-4 percent and those of other cereals by 8-10 percent. With grain stocks at record levels, pressure to export increased. Consequently, on the trade front the government took further measures to promote cereal exports, abolishing the minimum export price for durum wheat, setting a 1994-95 export quota of 500 000 tonnes for common wheat and raising that quota for 1995-96 to 2.5 million tonnes. Rice exports have remained free from restrictions since late 1994, while 1994-95 export quotas of 50 000 tonnes each for maize, sorghum and millet remained about the same as the previous year. Efforts to increase exports of value-added and higher value agricultural products as a means of transferring the benefits of the liberalization process to rural areas continue to show success with increased exports of fresh fruit and vegetables, meat and meat preparations, processed fruit and juices, other processed food and floriculture products.

Agricultural output in *Indonesia* grew by 2.5 percent, recovering from its flood- and drought-induced poor performance of 1994. Import tariffs were lowered or abolished on maize, sorghum and barley. Rice production benefited from a higher paddy support price and from the introduction of drought-resistant varieties, while the government announced a US$900 million programme to improve irrigation for rice production on over 1 million ha. In order to increase rice procurement, higher procurement prices, lower procurement quality standards and a higher transportation subsidy were introduced.

ASIA AND THE PACIFIC

The agricultural sector in *Malaysia* improved its performance in 1995, largely on the strength of the oil-palm, forestry and livestock (primarily poultry) sectors and as a result of improved export prices. Land under fruit production continued to increase dramatically. The price of wheat-flour was kept frozen during 1994-95, for the fourth year. As 1995 was the final year of the Sixth Malaysia Plan (five-year plan), major agricultural policy changes await the Seventh Plan in 1996.

Agricultural production in *the Philippines* suffered from poor weather and typhoons in the third quarter of 1995 are likely to have an adverse effect on agricultural results in fiscal 1996. With annual population growth of 2.4 percent, limited land available for cultivation and further economic growth and trade liberalization expected, agricultural imports are likely to increase rapidly. Domestic prices for rice, maize and sugar rose to at least double world prices in 1995, forcing the government to allow major imports of these sensitive commodities. Changes may be significant in 1996 as much of Philippine agricultural production (other than rice) that was formerly protected becomes exposed to world market forces through the implementation of the country's Uruguay Round access commitments.

The agricultural sector in *Thailand* grew by about 3 percent in 1995 with similar growth expected in 1996. Farm income has been rising as a result of the combination of firm primary product prices and increased productivity, while the continued boom in manufacturing is boosting consumption in urban areas. Import quotas have been raised for maize and rice, while a rice exporters' marketing subsidy has been implemented. In 1995 the government extended the coverage of its scheme of seed subsidies to promote increased use of high-yielding, hybrid rice seed. The Cabinet also approved a proposal to set up the country's first commodity futures exchange.

In *Viet Nam,* the agricultural sector grew more slowly than the industrial sector, but still increased by 3.5 percent. Further gains in the sector are likely to be greatest in industrial crops where export incentives continue to be exploited. New agricultural land-use tax policies, together with recognition of land transfer rights, should have a positive impact on the effective use of agricultural land.

In *Bangladesh,* bad weather conditions constrained

agricultural output which contributes more than one-third of total output. The government froze the 1994-95 minimum support prices for both paddy and wheat. A fertilizer shortage during the dry season *boro* crop, following a disappointing main *aman* rice crop, resulted in agricultural sector growth of only 0.2 percent in 1995, well below even the relatively stagnant growth of 1.8 percent in recent years. The decline in crop production, however, was largely offset by strong growth of non-crop agriculture, particularly in fisheries and livestock.

The Government of *Nepal* adopted an Agricultural Perspective Plan in May 1995, calling for substantial investment in irrigation, fertilizer use and rural infrastructure.

In *Pakistan*, the continued failure of the cotton crop for the third year in a row has kept GDP growth low and could jeopardize fiscal stability.

State procurements of paddy in *Sri Lanka* had been minimal in recent years, as market prices have generally exceeded the minimum support price but, following a bumper paddy harvest in 1994 and lower rice demand, the Paddy Marketing Board stepped in to procure roughly 10 percent of the harvest and the government implemented seasonal import tariffs. Meanwhile, the ban on wheat-flour imports was lifted in early 1995. Commodity prices for tea, rubber and coconut are not expected to rise significantly over the next two years, and this will have an adverse effect on the agricultural sector of Sri Lanka.

Issues and prospects for regional agriculture

The rapid economic growth throughout much of East Asia has come at a high environmental cost. In urban areas, pollution and congestion are common. In rural Asia deforestation or desertification, groundwater depletion or contamination, soil salinity in irrigated areas, loss of biological diversity and erosion are some of the problems endangering agricultural productivity. A clear understanding of the extent to which these are necessary evils of development remains elusive, and in most countries an unconscious decision is being implemented to delay environmental protection or enhancement until some future, unspecified level of development is achieved. The fact that environmental protection is much cheaper and easier than

ASIA AND THE PACIFIC

rehabilitation is often given little consideration in the rush for income growth.

The massive extent of poverty in Asia and the complexity of the interactions between poverty and the environment make it difficult to predict the environmental effects of income growth. With higher income, there is the potential for greater mitigation of negative environmental effects, but there is also likely to be greater consumption and waste of environmental resources.

The Asian environment sustains more than half of the world's population, the majority of its poor population who depend on the rural environment for their survival and a large share of the world's biological diversity. In the Asia and the Pacific region, Australia, China, India, Indonesia, Malaysia and Myanmar have been classified as "megadiverse" by the Parties to the Convention on Biological Diversity because of the range of their plant and animal species. In spite of poverty and declining rates of fertility, from 1990 to 2010 developing Asian countries will add almost 1 billion new consumers to those already straining the earth's carrying capacity. Even in 2010, over half of the economically active population of these countries will still be involved in agriculture, implying further intensification of land and water use, with more mineral fertilizers and pesticides.

Asia is already the region with the lowest per caput fresh water availability in the world and the shortage is expected to worsen. At the same time the region has experienced a high level of soil degradation. Both domestic and international demand for agricultural products in Asia can be expected to increase pressure on the environment.

Concerns have been raised that China, in particular, will face rapidly growing demand for grain for food and feed at the same time as the agricultural resource base is declining or being degraded and the potential for yield increases is uncertain. Given the massive population involved, there are predictions that Chinese demand for grain imports could overwhelm world grain markets.[21] Such studies are, however, generally based on little confidence in the ability of production to respond to policy reforms and market mechanisms. More carefully reasoned studies express greater optimism that world grain markets (and Chinese production) are not endangered.[22]

[21] For one of the more alarmist expositions of this view, see L.R. Brown. 1994. Who will feed China? *World Watch,* September/October 1994, p. 10-19.

[22] See Box 15 on Prospects for China's grain trade p. 276.

ASIA AND THE PACIFIC

Over the last two decades, as the economic and environmental interdependence of developing economies in the Asia and the Pacific region has increased, so have their efforts towards regional and subregional cooperation. Prominent among these are the Asian Pacific Economic Cooperation Council (APEC) forum, the Association of Southeast Asian Nations (ASEAN), the South Asian Association for Regional Cooperation (SAARC), the South Pacific Forum and the South Pacific Commission. Subregional cooperation arrangements in Asia include the Southern China Growth Triangle, the Singapore-Johor-Riau Growth Triangle, the Tumen River Area Development, the Indonesia-Malaysia-Thailand Growth Triangle, the Brunei-Indonesia-Malaysia-Philippines East ASEAN Growth Area (BIMP-EAGA) and the Greater Mekong Subregion. These cooperative efforts aim at promoting intraregional trade and investment, as well as more efficient resource use in order to benefit the environment. They also provide fora for the discussion and planning of cooperative efforts for sustainable agriculture and use of the environment.

Most of the larger cooperative efforts have an Asian trade liberalization focus. For example, the APEC forum has plans for trade liberalization among developed members by 2010 and among developing members by 2020, the ASEAN Free Trade Area (AFTA) is currently under implementation and recently plans have been made for a South Asian Preferential Trading Arrangement among the members of SAARC. Most of the efforts involve gradual liberalization, so there is likely to be a correspondingly gradual contraction of output in more protected industries and expansion in those less protected. In the Philippines, simulation results suggest that trade liberalization will increase national levels of pollution from production by reallocating output towards logging, mining and agriculture and, within manufacturing, towards more pollution-intensive industries such as food processing, beverages and wood products.[23]

Trade policies can have unintended environmental consequences, even when applied for environmental purposes. Rapid deforestation has led to bans on log exports from Cambodia, Indonesia, the Philippines, Thailand and Vanuatu. Export restrictions to favour local wood processors in Indonesia, however, have

[23] P. Intal Jr. and P. Quintos. 1994. *Adjusting to the new trade and environment paradigm: the case of the Philippines.* Paper presented at a symposium in honour of Dr Gelia Castillo, Quezon City, the Philippines, 27 to 28 September 1994.

ASIA AND THE PACIFIC

been found to promote greater use of logs in production by lowering the domestic timber price, resulting in even greater environmental degradation.[24] In this manner, proposals from richer, tropical timber importing countries to limit imports of tropical wood products to "save the rain forests" can actually lead to increased deforestation.

When property rights are poorly defined or when there is a common property resource, there is often a tendency to mismanage the resource because no proper price is paid for its exploitation. Even ownership and management by the government have not sustained healthy forest systems in much of Asia, while private, community-based tenure rights might improve forest management.

Property rights remain poorly defined in many areas of Asia and the Pacific. Inconsistencies in the treatment of squatters in the forests of Thailand have exacerbated deforestation both in that country and, through trade, in its neighbours. Land reform remains a critical issue to be addressed in the development of the Philippines.

Confrontation over the Spratley Islands, arguments over water flows to the Aral Sea and the 1995 seizing of Japanese fishing boats in the Pacific by the United States make clear that it is not only domestic but also international property rights that are unsettled. As populations grow and the demand for scarce resources increases, tensions over the assignment of property rights can be expected to increase.

The international efforts under way in various Asian and Pacific fora related to cross-border environmental interactions cover a wide range of activities, from capacity building and institutional strengthening to biological research, the control of cross-border movement of hazardous wastes, bans on driftnet fishing and efforts to slow global warming and protect the ozone layer. These efforts need to be intensified, given the urgency of many of the problems, their importance to regional and global food security and the tendency for international disputes to escalate if not resolved.

[24] C.A.P. Braga. 1992. **Tropical forests and trade policy: the case of Indonesia and Brazil.** *In* P. Low, ed. *International Trade and the Environment.* World Bank Discussion Paper No. 159, p. 173-194. Washington, DC.

ASIA AND THE PACIFIC

PAKISTAN
Economic developments

The political environment has been a continuing major influence in Pakistan's economic and social development. Lengthy periods of martial law have been interspersed with fragile elected coalitions since Pakistan's creation in 1947 when it split off from India. The country has borne a heavy financial and political burden from external and internal strife that continues today. Events which have greatly affected the ability to govern include the separation of the country in 1971 that created Bangladesh from East Pakistan, the influx of up to 3 million Afghan refugees seeking protection from the war with the former USSR, smuggling of drugs and other goods across borders, continuing disputes with India over Kashmiri allegiance and tensions among political factions, most recently in and around Karachi, Pakistan's major city and only port. The need to spend more than one-quarter of the government budget on defence in order to respond to these situations plagues Pakistan as it attempts to build much-needed public infrastructure, comply with lenders' demands for macroeconomic reform and address festering social and environmental issues.

Pakistan remains among the world's poorest countries, particularly in the rural areas where 70 percent of the population live. Real per caput income stands at US$430 (1993) despite having expanded at a healthy rate of 3.1 percent per year between 1980 and 1993. No official census of population has been performed since 1980, but the population is estimated at about 127 million (1995). The positive growth in per caput income has been achieved despite high population growth rates, but has not prevented the absolute number of poor in Pakistan from increasing.

Combating population growth has proved to be more difficult for Pakistan than for nearby developing countries because of the limited economic role and educational opportunities for women. At 6.2 percent, the fertility rate is the highest in the developing world outside Africa and the Near East. The female literacy rate is 20 percent nationwide, but much lower in some rural areas. One-third of girls enroll in primary school, but only 13 percent continue into secondary school. Pakistan is ranked 132 out of 173 countries in the UN Human Development Index and is particularly low in

educational and health measures. Physical conditions are also poor: 20 percent of the population has access to sanitation (10 percent in rural areas); 80 percent has access to clean water (45 percent in rural areas); and only about 10 percent of villages have electricity. In all of these measures, Pakistan is substantially behind other Asian countries identified by the World Bank as having similar circumstances.[25]

The social and food security pressures created by population growth and the slow rate of improvement in education and health systems available to the poor and middle-class segments of society are looming as major issues to be dealt with in the latter half of the 1990s.

Pakistan achieved high economic growth rates throughout the 1950s and early 1960s caused by an influx of foreign aid following the separation from India, a low base of output in both industry and agriculture and agricultural sector growth spurred by green revolution innovations. Overall GDP growth was 6.1 percent annually during the 1960s. During the 1970s, the government aimed at creating conditions for the development of domestic industry and, in the process, changing Pakistan from a primarily poor, agrarian nation to a rapidly growing, industrial economy using modern technology. The government intervened heavily in the economy to transfer resources from agriculture to the nascent industrial sector, which was expected to have higher overall growth potential. During this period, agricultural output grew by 3 percent per year, while industrial output grew by 5 percent and overall GDP by 4.9 percent.

The government's emphasis was on import-substituting production in an effort to achieve self-sufficiency. Policies included nationalizing most major industries, imposing high tariffs and other barriers to trade to provide absolute protection from foreign competition, controlling input flows, establishing price controls and subsidies on consumer goods, increasing wages and deficit spending on a large scale for public investment projects.

Macroeconomic conditions and trends
As in many other developing countries, Pakistan faced deteriorating macroeconomic conditions after the oil price rises and global recession of the 1970s. At the start of the 1980s, the government deficit was 5 percent

[25] World Bank. 1993. *Pakistan: Country Economic Memorandum, FY 1993.* Washington, DC.

ASIA AND THE PACIFIC

of GDP, the current account deficit was 3.5 percent and debt as a share of GDP was 40 percent.[26] A structural adjustment plan was devised with the World Bank and the International Monetary Fund (IMF) in 1982 to correct these problems and begin to orient Pakistan's economy towards exports and more liberalized markets. Specific progress was made in liberalizing trade and foreign payments, privatizing banks and industry, relaxing restrictions on investment (both domestic and foreign) and strengthening the financial system.

All manner of aid packages were provided to Pakistan by international donors (see Box 11 for details) and a political consensus developed around the economic reforms promoted by international lenders. The macroeconomy grew by an average 6.3 percent each year during the 1980s, raising hopes that Pakistan would be able to imitate the "tiger" economies of Southeast Asia. The growth was fuelled by two factors not common to those countries. First, Pakistan exported labour in large numbers to the Persian Gulf and elsewhere, receiving in return US$2-3 billion per year in repatriated earnings. Second, the country borrowed heavily which allowed government spending increasingly to dominate the economy. These factors allowed some development of physical infrastructure and a gradual improvement in incomes. Sectoral growth was especially fast in utilities, construction and mining.

In spite of progress in specific sectors, Pakistan's overall macroeconomic picture worsened after the reform programme was instituted. By 1987 the government budget deficit had reached 8.5 percent of GDP – twice the average of Pakistan's Asian neighbours. Internal government debt totalled about 43 percent of GDP, with a roughly equivalent amount of external debt. Pakistan was saving about 13 percent of GDP (the developing world averages 23 percent) and investing about 18 percent. The difference between domestic savings and investment must be derived from foreign borrowing and investment. Compounding the pressure on the external balance were Pakistan's growing import needs and shrinking workers' remittances.

The burdens of Pakistan's cumbersome planning apparatus and its protectionist industrial policies were difficult to overcome. Fundamental macroeconomic

[26] Pakistan's fiscal year is July to June, but output and budget figures in this report are cited using one year only. For example, the 1987-88 budget is referred to as 1987 in this report.

BOX 11
AID TO PAKISTAN UNDER STRUCTURAL
AND SECTORAL ADJUSTMENT PROGRAMMES DURING THE 1980s

Pakistan has availed itself of many types of loan packages available from multilateral donors. The main thrust of the programmes has been to achieve more market orientation, develop infrastructure, modernize and remove subsidies and trade protection. Specific lending packages included:

• IMF Structural Adjustment loan of US$1.6 billion in 1980;
• International Development Association (IDA) Sectoral Loan for Fertilizer of US$50 million in 1980;
• International Bank for Reconstruction and Development (IBRD) and IDA Structural Adjustment Loans of US$140 million in 1982;
• IBRD Sectoral Loan for Energy of US$178 million in 1985;
• IBRD Sectoral Loan for Export Development of US$70 million in 1986;
• IBRD Sectoral Loan for Agriculture of US$200 million in 1988;
• IMF Structural Adjustment Loan of US$515 million in 1988;

• Asian Development Bank (ADB) Sectoral Loan for Industry of US$200 million in 1988;
• IBRD Sectoral Loan for the Financial Industry of US$150 million in 1989;
• IBRD Sectoral Loan for Energy of US$250 million in 1989;
• ADB Sectoral Loan for Agriculture of US$200 million in 1989.

IBRD and IDA are lending arms of the World Bank.

_____

Source: Qureshi, Pakistan Institute of Development Economics, 1995.

conditions for sustained growth had not yet appeared. Bottlenecks in vital components of the economy and social deterioration began to be evident. Pakistan's manufacturing sector was heavily oriented towards the processing of basic commodities and the agricultural sector lacked the infrastructure and research base to maintain productivity growth. Both manufacturing and agriculture were dependent on a complex system of government-controlled inputs and inadequate infrastructure.

Recent years have seen fast growth in money supply, increasing inflationary pressures and declining confidence in government management. The inflation rate was kept in single digits during most of the 1980s, but has crept into double digits, hovering around 16 percent and more in the early to mid-1990s. The Pakistani rupee has steadily depreciated (by 52 percent between 1980 and 1992) since a managed float was adopted in 1982 and was further devalued in 1993 and 1995 as a result of continuing high domestic inflation rates.

Renewed IMF/World Bank structural adjustment programmes were instituted in 1988 and in February 1994 with the broad goals of improving the GDP growth rate, reducing the fiscal deficit, achieving full currency convertibility and reducing the current account deficit. The World Bank has also urged further deregulation and privatization of the economy, including more investment in social services and infrastructure for transport, communications, irrigation and energy. In addition, a Special Action Program (SAP), providing US$200 million from the World Bank and bilateral support from other donors, is intended to redress some of Pakistan's deficiencies in the important social and human resource areas. SAP focuses on basic education, primary health and nutrition needs, population planning and rural water supply and sanitation.

Two-thirds of the way through this programme some success is obvious on major macroeconomic variables. The budget deficit shrank to 5.5 percent of GDP in 1994, total expenditure dropped to 20 percent of GDP in 1994 and the current account deficit has almost halved to 3.6 percent of GDP. Savings and investment rates have improved slightly. While progress has been made, it has been slower than hoped. Interest and

defence expenditures are still high and debt service consumes 34 percent of foreign exchange earnings. A higher level of urgency has been imposed in the past year as the IMF threatened to withhold financial assistance until further reforms were in place. As a result, there have been recent price increases in essential food items and electricity as the government attempts to reduce its deficit by cutting subsidies and other expenditures.

Importance of the agricultural sector

The agricultural sector is crucial from a social and economic perspective in Pakistan. It still provides one-quarter of the country's economic output, 50 percent of its jobs and 13 percent of exports. Agriculture is also the only significant employer of women, who constitute 16.5 percent of the paid labour force in agriculture. It is the main driver in the economy, as illustrated in 1993 when severe flooding and a cotton virus combined to cause a 5.3 percent decline in agricultural output and slowed overall GDP growth to 1.9 percent from 7.8 percent the previous year. Some 60 percent of Pakistan's manufacturing output comes from processing agricultural products and 70 percent of its exports are clothing and textiles.

Pakistan has an excellent climate and natural resource base for agriculture. The very warm summers and moderate winters provide two growing seasons for many crops and the topography throughout much of the country provides good conditions for a variety of agricultural products. Of the 31 million ha suitable for agriculture, 22 million are currently under cultivation.

Agricultural output grew at about 3 percent per year between 1970 and 1995, but is highly variable from year to year. The variability of Pakistan's agricultural output can be attributed to several factors, some of which are preventable, although they have recurred with increasing seriousness in recent years. These factors are flooding, pests and disease, uncertainty of input supplies and resource degradation. Such issues must be dealt with relatively quickly for Pakistan's agriculture to remain viable as a source of food for the population and a source of raw materials for the manufacturing sector.

One of the main features of Pakistan's agricultural sector is the uneven level of development which

exacerbates weather-induced instability and creates wide gaps in productivity within the sector. Agriculture in Pakistan is still undergoing transition from traditional to modern methods of production. Government experts estimate that about 25 percent of farmers still use traditional methods such as oxen or hand-ploughs, about 55 percent use a mix of traditional and modern methods and the remaining 20 percent have adopted modern technology and equipment. As well as having an effect on the cost of production and, therefore, the government's level of support prices, the level of farming technology affects farmers' choice of crops, vulnerability to pests and disease, crop and livestock yields and, of course, income.

Past and recent trends in area, production and yields of major crops are shown in Table 4.

Pakistan is nearly self-sufficient in most crops and livestock, but is incurring growing import demand for wheat, edible oils, sugar and tea. Imports of major agricultural products are shown in Table 5. The share of GDP contributed by agriculture has been declining gradually from 53 percent in 1947 to its current 24 percent. Nonetheless, it is of vital importance to Pakistan's macroeconomy as it provides raw inputs to the growing manufacturing sector and essential earnings from exports.

In addition to the contribution agriculture makes to the macroeconomy in Pakistan, certain agricultural products are important for social and political reasons. Wheat consumed in the form of bread is the most important component of the Pakistani diet, providing almost one-half of total calories consumed. The government continues to provide subsidies to maintain low prices for wheat-flour, even when it means importing wheat in bad crop years. During 1994, the government spent about US$14.4 million on subsidizing the sale at low prices of imported wheat. This represents about 40 percent of total wheat subsidies. Wheat imports in 1995 were only about 200 000 tonnes as the result of a good wheat crop, but structural problems in the sector still need to be addressed if Pakistan is to prevent rising import demand.

Food production per caput has grown by an average of 1.2 percent per year since 1979, barely meeting the needs of the increasing population. Malnutrition is still

ASIA AND THE PACIFIC

TABLE 4

Average annual percentage change in area, production and yield of major crops (1947-1988 and 1990-1994)

	Area		Production		Yield	
	1947-88	1990-94	1947-88	1990-94	1947-88	1990-94
Wheat	1.68	0.62	2.35	1.24	4.02	0.63
Rice	2.35	1.15	4.52	7.00	2.17	5.82
Sugar cane	3.79	2.89	4.53	7.28	0.74	4.26
Cotton	1.94	0.61	0.14	-5.78	2.21	-6.36

TABLE 5

Imports of major agricultural products (1993)

	Quantity	Value
	('000 tonnes)	(US$ million)
Edible oils	1 131	491
Wheat	1 408	240
Tea	112	182
Pulses	154	44
Sugar	48	15

apparent in about 40 percent of children under five years. Per caput fat consumption is rising and adult nutrition meets minimum standards, but protein and calorie consumption have been stagnant since 1989. Inadequate consumption of dairy products and fruit occurs widely, although rural populations have better access to buffalo milk and cereals than urban dwellers, while the latter consume more meat. Milk and butter from buffalo are important in people's diets, especially the rural poor, and contain a higher fat content than cow milk products so provide a substantial share of dietary intake.

Other major agricultural products are livestock and dairy products, rice, sugar and cottonseed. While crops dominate the sector, livestock accounts for 33 percent of agricultural output. Minor agricultural products in Pakistan are pulses, fruits, vegetables, fish and forestry products.

Cotton plays a major role in earning foreign exchange for Pakistan by supplying the large textile producing industry. Output peaked in 1991 at 12.8 million bales but has suffered in recent years from flooding and then a serious infestation of cotton curl virus that the government is still attempting to eradicate. The government has had difficulty dealing with the problems in the sector caused by pests. It has tried and failed to introduce more resistant seed varieties and pesticides in a timely manner. Furthermore, while being cheap on export markets, Pakistan's cotton is not high quality and the sector faces growing competition in its export markets from India, China and Thailand.

Cotton manufactures have been under serious strain because of shortages of raw cotton. The cotton crop was 8.6 million bales in 1994 and Pakistan was forced to import a small amount. The combined capacity of 1 100 ginneries and 1 200 presses is about 12 million bales per year. Domestic cotton prices are high, but higher international prices have prevented companies from importing enough quantities to keep mills operating. As a result, there have been many temporary shutdowns of manufacturing facilities as companies have attempted to negotiate higher prices for their finished products.

Government intervention in the agricultural sector
As in other sectors of the economy, agriculture in Pakistan has been subject to a high degree of government influence and intervention. A combination of sector-specific, trade and macroeconomic policies has been used in an effort to maintain low consumer prices, achieve price stability for farmers and support the agricultural processing industries. Agricultural prices in Pakistan have traditionally been set below world prices and maintained through trade barriers. Since 1988, the government has renewed efforts to deregulate, privatize and increase exports. The economic reforms have concentrated on removing price and quantity controls and some of the rigidities caused by government involvement in transportation and distribution. Progress has been made in phasing out subsidies and directing a greater share towards consumers rather than farmers.

Nonetheless, the government remains an important force in the economy, both through its direct

intervention and because of the lack of private-sector capacity to replace it for needed functions. Of all investment in the agricultural sector, the government contributed 33 percent in 1994, while the private sector provided the rest. The government share has increased since the mid-1980s as a result of the private sector's failure to take over some of its activities. Even with recent reforms, many prices remain fixed and provincial authorities often impose controls when they perceive commodities to be in short supply. The price support policy for major commodities remains an important instrument determining resource allocation and production levels.

The Agricultural Price Commission recommends support prices for all the major agricultural commodities (wheat, rice, cotton, sugar cane, grams, non-traditional oilseeds, potatoes and onions) each year before the planting season. The intention is to encourage production and protect farmers from cost increases. In establishing recommended prices, the Commission considers domestic and international market conditions, productivity trends, the cost of production and crop substitution potential, as well as the production targets set by the Ministry of Agriculture. For wheat price supports, the Commission also considers the impact of any price change on consumer budgets and the overall price level.

The support prices are intended to be minimum guarantees but can end up being the market prices faced by farmers because of the rigidities and market power held by the government in providing inputs and purchasing outputs of the sector. For instance, farmers generally have little storage capacity and will sometimes sell their products to the government at harvest when prices are low rather than risk losses from spoilage. On average, the government purchases 20 percent of wheat output each year and resells it to flour mills.

In addition to the support prices available to farmers, the government is still involved in setting some consumer and input prices. Both wheat and edible oils are subsidized to consumers. Wheat prices in particular have remained low relative to import prices and other grains. Much of the benefit of cheap wheat is received by foreign producers and flour millers, rather than consumers. This is because the price of wheat received

by the farmer is determined by government decisions on import quantities. It has risen far more slowly than have the flour prices received by the mills.

Subsidies on pesticides and seeds have been gradually phased out, but water, credit and electricity are still subsidized. Subsidies were reinstated for fertilizer in 1995. Operation and maintenance of the irrigation system is to be paid for by charges levied by land area, but farmers have not been responsible for the capital costs of the irrigation system. Subsidies are provided for tubewell installation to farmers owning at least 5 ha of land. The government is also heavily involved in the provision of credit to the sector through determining the allocation of credit and interest rates and terms charged on agricultural loans.

The general level of tariffs and trade restrictions has been reduced (the maximum tariff rate was lowered to 65 percent in 1995 and is scheduled to be 35 percent by 1997), but specific trade price distortions are in place to help meet domestic needs. A growing demand for edible oilseeds has led to the imposition of an import duty as the government hopes to encourage domestic production, while the sugar processing industry is also protected through import duties. Wheat imports are subsidized and, until recently, rice and cotton exports were taxed as a means of earning revenue for the government. A special duty was imposed on cotton during 1994 because of the domestic shortfall.

The productivity problem

Pervasive government intervention has impeded the development of Pakistan's agricultural sector. The sector has achieved strong growth and kept up with demand because of favourable natural conditions and a large agricultural labour force working under poor social and economic conditions. Nonetheless, productivity in most products has lagged severely since the early 1980s.

There is potential for Pakistan's agricultural output to increase substantially from current levels, based on comparisons of average yields with international crop yields and those achieved by progressive farmers within the country. According to a study sponsored jointly by FAO and Pakistan's Ministry of Food, Agriculture and Livestock, wheat yields would rise by 50 percent if the practices of the progressive farmers were widespread.[27]

[27] FAO. 1995. *Strengthening wheat productivity enhancement programme.* In collaboration with the Pakistan Ministry of Food, Agriculture and Livestock, Islamabad.

ASIA AND THE PACIFIC

Another study claims that average farm productivity could be improved by at least 15 to 20 percent with proper application of inputs and improved farm practices.[28] Yields from most crops have become relatively stagnant, except for rice, where new varieties were introduced, and sugar, which is heavily protected. Seed cotton is Pakistan's only major crop with yields close to average world levels.

Pakistan's agricultural sector has struggled to achieve the needed improvements in output to assure an adequate supply of food for the country's growing population. Beyond the price and trade policies that have generally penalized agriculture, other factors are important in determining the productivity of Pakistan's agricultural sector. They include:

- fragmented landownership;
- limited irrigation supplies;
- inadequate social and physical infrastructure;
- unavailable and low-quality inputs;
- lack of information;
- environmental degradation.

These conditions are at the root of Pakistan's comparatively low agricultural productivity and its poor prospects for maintaining self-sufficiency under conditions of growing demand. Each is briefly discussed below. The aggregate effect of these problems is a high level of on-farm and off-farm output losses, low yields in comparison with competing countries and a low level of responsiveness to government reforms and price changes. Total on-farm losses are estimated to be about 35 percent of output from a combination of uncertain and badly timed water, electricity and fertilizer supply and generally non-existent storage facilities. It is estimated that the poor quality of farm-to-market roads adds 30 percent to the cost of farm products as only about 18 percent of paved roads are in good condition.

To make matters worse, the agricultural sector faces tightening of some of these constraints. Growth in output of 55 percent over the decade of the 1980s was derived from a 13 percent increase in cultivated area, a 20 percent increase in water availability at the farmgate, an 80 percent increase in fertilizer use and a 260 percent increase in the number of tractors.

[28] A. Mahmood and F. Walters. 1990. *Pakistan Agriculture.* Islamabad.

Cultivatable land and farmgate water are constraints that have little potential for further increase, while fertilizers and the use of tractors appear to be reaching the limits of their high returns. In fact, excessive use of these inputs may be contributing to problems of soil erosion and degradation that could inhibit production.

Fragmented landownership. In spite of Pakistan's highly concentrated landownership overall, fragmentation of landholdings is becoming a major problem. Some 80 percent of farms are less than 5 ha and 47 percent are smaller than 2 ha. The sharing out of land to many children increases the number of farms, thereby reducing the efficiency and deliverability of services. In general, the smaller farms have less access to credit, machinery and other productivity-enhancing inputs. In addition, they are risk averse, less diversified in crops and have less marketing flexibility. A limited availability of land titles, high transfer taxes, non-availability of credit for consolidation of land and restrictions on subdivision all inhibit change. There have been several half-hearted attempts at land reform since 1958, but little actual change. Understandably, people place high value on landownership for food security and because of insecurity about future government policies.

Limited irrigation supplies. Pakistan's weather would allow close to 200 percent cropping intensity in many areas but water limitations reduce it to an average of 116 percent. Rainfall is highly variable and seasonal, so Pakistan relies on irrigation fed by the Indus River. Pakistan possesses the world's largest contiguous surface distribution system with 36 000 miles (58 000 km) of canal conveyance and more than 1 million miles (1.6 million km) of water courses, channels and ditches reaching an area of 10.4 million ha. Some 78 percent of cultivated land is irrigated and the rest is rain-fed (*barani* lands). At present, 90 percent of output comes from irrigated areas, but estimates are that no more than a 10 percent expansion in irrigated area is possible and only at great cost. Even irrigation does not prevent seasonality; 85 percent of the system flow is in the *kharif* season and 15 percent occurs during the *rabi* season.

Reliance on the Indus River basin results in little

control over supply, an inability to charge based on usage and high losses from uncontrolled flows. Water losses occur in three main ways; along the canal system, in the watercourses and on the farm. The efficiency of the system is estimated at about 35 to 40 percent. This figure compares favourably with irrigation systems in other countries, but degradation and lower recycling reduce what is available in Pakistan. Farmers are responsible for the maintenance and operation of the water courses, which are being lined through cooperative projects involving farmers and the government. About 25 percent of the water courses have been lined over a 20-year period.

Both water quantity and quality pressures are rising. Agriculture consumes more than 90 percent of current water supplies, but urban and rural residential, commercial and industrial needs are growing. In addition, water quality is degraded by agriculture, as well as by other uses. About 25 percent of urban areas are not equipped with adequate sanitation and only 3 percent of industrial users treat their effluent to international standards.

Farmers are becoming more aware of conservation and efficiency from intercropping, but many are at the mercy of a water supply provided by the Indus River. Most of the area where fresh groundwater is available has already been exploited with tubewells and private investment in tubewells is at about replacement levels. There is growing concern as well about infiltration from saline aquifers into fresh groundwater supplies because of the extent of pumping from tubewells. About 10 percent of cultivatable land is out of production as a result of severe salinization, while 5 percent of cultivated lands are in the same condition, leading to a total loss of crops. Another 10 percent of cultivated area is slightly or moderately saline with a resulting crop loss of one-third to two-thirds. Some secondary salinity is occurring.

The topography is relatively flat in many areas and the irrigation system was not designed to follow the land contours so water is not used in an optimal manner and drainage is poor. As a result, waterlogging of the soil is a serious problem. Over 20 percent of cropped land is somewhat or very waterlogged. System drainage construction is occurring slowly but increasing demand is outpacing the gains from improved drainage.

Other measures being taken are programmes of soil conservation and watershed management but these are still small-scale.

Soil erosion is causing siltation in the reservoirs at a rate of 60 million tonnes per year. An estimated 11 percent of the reservoirs' combined storage capacity is expected to be lost by 2000. Storage capacity is important to the system as it is the only way to control water flows in heavy rain systems and to deliver water in a controlled manner.

Inadequate social and physical infrastructure. Social and physical infrastructure in rural areas is starkly inadequate in Pakistan and the services available in provinces and villages vary widely. Where education and health care are available, they often lack essential materials and trained personnel. A complex division of duties between the provincial governments and the national government in providing services and materials to agriculture exacerbates an already inefficient transportation and distribution network. Lack of physical infrastructure such as roads, stores, refrigeration units, refrigerated transport and cargo services at airports limits the ability of the private sector to modernize agriculture and deliver benefits back to farmers.

Unavailable and low-quality inputs. Power, credit, seeds, fertilizer and pesticides have been provided to farmers at subsidized rates, but are frequently not available when farmers need them and are of poor quality. Furthermore, widespread corruption, diversion and adulteration of materials have inhibited the development of efficiently functioning input markets and have led to the inefficient and inequitable delivery of essential inputs. Subsidies have been or are being phased out and farmers face rising prices without yet receiving the benefits of improved supply.

Agricultural credit continues to be heavily subsidized but inefficiently and inequitably. The problems include low allocations of credit (only 30 percent of demand is being met), improper and cumbersome disbursal mechanisms (only 75 percent of the funds allocated were distributed in 1994), corrupt banking practices, lack of technical expertise and antiquated systems. A combination of negative real interest rates and little

enforcement of payment results in incentives for waste and the use of funds in an inefficient manner. On a broader level, the provision of about US$300 million in agricultural credit by the government at negative interest rates increases the money supply, worsens inflation and discourages saving.

Other credit policies affect agricultural productivity more directly. For instance, the same rates are charged on all banking loans and have in the past been made only with land as collateral, limiting availability to landowners. More recently, farmers with long-term leases are able to get credit on the basis of lease rights and have incentives to increase their output, while only 6 percent of sharecropping households have access to bank credit and have less incentive to invest in productivity-enhancing tools. Collusion between banking officials and large farmers has allowed the bulk of credit to be directed towards the large landholding families and farmers with greater political influence. The Agriculture Development Bank of Pakistan (ADBP) has recently streamlined its loan-making process, especially for small farms, through a "one-stop shopping" credit window and increased outreach to villages.

Another innovation to support rural development is a programme of small loans to women for cottage industry activities. The programme began in 1993 with 150 million rupees (US$4 million) available for loans. The use of female loan officers to seek out women interested in commercializing their handicrafts or other activities has successfully overcome the cultural barriers preventing women from obtaining credit and engaging in business. As with the Grameen Bank of Bangladesh, the repayment rate of almost 100 percent is far higher than the 60 to 80 percent for typical agricultural loans made by ADBP.

Lack of information. There is a serious information gap throughout the sector. Starting from a large cohort of semi- or illiterate farmers, who have few means of communication available to them apart from the extension agent on a motorbike, and ending with the agricultural research and teaching institutions that are rigid in their structure and completely autonomous in their operations, there is little sharing of knowledge. Information is shared primarily when farmers

themselves gather after sunset to exchange progress reports. They are eager to replicate successes, but lack the technical expertise to find out why there are differences in yields among themselves. One study showed that the main sources of farmer information about crop technology are the radio and other farmers.

The agriculture extension programme is very bureaucratic. Subject matter specialists with training are not mobile and generally use field days to convey information. These are followed up by grassroots agents who are underequipped and have little education. They are required to visit large areas on motorbikes, which is slow and difficult during the rainy seasons. Even more of a problem is the lack of training and expertise they have. One-way information transfer is common and women and small farmers are often ignored.

Environmental degradation. A final problem that derives from most of those discussed above is environmental degradation. Its toll on agricultural production has not yet been quantified, but it appears to be increasingly responsible for poor results in the sector.

There is concern about aquifer contamination from heavy use of nitrate fertilizers and pesticides, and 75 percent of farmgate water is brackish. Farmers have had little training in fertilizer use, soil and crop requirements. They often apply whatever they receive; fertilizer use doubled between 1980 and 1993. As a result there is less application than is required for most crops, but excessive fertilizer use for cash crops such as cotton, rice, sugar cane, fruits and vegetables. Regulations about application are not enforced. Pesticide use has increased fivefold since 1981, but the low quality of the pesticides applied may be causing pest immunities.

Siltation and erosion may be factors in the flooding that destroyed the cotton crop in 1994/95. Unrestricted grazing adds to the problem. Most farmers do not have access to facilities for testing their soil, seeds, crops or livestock. This gives rise to recurrence and persistence of pests, disease and poor soil – problems that are undermining Pakistan's efforts to increase productivity.

In sum, slow growth in productivity is a complex issue requiring many different types of responses. Some experts in Pakistan are not optimistic, pointing out that

ASIA AND THE PACIFIC

even if government targets are met every year, food output may not keep pace with population growth. They estimate that production must rise by 4 to 5 percent annually to provide adequate food, excluding provision for losses. Others have pointed to the clear opportunities for improving yields and the management of farm systems.

The Government of Pakistan is taking measures to address these issues. It is focusing on introducing new high-yielding varieties to more areas, bringing irrigation to rain-fed areas and improving the availability of inputs. A high-level Agriculture Ministry official has declared that self-reliance in wheat can be achieved in three to four years by taking marginal lands out of production, more intensive cropping, efficient input use and encouraging wheat production while discouraging sugar production. The government retains primary responsibility for the provision of inputs, while relying increasingly on the private sector for output distribution. A high-level National Agriculture Coordination Committee is being established to accelerate current plans, such as the existing water management programme, and implement new ones.

It is clear that Pakistan's agricultural experts are aware of the steps necessary to improve productivity. At the same time, they face declining budget allocations to the sector, mandates to reduce government intervention and tightening resource constraints. The government recognizes that allowing prices to reflect comparative advantage better is a necessary but not sufficient condition for an efficient agricultural sector. It is also developing non-price policies to provide appropriate assistance in the form of increased information, research and testing tools and pollution prevention measures.

Progress and problems

As Pakistan moves through its second decade of economic reform, it faces significant opportunities amid growing obstacles. Major changes in economic policies and institutions have been accomplished and these will lead to the rationalization of prices and resource use, a stronger private sector and the ability to integrate into the global economy if they are maintained. The end result will be improved economic performance and increased investor confidence. The challenge is for the

long-term benefits of economic reform to appear before the short-term problems of social, political and environmental deterioration become overwhelming.

Calls for increased social and development expenditures have been getting louder for several years as the country's economic conditions worsen and poverty grows. Nonetheless, many of the economic reforms pursued under the conditions imposed by international lenders have squeezed the bloated government sector. The plan has been to increase expenditure gradually in the needed categories while reducing expenditure on subsidies, defence and, eventually, interest payments. Cuts in government budgets are taking a heavy toll on agriculture. The allocation to agriculture has dropped in each of the five-year plans and the Eighth Five-Year Plan (1993-98) allocates only about 1 percent of the total to agriculture.

Rationalization of input prices and the trade regime will help agriculture survive the cuts in subsidies, but it will be effective only if the institutions for participating in the market economy are allowed to develop. The programme to remove trade barriers and protection for some commodities must be matched with provision of essential public goods and services. The most important of these are plant research and extension to reduce the devastating effects of disease on the sector, provision of insurance, credit and non-distorting price or income support to reduce vulnerability to supply-shocks and infrastructure for marketing and delivery of inputs and outputs. Other opportunities have been identified to develop production of fruits and vegetables, non-traditional edible oils and other crops that can tolerate the vagaries of water and soil conditions in certain parts of Pakistan.

Social and environmental problems are mounting in both rural and urban areas. They affect Pakistan's ability to produce and deliver food, as well as weakening confidence in the government. The highest priorities for the government are again in the area of basic public goods, such as education and health services; access to sanitation and clean water; development and distribution of technology and information for pollution prevention; and population control. There is some concern that an urban bias is increasingly depriving agriculture of adequate land and water resources in

Pakistan. Regardless of the reason, social tensions are likely to mount as these natural resources become scarcer.

Pervasive problems affecting agriculture and other sectors which must be dealt with include smuggling, incentives for corruption and diversion of goods and bureaucractic inaction, including the enforcement of laws. The increasing political violence in Karachi and elsewhere presents a serious deterrent to foreign investment, as well as an uncertain trading environment at the port.

The government has taken action to resolve some of these problems, but this has not yet been enough. Spending on social programmes increased in 1994 by 33 percent to 2 percent of GDP, 72 percent of targeted industries have been privatized and investment is now allowed in previously closed sectors, such as banking, transport and power. There is a clear intention to improve the quality of public services and develop systems of resource protection and management. These efforts must all be continued and accelerated as population growth, economic reform and poverty are simultaneously addressed.

LATIN AMERICA AND THE CARIBBEAN

REGIONAL OVERVIEW
Economic developments

The economic environment in Latin America and the Caribbean in 1995-96 has been strongly influenced by the effects of the financial crisis that took place in late 1994 in Mexico and successively in Argentina. The deep recession that followed the crisis in these two countries was largely responsible for a significant slow-down in the region's rate of GDP growth. The reduction of capital flows to the region was not as pronounced as initially feared, however; growth in most other countries slowed only slightly, inflation continued to decline – with the major exception of Mexico – and exports remained buoyant. Nevertheless, there are concerns over current account deficits which, particularly in Brazil, have reached extremely high levels, as well as over the sustainability of capital inflows, competitiveness problems linked to currency overvaluation and the deteriorating social conditions in several countries. In this general context, the performances of regional agriculture have remained disappointing despite remarkable success stories, particularly in the agro-export sector, in some countries.

After a healthy 3.6 percent average annual economic growth rate between 1991 and 1994 – with the 5 percent of 1994 being the highest since the late 1970s – the region's economic growth slowed sharply to less than 1 percent in 1995. The financial crisis and measures to reduce macroeconomic imbalances and regain international credit resulted in strong economic recession in Mexico (-7 percent) and Argentina (-4.4 percent). Uruguay also experienced a reduction in economic activity that was caused mainly by the growing interdependence with the Argentinian economy within the framework of the Southern Common Market (MERCOSUR). In Brazil, on the other hand, the remarkable success of the Real stabilization plan favoured a substantial reactivation of the productive activity in 1994 and 1995. Although lower than the previous year, GDP growth was still a healthy 4.2 percent in 1995, thanks in particular to very good performances in the agricultural sector. Estimates for 1996, however, point to a significant deceleration in Brazilian growth, to 2 percent or less, with agriculture being again a major, this time negative, factor in the overall performance. Venezuela recorded a slight

improvement after the deep recession of 1994 which reflected favourable results in the oil sector. Chile and Peru achieved growth rates above 7 percent.

Growing unemployment and lower real wages were recorded particularly in Argentina, Mexico and Uruguay. The need to respond to the financial crisis forced Argentina and Mexico to implement painful fiscal adjustments including substantial rises in taxes and public-sector service fees and, in the case of Argentina, public-sector wage cuts. These measures had the inevitable effect of aggravating situations of poverty and social tension.

From 1994 to 1995 the average regional inflation rate fell from about 337 percent to 25 percent, the lowest in 25 years. Such spectacular progress reflected mainly the success of anti-inflationary policies in Brazil, strict monetary management in Argentina and other successful stabilization efforts throughout the region. By February 1996 the annual inflation rate in Argentina had fallen to a negligible 0.3 percent and the monthly rate in Brazil to 0.7 percent, the latter being the lowest in over 20 years. In Mexico, by contrast, the financial crisis and new peso devaluation caused an upswing in inflation to 52 percent in 1995. Venezuela's inflation was also around 50 percent.

In the external sector, a significant improvement was achieved in the trade balance, with the region recording a US$8 billion surplus in 1995. This was the result of a 13 percent increase in real exports, with those of Argentina rising by 30 percent and eight other countries in the region reporting rates of over 10 percent. Improvement in the export performance was caused largely by higher commodity prices, in particular for copper, cotton, wheat and wool, which enabled a improvement of nearly 2 percent in the region's terms of trade. In the case of Mexico, the gains in competitiveness brought about by devaluation strongly boosted exports and this, together with a contraction in imports, contributed to a virtual balancing, by end-1995, of the previous large deficit in current accounts.

Agricultural performances and issues

For the region as a whole, agricultural (crop and livestock) production was estimated to have increased by 1.8 percent in 1995, a significant drop from the 4.0 percent growth recorded the previous year and only slightly better than the mediocre average growth of 1.4 percent during 1990-94. This overall result stemmed from widely varying country situations. Among the largest producers, output in *Argentina*

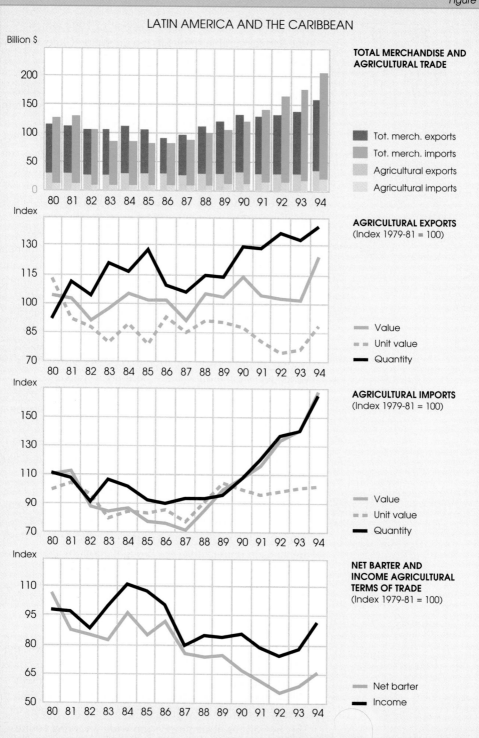

Figure 9A

LATIN AMERICA AND THE CARIBBEAN

Billion $

TOTAL MERCHANDISE AND AGRICULTURAL TRADE

- Tot. merch. exports
- Tot. merch. imports
- Agricultural exports
- Agricultural imports

Index

AGRICULTURAL EXPORTS
(Index 1979-81 = 100)

- Value
- Unit value
- Quantity

Index

AGRICULTURAL IMPORTS
(Index 1979-81 = 100)

- Value
- Unit value
- Quantity

Index

NET BARTER AND INCOME AGRICULTURAL TERMS OF TRADE
(Index 1979-81 = 100)

- Net barter
- Income

Source: FAO

Figure 9B

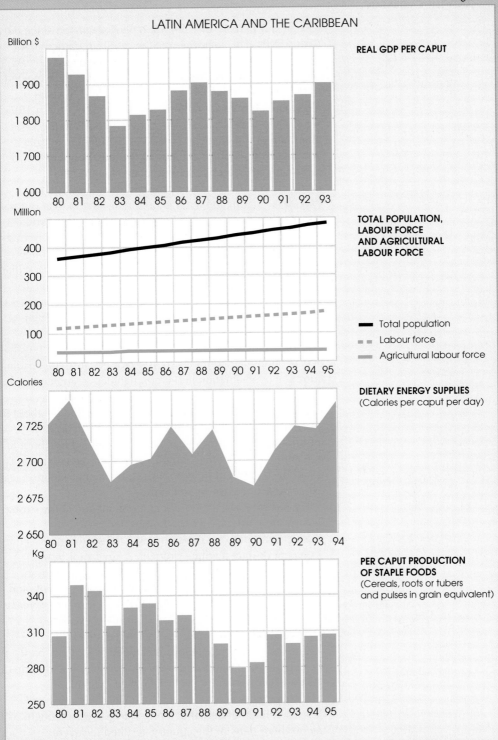

LATIN AMERICA AND THE CARIBBEAN

REAL GDP PER CAPUT

**TOTAL POPULATION,
LABOUR FORCE
AND AGRICULTURAL
LABOUR FORCE**

Total population

Labour force

Agricultural labour force

DIETARY ENERGY SUPPLIES
(Calories per caput per day)

**PER CAPUT PRODUCTION
OF STAPLE FOODS**
(Cereals, roots or tubers
and pulses in grain equivalent)

Source: FAO

rose by 5.5 percent in 1994-95, having stagnated since the early 1990s. This increase was the result, in particular, of good rice, wheat and sunflower crops. The recovery was short-lived, however, and agricultural output was expected to fall in 1995-96 after the worst drought for 20 years affected extensive agricultural areas of the country in 1995. Agriculture was also hit by higher credit costs in the aftermath of the financial crisis. While the international competitiveness of Argentinian agriculture continued to be negatively affected by the peso overvaluation, the elimination of export taxes provided compensation to exporters. Among the main export items, the market outlook for meat appeared especially bright in view of the progress achieved in eradicating foot-and-mouth disease, increased demand for Argentinian meat in Europe following concerns over "mad cow disease" and preferential access to Brazilian markets in the context of the MERCOSUR agreement. The prospects for grain exports also appear favourable in view of the current tight international market situation and high prices for these products.

In *Brazil* the stabilization plan seems to have had negative effects on the agricultural export sector because the ensuing currency overvaluation and credit tightness coincided with weak prices for some important export products. Agricultural production was expected to decline by about 5 percent in 1996, largely reflecting credit restrictions introduced the previous year, having expanded by about 6 percent in 1995. Cereal and oilseed output were expected to fall by 10 percent in 1995-96, while meat production was expected to increase significantly.

In *Chile,* the agricultural sector continued to show strong dynamism, particularly export crops, led by forestry products and pulp for paper. In 1995 the sector increased by 5 percent despite a winter drought. A key factor in the expansion of agriculture was the strong rise in prices, in particular of fish-meal, which rose by over 20 percent, and woodpulp by over 60 percent relative to the previous year. For the first time, exports of forest products exceeded traditional agricultural exports, while the area under commercial forest plantations continued to expand, partly at the expense of traditional crop area. Production and trade of fresh and processed fruit also remained dynamic.

In *Mexico* the economic and financial difficulties and depressed internal demand, along with a severe drought in the northern parts of the country, resulted in severe production shortfalls, particularly for cereals and oilseeds.

**LATIN AMERICA
AND THE CARIBBEAN**

Restrictive monetary policies led to a 36 percent decline in total agricultural financing during the first months of 1995. Interest rates rose to exceptionally high levels before stabilizing at 30 to 40 percent by the end of the year. The peso devaluation favoured exports of vegetables and fruits, which had already been enjoying good competitive positions in international markets, but also resulted in higher costs of, and reduced demand for, imported inputs.

The agricultural sector in *Peru* continued to show dynamism, despite a marked slow-down from the 14 percent growth recorded in 1994, thanks to good climatic conditions, a strengthening in internal demand and an improved environment for investment. Potatoes, sugar, coffee and livestock products had the strongest production performances, while rice crops declined. In the case of potatoes, good production conditions actually led to some overproduction and depressed prices, damaging small producers and emphasizing the need for better crop programming and management, market information and crop diversification.

In *Cuba*, reform measures contributed to the revival of a number of subsectors including meat, tobacco and vegetables, which showed booming performances in 1995. The key sugar-cane sector is facing a deep crisis, however, with production in 1995 having fallen to 3.3 million tonnes, the lowest in decades. Shortages of machinery and fertilizers, as well as labour problems during the harvest period, contributed to the crisis.

Agricultural performances in the Central American and Caribbean subregions ranged from mediocre to poor in most countries. Indeed agricultural production in 1995 fell from the previous year's level in Antigua and Barbuda, Belize, Cuba, El Salvador, Dominica, Haiti, Panama and Trinidad and Tobago, although in the latter country the decline took place after an exceptionally favourable crop year in 1994. Only a few countries, including Guyana, Guatemala, Honduras and Nicaragua, achieved agricultural production increases significantly above population growth. Such generally disappointing performances occurred against the background of already poor trends since the early 1990s. (The experience of Central America is discussed in *The State of Food and Agriculture 1995*.)

The role of agricultural policies
Agricultural policies in the region have been strongly influenced by the general economic policy environment. In

general, the process of agricultural market liberalization and external opening has been pursued, but with varying degrees of policy commitment ranging from the example of Argentina, where the process has been radically pursued, to that of Venezuela where state intervention in market and pricing mechanisms has remained significant.

In the case of *Argentina* all forms of subsidies, market intervention and export taxes were eliminated. Only minor support measures to agricultural production subsisted, such as a special credit line introduced in mid-1995 through the national bank for financing oilseed and maize crops, although at conditions close to those of the market. Such measures were intended to ease the credit shortages and high lending costs arising from the rigid financial control policy. The other remaining form of direct support is a special fund for tobacco production, although its elimination is also under discussion.

In *Brazil,* one of the elements of the ongoing stabilization programme has been the replacement of the old system of indexed interest rates by a system of variable interest rates, which are also applicable to agricultural loans. Following the dramatic abatement of inflation, interest rates declined by half, but many farmers still considered agricultural credit availability too limited and its cost too high. New loans at fixed interest rates have been created for maize production, however, and special lines of soft lending have been introduced for small farmers and selected products (cotton, rice, manioc). Moreover, the government requests the banks to devote part of their portfolio to agriculture and is also pressing large producers to enter commodity futures markets. Support to the Real resulted in currency overvaluation which reduced external competitiveness for exports and created greater incentives for imports. This caused protests from agricultural producers, especially because compensation from subsidized support programmes were no longer available. Complaints were also raised about the high taxation of primary product exports, which diminishes according to the product's degree of processing. The harmonization of phytosanitary regulations and the adoption of common tariffs under the MERCOSUR agreement have represented enhanced opportunities but also challenges to the competitiveness of Brazilian products. Tariffs have been reduced to an average 20 percent, although for some products they were raised; in the case of rice, for example, from 10 to 20 percent. For the first time, cocoa will be imported in competition with local production.

LATIN AMERICA AND THE CARIBBEAN

Agricultural policies in *Chile* include support for some products, credit for disadvantaged farmers, export promotion and investment in infrastructure and services for agricultural production and marketing. In particular, support measures were introduced or strengthened in response to the competitive losses associated with currency appreciation since end-1994. Among the most significant measures were the establishment of an export promotion fund with an initial US$10 million capital and the introduction of additional duties on imports of some products, including wheat, sugar and vegetable oils, when prices fall below predefined levels and during certain periods of the year. A number of phytosanitary restrictions are also applied on imports. Chile has a diversified tariff system that varies according to the existing agreements with trading partners. A recent study by agricultural entrepreneurs concluded that the entry of Chile to the North American Free Trade Area (NAFTA) and MERCOSUR would reduce traditional crop production significantly. MERCOSUR would have negative effects on Chilean agriculture overall, while NAFTA would benefit exporters, especially of processed products.

An issue of considerable concern in Chile is forest management. A recent study by the central bank estimated that, at the current rate of deforestation, only half of the current 7 million ha of forest land will subsist over the coming 25 to 30 years. The results of the study have been challenged by industrial organizations. Another study, sponsored by the French forest agency, concluded that under current rates of exploitation all perennial tree species will have disappeared in 30 years. The seriousness of the problem prompted the government to introduce new legislation to regulate forest exploitation.

The entry into force of NAFTA has considerably influenced agriculture in *Mexico*. Trade liberalization under the Agreement had resulted in a 17 percent increase in agricultural imports from, and a 7 percent increase in exports to, the United States in 1994. The financial crisis and devaluation of the new peso radically changed the picture; in 1995 agricultural exports to the United States rose by 35 percent, and imports fell by a similar amount. Along with the process of tariff elimination, for which a 15-year transition period has been established,[29] negotiations have been pursued on the harmonization of phytosanitary and labelling standards.

After a probationary period, the Procampo programme of

[29] See FAO. 1994. *The State of Food and Agriculture 1994*. Rome.

direct income support to farmers, which replaced the old system of price support, entered a permanent phase of implementation in 1995. It recognized a contribution per hectare (440 pesos in 1995) and according to type of product (grains, cotton, rice). The government also announced a new scheme to restructure agricultural debt in the face of problems arising from the financial crisis, although such a scheme may involve public expenditure costs and inflationary pressure.

Following the presidential elections in April 1995, the Government of *Peru* has adopted important measures in favour of agriculture. In July 1995 a new landownership law was promulgated that was expected, *inter alia,* to provide a better climate for credit and investment. At the same time, new regulations were issued to protect small farmers and indigenous communities who had, or were at risk of having, their land occupied by other groups. New legislation was also being studied to reduce the inefficiencies and abuses that characterize water use through the sale of utilization rights. A new law was also being discussed in Parliament that aimed at environmental protection as well as addressing employment and investment concerns. The introduction of an 18 percent tax on the sale of agricultural inputs has been the object of intense debate. The Ministry of Agriculture is undertaking a major programme to regularize landownership titles, which will enable landownership to be used as collateral for agricultural loans. Inadequate credit availability is, indeed, a major limiting factor to agricultural development in Peru. The government offers special credit lines for the purchase of inputs, but their scope is inadequate to meet demand. Some agricultural associations have proposed the creation of a rural bank to complement the role of existing rural financing funds by offering long-term credit. Another government initiative, so far little used by farmers however, has been the establishment of a market information network.

Agricultural policies in *Venezuela* differ from those in most other countries in the region in that they have maintained a strong interventionist and protectionist character, despite various attempts at liberalization between the years 1988 and 1993. New legislation for agricultural development is currently under discussion to provide the legal framework for agricultural policies in the coming ten years. The general aim is national self-sufficiency in food, to be achieved through various mechanisms of state protection of the sector. Temporary foreign exchange control measures,

aimed at limiting imports, were being applied in 1995. A number of import priorities were established, including some essential foods and inputs for agricultural and agro-industrial production. A price band system was adopted in May 1995 in line with Andean Pact (AP) provisions and aimed at stabilizing domestic market prices and ensuring a certain protection to agricultural producers when international prices fall below predetermined levels. Rigid phytosanitary controls and regulations, implemented on the basis of over 300 obligatory standards, have been established by the competent agency as a means of regulating imports. Price controls on over 120 consumer items, including foodstuffs, have been enforced since 1994. Attempts were made in 1995 at liberalizing prices within the framework of an anti-inflationary pact between the government and enterprises, but these did not reach any concrete result. One of the most important programmes of government support to agriculture concerns debt refinancing at subsidized interest rates. In addition, subsidies are granted for the purchase of food by poor and vulnerable groups (schools, children, lactant mothers). In December 1995 a new pilot programme was introduced in five cities to enable poor population groups to purchase essential foods at prices below those officially controlled.

In *Cuba*, the government has been pursuing economic reform slowly, within a context of major economic and financial difficulties. An important element of the reform in agriculture has been the accelerating decollectivization of the land. Less than one-third of the cultivatable land remains under state farms (about three-quarters in the early 1990s), the rest having been progressively allocated to various forms of cooperatives and private small farms. While the state still provides production requisites on preferential terms and establishes production quotas for public procurement, the private sector is allowed to sell any amount of production in excess of the quota on the free market.

Prospects and emerging issues

The outlook for the region's agriculture will be largely determined by the ability to overcome the problems and uncertainties that cloud the macroeconomic environment. The severe shock represented by the Mexico crisis showed, on the one hand, considerable resilience within the region's economies, in sharp contrast with the events that followed the crisis of the early 1980s. On the other hand, it also

underlined the risks involved in capital flow volatility and the importance of maintaining international confidence through unflinching commitment to economic stability and reform. If the region's economies emerged relatively unscathed from the recent crisis it is to a large extent because Argentina and Mexico, as well as some other countries, proved such a commitment to exist. In addition, two major elements of the reform effort played an important role: the economic opening, which enabled exports to become central parts of the post-crisis adjustment; and the economic liberalization and integration, notably within the NAFTA and MERCOSUR agreements, which proved to be major elements of stability.

While the need for pursuing and deepening economic reform is beyond question, there are, however, elements of the process that raise concern, notably for agriculture. The actual or perceived consequences of the deregulation of the agricultural and rural economy are subject to considerable controversy. One theme fuelling the debate is the disappointing performance of the agricultural sector since the early 1990s, in coincidence with the accelerated process of market liberalization. The 1990s have witnessed significant improvements in average yields, which have risen by 3.3 percent per year compared with 1.3 percent during the 1980s; the cultivated area, however, far from expanding as it did during the 1980s, has declined by 2.2 percent annually, the result being a 1.4 percent annual increment in production. This rate of growth, below even that of the depressed 1980s (2 percent), is clearly insufficient to allow agriculture to contribute adequately to the food security and economic growth of the region. Obviously, such overall mediocre performance reflects many factors not necessarily related to the reform but, as reviewed above, a number of features stemming from recent policies – such as overvalued exchange rates, the reduction of public support, higher credit costs, and the overall demand-compressing effects of fiscal and monetary restraint – have undoubtedly played an important role.

Another debated issue is the extent to which economic liberalization has contributed to accentuating income inequalities, overall and in rural areas. Economic Commission for Latin America and the Caribbean (ECLAC) estimates suggest that the already notoriously unequitable income distribution patterns in the region have tended to get worse in many countries throughout 1980-1992. How this phenomenon has affected the rural sector in recent

years has not yet been fully assessed, but evidence points not only to an accentuation of income inequality, but also to cases of growing pauperization in rural areas, where over half of the people live in absolute poverty. This is largely attributable to the deregulation of the rural economy which favours primarily the larger producers and traders who already enjoy conditions of competitiveness and are better able to capture the opportunities offered by unrestricted markets. By contrast, the progressive retreat of the state has translated into serious problems for large segments of the traditional peasant sector for whom economic viability was strongly linked to state support. The recent financial difficulties faced by several countries further restricted the ability to help small producers in such areas as technical assistance, credit and debt alleviation.

These features underline how difficult it is to find a policy blend that simultaneously addresses the needs to consolidate macroeconomic stability, resume sustainable growth and share equitably the benefits of growth among all segments of society. Furthermore, they point to the need for coherent policies to facilitate an orderly transition to a deregulated rural economy. Such policies should encompass restructuring of factor ownership in conditions that ensure equitable sharing of resources, safety of investment, dynamism of land markets and efficient use of resources. Experience has shown, most recently in the example of Peru, that this form of policy action can compensate effectively for the reduction or elimination of previous forms of direct support. At the same time, fiscal policies should orient economic activity towards rural areas with productive potential. Such policies are needed in order to avoid a process of rural transformation that merely takes the form of an abandonment of the land.

COLOMBIA

In a region where economic volatility is the norm, Colombia stands as an island of relative economic stability. This result is a consequence of decades of prudent and stable fiscal, monetary and foreign exchange rate policies. Such policies have kept the economy insulated from the great booms and recessions experienced by other Latin American countries. As a result, the Colombian economy remained virtually unaffected by the debt crisis of the 1980s displaying instead the region's highest growth in GDP for that decade.

Stability in economic performance has been achieved simultaneously with substantial changes in economic structure. After a large coffee boom in the mid-1970s, economic growth was led by the service sectors of the economy until 1982. In the 1980s, the mining sector accelerated dramatically, as a consequence of important findings of coal and petroleum. In the latter half of the decade, after a mild macroeconomic adjustment programme, agriculture and manufacturing both outpaced the service sectors, spurred by the devaluation of the real exchange rate.

From 1986, a new attitude of "internationalization" of the economy took form in a programme of gradually increasing exposure to world market forces. The pace of the programme accelerated rapidly in 1990, when major economywide reforms were announced as part of the *apertura* (opening) of the economy. *Apertura* was the Colombian version of the programmes of trade liberalization and increased reliance on market forces that took place throughout the region from the mid-1980s onwards. In Colombia, the reforms were presented as the antidote to slowing rates of productivity growth recorded in several sectors during the 1980s and to the limitations stemming from the relatively small size of the domestic market.

The economy responded well to the new policy regime. Rates of growth have surpassed 5 percent per annum since 1993. Private investment increased to record levels and unemployment has exhibited a continuous decline since 1990. However, some of the reforms posed difficulties in certain sectors that had traditionally been protected from world market volatility, including tradable agricultural crops. Falling profitability in these sectors was exacerbated by the appreciation of the exchange rate caused by the massive inflow of capital from abroad attracted by high domestic interest rates, the discovery of large oil reserves and increased confidence in the economy.

Agriculture as a whole benefited from trade liberalization, since import barriers for manufacturing had traditionally favoured the allocation of resources to non-agricultural activities. Nevertheless, immediately after the trade and marketing reforms, many tradable crops suffered a sharp fall in profitability as a result of lower tariffs, falling world prices and an appreciating exchange rate. On the other hand, non-tradable crops such as tubers, vegetables and meat products benefited greatly from increased domestic demand and new intraregional trade opportunities with Ecuador and Venezuela, albeit after suffering harvest losses during the intense drought of 1991-92. The negative results of 1991-92, however, turned farmer opinion against the reforms and generated pressures for compensatory measures.

Since 1993, planted areas and production levels have displayed uninterrupted growth, partly as a result of the implementation of emergency government measures, better meteorological conditions and increasing international prices. In spite of the rapid growth of agricultural imports, after the adjustment to lower real prices, domestic producers are now in a better position to compete with foreign suppliers. Public and private efforts have concentrated on carrying out the research and infrastructure development required to guarantee long-term profitability. As a result, Colombian agriculture is better prepared to face the challenges of the next century than it was before 1990.

Macroeconomic performance
Economic setting: 1985-1990. After a period of recession and growing economic imbalances since 1981, the Colombian economy was subjected to a mild adjustment programme starting in 1985. Public expenditures were reduced, the tax burden was increased and measures to devalue the exchange rate were put in place in order to correct the overvaluation accumulated since the late 1970s. As a result of these measures, the fiscal accounts improved rapidly and the current account switched from a deficit in 1985 to a surplus by 1986. GDP growth strengthened to an average 4.4 percent per annum in the 1985-89 period, after having grown at only 2.5 percent per annum from 1980 to 1984.

Export growth was particularly rapid in the second half of the 1980s, generating a sizeable trade account surplus as a result of favourable terms of trade and devaluation of the real exchange rate (after falling by 20 percent in 1985, the real exchange rate continued to depreciate at an average

rate of 4.5 percent annually until 1989, when it was further devalued by 13.5 percent). As a consequence, non-traditional exports grew at an annual rate of over 20 percent. Export growth was further enhanced as from 1988, when measures were taken to implement a plan of internationalization of the economy.

The new policy framework:* apertura *policies. In August 1990, the pace of liberalization was quickened with the announcement of structural reforms in the trade, financial and foreign investment regimes. These measures were followed, over the following three years, by the passage of new legislation pertaining to, among others, foreign exchange, monetary and labour regimes.

On the trade front, the gradual liberalization process that commenced in the final years of the 1980s was accelerated in 1990. In that year, import quotas and other trade restrictions were abolished. A timetable for tariff reduction over a three-year period was announced, although its targets were met in less than 24 months. Tariff rates were reduced from 36.3 percent in 1990 to 11.6 percent in 1993. Additionally, an aggressive agenda of trade negotiations led to special agreements with Venezuela, Ecuador, the Andean Pact, G3 (Mexico, Venezuela and Colombia) and Chile. Colombia also benefited from the Andean Trade Preferences Act granted by the United States in 1992, which allows most Colombian goods tariff-free access to the United States market until 2001. A similar scheme was negotiated with the European Union (EU), with preferences lasting until 2004.

A new financial regime was approved in 1990, designed to stimulate competition and the entry of new participants, including foreign investors, into the financial services arena. Under the new scheme, the segmentation of financial markets into specialized institutions was replaced by universal banking provisions. Forced investments were reduced and the government announced a rapid timetable for the privatization of a number of state-owned banks. The new regime also strengthened banking supervision norms and increased capital standards to international levels.

Provisions limiting the presence of foreign interests in the Colombian economy, which had been established in the early 1970s, were eliminated in 1990. Controls on foreign investment were lifted for most areas of the economy and investors from abroad were guaranteed equal tax treatment. Controls on remittances were also relaxed.

In 1991, controls on the capital account were abolished

**LATIN AMERICA
AND THE CARIBBEAN**

and Colombian nationals were allowed to contract debts directly from foreign lenders. The monopoly on transactions in foreign exchange held by the central bank was abolished and the market for foreign currency was transferred to the private financial system. The "crawling peg" regime of exchange rate management was replaced at the end of 1991 by a "dirty" float and, since 1994, a pre-established band has been in operation in order to allow greater influence of market forces in the determination of the price of the currency.

The labour reform of 1990 removed uncertainties about the costs of hiring personnel and made contracting procedures more flexible. The social security system was changed in 1993 from a pay-as-you-go system to one of private capitalization. The new legislation expanded coverage of pension and health benefits to a greater share of the population and allowed private pension funds to compete with the public agency in charge of social security. In addition, a new universal health system was introduced, according to which all workers are entitled to a mandatory health plan, to which they must contribute 12 percent of their wages.

In 1991, a new constitution made the central bank independent from the executive branch. The mandate of the new monetary authority emphasizes inflation reduction goals. The focus of monetary policy shifted from the growth of monetary aggregates to regulation of interest rates through open market operations. The constitution also mandated an ambitious fiscal descentralization regime, with increasing shares of central government revenues transferred to local levels. To compensate for revenues lost through these transfers and from the lowering of tariff rates, the income, sales and gas tax regimes were modified in 1992. The government achieved a neutral fiscal stance in the 1990-94 period, reflecting the high priority awarded to maintaining macroeconomic stability.

Performance. In spite of fears of an economic crisis as a result of the trade liberalization, the Colombian economy performed surprisingly well in the 1990-95 period. GDP growth increased continuously from 2.0 percent in 1991 to 5.7 percent in 1994 and 5.3 percent in 1995. After falling in real terms in 1991, investment grew at an average real rate of 19.0 percent in the 1992-94 period, spurred by the lower costs of capital goods brought about by tariff reductions, the appreciation of the exchange rate and confidence in the

future of the economy. Urban employment increased at a fast pace, offering job opportunities to the growing labour force and reducing the levels of unemployment and informality of employment.

As a result of the appreciation of the exchange rate (discussed below), the fastest growing sectors of the economy were concentrated among non-tradables. Aggregate economic activity was led by growth in construction of urban housing, oil and coal production, public and private services and financial activities. In agriculture, production levels of meats, vegetables, tubers, sugar and oil-palm exhibited the highest rates of growth.

In contrast with the 1985-89 period, the exchange rate appreciated by 13 percent between 1990 and 1994, in response to the increasing inflows of foreign exchange. The causes of this phenomenon have been a subject of heated debate among Colombian economists. Among the factors that seem to have played an important role were an increased confidence about the future of the Colombian economy after the structural reforms, the difference between internal and external yields on short-term investments and the doubling of known oil reserves. This last factor was a result of the massive findings of high-quality crude in the Cusiana and Cupiagua oilfields in 1992, which increased known oil reserves from 1.8 billion to almost 4 billion barrels.

The appreciation of the exchange rate was accompanied by a surge in imports, which grew at real rates of over 40 percent in 1992 and 1993. Export performance suffered from falling profitability and low international prices, particularly in traditional areas such as coffee. As a result, the current account switched from a surplus of 5.6 percent of GDP in 1991 to a deficit of 4.5 percent in 1994.

Policies 1994-1995. In August 1994, the incoming administration reaffirmed its broad commitment to furthering the reforms initiated in 1990, including the trade liberalization. However, a new emphasis was laid on arresting the exchange rate appreciation process and on using growing tax revenues from oil production to raise spending on social programmes and infrastructure. Employment generation is also an important objective, to be promoted by public programmes that foster the development of small private-sector enterprises.

In spite of growing political uncertainties, GDP growth was 5.3 percent in 1995, the result, in great part, of large

increases in oil production and government services. The central bank applied a tight monetary policy in order to neutralize inflationary expectations in the context of a more active fiscal policy. Strong signs of an economic slow-down were evident in the second half of the year and growth is expected to decline for 1996.

Sectoral policy changes and performance
The role of agriculture in the economy. In Colombia, agriculture has traditionally accounted for a higher share of GDP than in most economies of the region. This share was about 19.9 percent of GDP in 1980; a result that is associated with the large natural endowment of lands suitable for agricultural cultivation and with the absence of alternative sources of foreign exchange such as oil or other minerals. By 1990, the sector still accounted for nearly 17 percent of GDP, with nearly 25 percent of the population still living in rural areas. About 20 percent of the labour force is employed in the agricultural sector.

As a result of widely differing agro-ecological conditions and land tenure structures, Colombian agriculture is highly heterogeneous. Exportables account for about 30 percent of the value of production and include a smallholder crop, such as coffee, and several plantation crops, such as bananas, flowers, sugar and cotton. Importable crops contribute nearly 35 percent of the value of agricultural production and include those produced by *minifundia* farmers (barley, wheat, maize) as well as cereals and oilseeds grown in medium- and large-sized farms (sorghum, soybean, oil-palm). Traditional non-tradable items account for about 45 percent of agricultural GDP and include the large-farm dominated livestock sector, as well as vegetables, fruits, tubers and other staples produced in small operations.

The share of GDP accounted for by agriculture has been declining over the past three decades. The sector grew at an average annual rate of only 1.6 percent in the 1980-84 period, as a result of falling prices, an appreciating exchange rate, declining public-sector investments and growing rural violence. However, sectoral growth more than doubled to 3.7 percent from 1985 to 1989, as a result of higher prices, a depreciating exchange rate and policies that protected producer prices by restricting food imports. In particular, the sector benefited from the Plan de Oferta Selectiva (selective supply plan), implemented in 1988 and 1989 to promote production of cereals and oilseeds by guaranteeing high prices to producers.

The growth pattern of Colombian agriculture has entailed more intensive use of land and capital than labour. Employment opportunities in agriculture have not grown significantly since the 1960s, a result of policies oriented towards fostering the subsectors of livestock and mechanized large-farm operations. The bias has been implicit in the pattern of public investment in agriculture, the orientation of the trade regime and the allocation of subsidies.

Apertura *measures.* Sectoral policies changed dramatically as part of the economywide programme of trade liberalization implemented since mid-1990. The new regime removed the emphasis from the need for sectoral policies, focusing instead on establishing a neutral macroeconomic environment that would allow sectors with comparative advantage to flourish. It was argued that agriculture would benefit because of the overwhelming resource advantage and the removal of the traditional policy bias in favour of manufacturing.

The largest policy shift came in trade-related policies. Import restrictions were eliminated, including the government monopoly on imports of most grains and oilseeds. Tariffs on farm goods were reduced sharply from an average of 31 percent in 1991 to 15 percent in 1992. In the same period, tariffs for agricultural inputs fell from 15 percent to 2 percent. Some importable crops (rice, maize, sorghum, soybean, wheat, barley and milk) and one exportable (sugar) were granted exceptional treatment through a variable tariff system linked to a price band system. This system was designed to filter out large swings in international prices, providing only medium- and long-term market signals to local producers.

The direct intervention activities of the public agency in charge of agricultural marketing, IDEMA, were sharply curtailed. Purchases were restricted to marginal areas where farmers faced severe difficulties in taking their crop to market. Public stocks of grains were drawn down. Guaranteed producer prices for grains and oilseeds were replaced by minimum prices set according to recent world market trends. These measures were complemented by the elimination of all consumer price controls.

A special programme for the modernization and diversification of lagging sectors was designed in 1991. The aim of the programme was to cushion the blow of external competition and help accommodate required resource shifts

in certain crops where local farmers were especially uncompetitive. The programme focused on four smallholder crops (wheat, barley, dark tobacco and *fique*, a type of jute). It included technical assistance, temporary price supports and the encouragement of alternative crops. In practice, implementation of several key components of the programme was delayed and this was later blamed for some of the difficulties faced by farmers in 1992.

Special attention was given to opening new markets for Colombian crops through trade agreements. Many non-traditional agricultural exports benefited from the trade preferences obtained from the United States and the EU. The enhanced integration with Andean Pact nations opened new possibilities for farmers because Colombia enjoyed greater comparative advantages in agriculture than other Andean partners. Some of the potential gains from greater trade within the Andean Pact, however, were thwarted by the lack of harmonization among member countries in their respective systems of price bands for importable crops.

Agricultural credit reforms initiated in 1989 were aimed at increasing the volume of resources available to farmers by creating a new rediscounting fund, FINAGRO, and increasing market forces in the determination of the cost and destination of credit. FINAGRO sought to supplement the banks' own funds for medium- and long-term investment credit. Starting in 1990, interest rates for medium- and large-scale farmers were increased to market levels. A four-year schedule was announced for the liberalization of interest rates on loans to smallholders. In spite of these measures, credit flows to farmers were severely disrupted from 1991, when accumulated losses of Caja Agraria, the agricultural development bank, paralysed the issuing of new loans.

In the 1990-94 period, a number of significant reforms were also undertaken with respect to key aspects of sectoral policy. A new policy for public support for irrigation investments was designed in 1991 to increase the role of the private sector in building and maintaining irrigation districts. A ten-year plan was adopted to increase public support for irrigation and drainage investments, with emphasis on large-scale projects.

Agricultural research responsibilities were transferred from ICA, a public agency, to CORPOICA, a new corporation created with public and private funds. The aim was to increase private-sector participation in the definition of research priorities and funding. The reform was

complemented by the creation of many crop-specific funds, financed by contributions from farm revenues. The main objectives of the funds were to sponsor research and to promote better marketing practices. Responsibilities for extension and technical assistance for small farmers was transferred from central agencies to municipal governments.

Land reform policy underwent a radical change with the approval of legislation to use state funds for direct subsidies to beneficiaries, who are now responsible for selecting the plots of land that they wish to acquire. Participation of the state agency (INCORA) is now limited to selecting beneficiaries, overseeing private negotiations and price levels and providing some technical assistance to beneficiaries. The design of detailed norms to regulate the private negotiation process delayed the application of the new methods until late 1995, when the first direct acquisitions by beneficiaries were announced.

To complement the implementation of the sweeping reforms outlined above, several sectoral agencies underwent radical reforms; these included the irrigation agency (INAT), the research and sanitation control body (ICA), the land reform institute (INCORA), the marketing parastatal (IDEMA) and the integrated rural development fund (DRI). In addition, the Ministry of Agriculture and its natural resources agency (INDERENA) transferred their functions in the protection of natural resources to the newly created Ministry of the Environment in 1993.

Reforms and agricultural performance. Starting in the second half of 1991, production levels for a number of important subsectors of Colombian agriculture, chiefly import crops (cereals and oilseeds), fell precipitously. Depressed prices for export crops also contributed to the crisis, which deepened in 1992 when agricultural GDP fell by 1.5 percent. Many farmers then turned against government policies and discussion about the causes of the crisis generated a national debate. Associations of grain and oilseed producers blamed trade liberalization and the withdrawal of marketing support from IDEMA. The government argued that the crisis was caused by the effects of drought and the collapse of international prices, factors that were out of its control.

While still controversial, it seems that the factors behind the reduced harvests and/or profits of 1991-92 varied depending on the crop under question. For coffee and cotton, collapses in world prices were the critical element (coffee crops rose strongly from 1989 to 1993), perhaps

compounded by the early stages of the appreciation of the exchange rate. Falling producer revenues for wheat, barley, rice, maize, soybean, oil-palm and sorghum seem to have been the combined result of the effect of the marketing reforms on producer prices and poor harvests caused by the most intense drought in three decades, which affected most of the country in late 1991 and 1992. Real producer prices fell in response to the combination of falling world prices, an appreciating exchange rate and increases in protection that were not sufficient to counteract the above factors. The shortfall in production caused by the drought seems to have been the determinant factor of the reduction in farmer income for vegetables, fruits and tubers. The only major production line that showed excellent conditions of production and profitability throughout 1990-95 was sugar. As a consequence of the crisis, aggregate rural incomes fell by 15 percent between 1990 and 1992.

Using general equilibrium analysis, it has been estimated that the decline in world prices and the relaxation of domestic agricultural price supports explained 70 percent of the observed deterioration in rural incomes. By contrast, trade liberalization benefited both rural and urban populations, raising farm revenues and promoting a more equitable income distribution.

The developments of 1991 and 1992 took a heavy toll on the living standards of the rural population. The share of the rural population living in absolute poverty increased from 26.7 percent in 1991 to 31.2 percent in 1992. The difference between rural and urban wages, which had been declining almost uninterruptedly since the early 1970s, increased substantially. After growing by 4.1 percent annually between 1988 and 1991, rural employment fell by 3.7 percent in 1992, representing a loss of some 200 000 jobs. Overall unemployment rates did not change considerably, because there was a decrease in participation rates combined with an increase in migration to urban centres, where the construction sector offered employment opportunities to displaced rural workers.

Agricultural trade patterns were greatly affected by trends in the exchange rate and international prices. Exports, excluding coffee, reduced their rapid expansion rate of the late 1980s, growing in value by 15.7 percent annually between 1990 and 1992. By contrast, the removal of import restrictions and the rapid growth of domestic demand resulted in accelerating agricultural imports, which grew at a rate of nearly 30 percent per year between 1990 and 1992.

Reactivation measures: 1993-1995. The extent and magnitude of the deterioration of rural incomes in 1992 exacerbated tensions between some farmer groups and the government. Producers of crops most affected by the crisis demanded an end to all trade liberalization measures and the provision of direct subsidies. Others supported the reforms but called for temporary measures to alleviate the effects of the crisis.

Starting in mid-1992, the government adopted ad hoc emergency measures that were consolidated into a reactivation plan by early 1993. This plan included a number of emergency trade-related measures, such as modifications to the price band scheme to increase protection levels moderately. Purchases of grains and oilseeds by IDEMA at above-market prices were resumed. An emergency employment programme was implemented, focused on areas where job opportunities had been most dramatically reduced. Regions receiving the most attention were those infested with coffee-borer and those where cotton plantations had been replaced by livestock grazing operations. Emergency credit measures were adopted to refinance overdue debts in crops affected by the crisis and provide government funds to an insolvent Caja Agraria. Public investment levels in agricultural agencies were also increased sharply.

In late 1993, tensions between the government and farmer groups led to the passage of a new General Agricultural Development Law by a Congress sympathetic to the interests of producers. Arguing that rural violence justified special treatment for agricultural production, the new legislation supported more active government marketing efforts; stronger countervailing and antidumping duties action to prevent the entry of subsidized food imports; the creation of commodity stabilization funds; the provision of loans for agriculture at below-market costs; and funding for an agricultural insurance scheme. The law also created a new investment subsidy scheme to support rural capital expenditures by the private sector. A fund (EMPRENDER) was created to stimulate the creation of new marketing and processing enterprises of special interest to small producers, in joint venture with the private sector. In spite of the law, in late 1995 only a few selected items included in its provisions had actually been implemented.

Application of the measures outlined in the reactivation plan was continued after the change of administration in

August 1994. The new government complemented the measures of 1993 with implementation of the investment subsidies created by the Agricultural Law. Subsidies were authorized for investment in irrigation projects and purchases of new machinery. A new programme to refinance and lower interest costs of overdue debts for small producers was also implemented in 1995.

The government also initiated a temporary programme of absorption agreements, in which processor industries, such as feed manufacturers and oilseed crushers, agree to purchase all domestically produced commodities at specified prices. The programme was complemented by direct subsidies to producers in the purchase of the soybean, cotton and rice harvests. In 1995, the price supports and the restrictions to imports implicit in the scheme increased protection levels for rice by 65 percent, for yellow maize by 25 percent, for white maize by 60 percent and for barley by 25 percent.

Production levels of most of the crops affected by the 1991-92 crisis displayed a slow recovery during the 1993-95 period. A Ministry of Agriculture study found that profit margins started to increase in late 1993, with the fastest rates of growth concentrated among exportable annual crops. Prices of all crops excluding coffee grew by 36 percent in 1994. In the same year, agricultural exports increased by 18 percent (excluding coffee), after falling by 4 percent in 1993. However, the value of imports continued to grow at fast rates, reaching 38 percent in 1994, caused, in great part, by higher prices of grains. The production of cotton displayed a significant recovery, yielding an exportable surplus by 1995, as a consequence of increasing international prices and government supports. Of all exportable crops, only bananas have continued to display stagnant production levels, as a result of global oversupply, the implementation of import quotas in the EU and growing violence in the Urabá region.

In 1995, agricultural production (excluding coffee) grew by 2.9 percent. Growth was concentrated in perennial crops, while annual crops fell by 0.1 percent as a result of the lacklustre performance of importables such as sorghum, soybean and maize. Smallholder crops presented high growth rates, particularly in plaintains, yuca and *ñame*. For the first time since 1990, agricultural exports grew faster than imports, in large part the result of higher world prices for Colombian exports and a faster rate of devaluation.

Future prospects

The bold economic reforms of 1990-93 yielded positive results for the Colombian economy. In agriculture, however, the record has been mixed. In the short term, the reforms to promote greater market orientation were partially accountable for the crisis of 1991-92 that was faced by most tradable crops. Trade liberalization and the removal of import controls exerted the most damaging influences on profitability for importable grains and oilseeds. The timing of the reforms was unfortunate, however; production levels had been buoyed by high international prices and a devaluating exchange rate in the 1985 to 1990 period. Implementation of the reforms coincided with the onset of a period of extremely low international prices and with a surge in capital inflows that further depressed producer incentives through the appreciation of the exchange rate. The effect of low producer prices was compounded in 1992 by shortfalls in production in many areas of the country that were affected by the most intense drought in three decades.

In spite of the setbacks, emergency measures were taken and most of the sectors that suffered the effects of reduced profitability between 1991 and 1993 have gradually recovered. Some of the measures have implied the abandonment of the free market spirit of the original reforms, as more pragmatic considerations have reigned. However, broad policy goals remain consistent with maintaining an open trade system in agriculture and most support measures implemented since 1993 have been temporary. In spite of the initial difficulties, farmer groups have accepted the basic principles of the new approach and have undertaken actions to improve their competitiveness for the future.

After the remarkable recovery of 1993 to 1995, Colombian agriculture seems poised to pursue a more sustainable growth pattern in the long term. Competition with imports has raised the level of awareness among farmers of the need to increase productivity levels and shift crop mixes towards the demands of the market. As a result, productivity levels are increasing and investments in infrastructure and research are laying the foundations for future growth.

Success for Colombian agriculture will, however, require that some remaining obstacles are overcome. Colombian farmers continue to face extremely high levels of rural violence, a factor that has checked the growth potential of Colombian agriculture for decades. According to a

government (National Planning Department) study, farmers lost between 10.6 and 17 percent of agricultural GDP annually during the 1980s as a result of kidnappings, extortions, crop losses, theft and general lack of security. Better growth prospects for agriculture will require that rural violence be sharply reduced.

The oil bonanza that is expected to last until the first half of the next decade may increase pressures on the profitability of tradable agriculture. As oil revenues are absorbed into the economy, the exchange rate is likely to appreciate even further and relative prices will move in favour of non-tradables. Most of the income gains of the boom are expected to be captured by the urban sector. In order to decrease the negative effects on production of tradables, in 1995 the government created an oil stabilization fund to reduce negative impacts, and this is expected to limit the rate of appreciation. For agriculture to reap benefits from the bonanza, public investment will need to be raised in key areas, such as research and transport infrastructure, that might increase the competitiveness of Colombian farmers.

Finally, Colombian agriculture will not take full advantage of its natural potential until measures are taken to improve the pattern of resource use. The intensity with which agricultural land is used continues to vary sharply from region to region; parts of the Andean highlands are overexploited whereas large areas in the Atlantic and Central Magdalena region are underexploited. This pattern of resource allocation will continue to generate significant efficiency, equity and natural resource losses until policy biases that favour large mechanized farming units and livestock operations are removed. This should expand employment opportunities in the countryside and reduce rural poverty as well as the reasons for violent actions.

NEAR EAST AND NORTH AFRICA

REGIONAL OVERVIEW
Economic developments

The countries of the Near East and North Africa region continue to face acute macroeconomic problems arising from fiscal deficits, inflationary pressure, deteriorating external terms of trade and a sizeable external debt. Furthermore, the region has been slow in adopting the reform programmes needed to provide an environment that enables sustainable development. These factors, together with episodes of civil war and recurrent droughts, have translated into generally slow and unstable rates of economic growth over the last decade and a half, even in those countries that introduced reform programmes more decisively. Progress has remained slow in such key areas of reform as the reduction of trade barriers, the reformulation of the regulatory framework and privatization of the large public sector. In particular, accelerating the process of privatization represents an arduous task in Egypt, Algeria, the Islamic Republic of Iran and the Syrian Arab Republic, where public enterprises retain dominant roles in industrial activity. There is also much scope for trade liberalization in these countries.

Economic growth in the region as a whole reached a modest 2.4 percent in 1995, after having stagnated the previous year. The oil prices in 1995 remained depressed, despite a notable spur in demand in the importing countries which was met primarily from non-members of the Organization of the Petroleum Exporting Countries (OPEC). Although demand-contracting policies were instrumental in mitigating inflation, weak oil prices continued to restrict growth. Nevertheless, several countries such as Turkey, Iran, Algeria and, to a lesser extent, Egypt, recorded significant improvements in economic growth after the depressed year of 1994. Jordan's economy continued to grow at a sustained pace.

Prospects for the short term appear mixed. On the one hand, improved regional stability may stimulate confidence and activity throughout the region; on the other hand, large macroeconomic imbalances and weak oil prices are expected to continue clouding the prospects for rapid growth in net oil-exporting countries. One major area of positive expectation is in regional cooperation. In particular, the process of peace among Jordan, Israel and their

Palestinian neighbours can pave the way for future cooperation in a number of economic areas. Notwithstanding past ineffectual attempts at intra-Arab trade (which accounts for only 8 percent of the total trade at present), the emerging regional trading group comprising these countries and including Egypt can, in the future, be one of the most important areas of regional trade and cooperation. This will require removal of the economic, political and institutional impediments facing regional cooperation at present. In agriculture, one of the more important areas within the ambit of regional cooperation is technology transfer. Israel at present is capable of producing innovative, regional and climate-specific technology, especially in the area of water management, which could be particularly useful elsewhere in the region. On the other hand, progress in regional agricultural trade will also be dependent on Israel removing domestic support and opening up its markets to allow for greater imports of agricultural commodities from its neighbours.

Agricultural performances and issues

Agricultural production growth in the Near East and North Africa region slowed from an already modest 2 percent in 1994 to 1.7 percent in 1995. Overall cereal production, at around 22 million tonnes in 1995, was estimated to be about 18 percent lower than the previous year's above-average harvest. In spite of the improved incentives provided through domestic agricultural policies and higher international prices, the region achieved limited success in the production of strategic crops, the diversification of the agricultural base and the enhancing of productivity of land and labour in the agricultural sector. Wheat production in North Africa, which depends largely on rainfall, was estimated to fall by 22 percent from 11.3 million tonnes in 1994 to 8.9 million tonnes in 1995 as a result of poor rainfall, especially in Morocco.

After a bumper crop in 1994, poor rainfall adversely affected agriculture in *Morocco* in 1995. Water levels in the country's reservoirs were depleted as a result of the drought in three out of the last four years, which seriously affected water availability for agriculture and other uses. The area planted to cereals was 37 percent less than it had been in 1994 and the production of cereals in 1995, at about 1.9 million tonnes, was estimated to be the lowest in 30 years. Wheat production fell by 80 percent (to 1.1 million tonnes) and that of barley by 84 percent in 1995. Consequently,

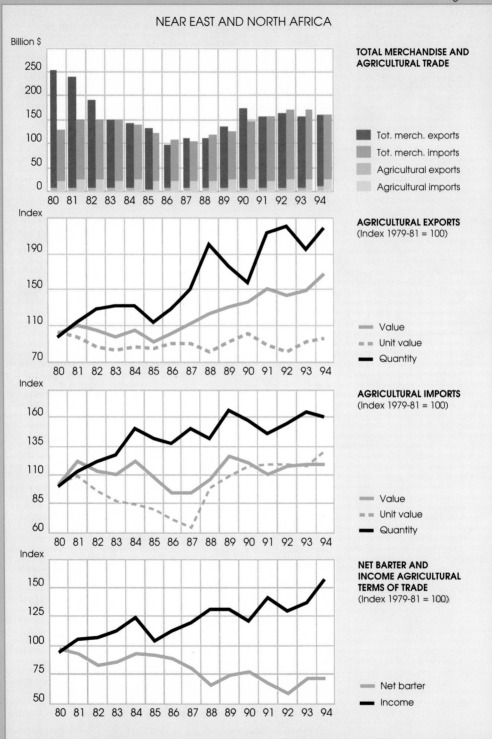

NEAR EAST AND NORTH AFRICA

Billion $

TOTAL MERCHANDISE AND
AGRICULTURAL TRADE

■ Tot. merch. exports
■ Tot. merch. imports
■ Agricultural exports
■ Agricultural imports

Index

AGRICULTURAL EXPORTS
(Index 1979-81 = 100)

Value
Unit value
Quantity

Index

AGRICULTURAL IMPORTS
(Index 1979-81 = 100)

Value
Unit value
Quantity

Index

NET BARTER AND
INCOME AGRICULTURAL
TERMS OF TRADE
(Index 1979-81 = 100)

Net barter
Income

Source: FAO

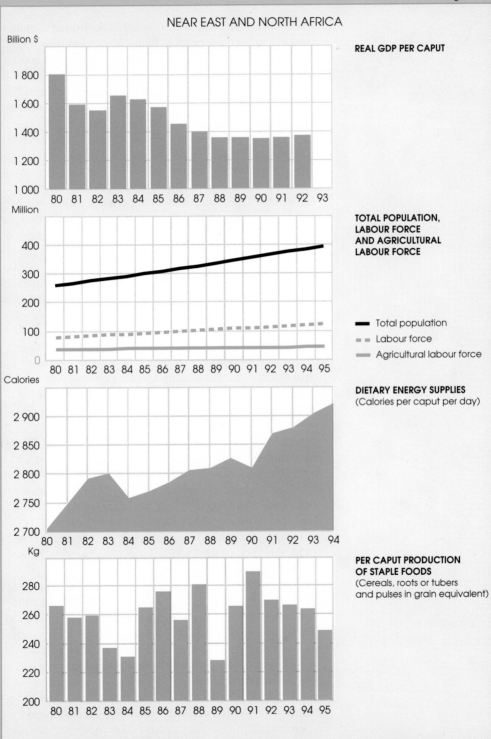

NEAR EAST AND NORTH AFRICA

REAL GDP PER CAPUT

TOTAL POPULATION, LABOUR FORCE AND AGRICULTURAL LABOUR FORCE

— Total population
- - Labour force
— Agricultural labour force

DIETARY ENERGY SUPPLIES
(Calories per caput per day)

PER CAPUT PRODUCTION OF STAPLE FOODS
(Cereals, roots or tubers and pulses in grain equivalent)

Source: FAO

wheat imports in 1996 are expected to be around 3 million tonnes – an increase of more than 150 percent over 1995. To spur production, the government increased the support price of sugar beet, sugar cane and cotton.

In *Egypt,* agricultural production increased by about 2.5 percent in both 1994 and 1995. The production of wheat was estimated to increase by 28 percent to 5.7 million tonnes, mainly because of better seed variety and a greater incentive structure. In spite of expanded production, increasing domestic and international prices are beginning to have a negative effect on domestic demand. Egypt remains the region's largest net importer of wheat, however. At the same time, both rice and cotton crop production are responding to favourable prices and market liberalization, particularly since cotton is now being traded by the private sector.

Historically, *Turkey* has been one of the few countries in the region to enjoy self-sufficiency in food. The government price policy under the current structural adjustment programme provides support to cereals, sugar beet and tobacco with price increases of 100 percent for cereals (barley, rye and oats). Agricultural policies in the recent past have led to Turkey becoming a net importer of wheat. Wheat production in 1995, although higher than the previous year's poor crop, was much lower than the projected 21 million tonnes, in part because of the damaging effects of unseasonable rainfall and pests. To meet the domestic demand, the government abolished the US$20 per tonne import levy on wheat to enable the private sector to import high-quality wheat. In 1995, Turkey imported significant quantities of wheat, sugar and beef; in 1996 it is expected to import about 1 million tonnes of wheat.

In *the Sudan,* after an exceptionally good cereal harvest in 1994, the forecast for 1995 is 3.3 million tonnes – 26 percent lower than in the previous year. Production of sorghum and millet are expected to decline by 12 percent and 46 percent, respectively, mainly as the result of a drop in the area devoted to these crops in both the mechanized and the irrigated areas. In addition, yields for these crops were affected by poor seasonal rains, pest damage and weed infection. Nonetheless, the overall prospects for wheat and coarse grain in 1996 are favourable following good rainfall, timely control of the desert locust and an increase in the area planted. Favourable domestic and international prices coupled with other incentives are also expected to boost production. Inadequate marketing and

transportation infrastructure remains one of the main constraints to the objectives of self-sufficiency in food and food export generation.

In *Algeria,* cereal production returned to the average level of 2.2 million tonnes in 1995, with wheat production growing twofold and barley threefold. The government took a number of steps to boost long-term agricultural production in view of the increasing food import bill which is one of the highest in the region. The new strategy is based on higher support prices and low interest rates for farmers, as incentives for boosting domestic production of grains, pulses and milk; enhancing production from existing land by improving extension services; and developing dryland agriculture in southern Algeria.

The sanctions on *Iraq* continue to affect both producers and consumers acutely. In spite of favourable weather conditions, cereal production decreased primarily by 10 percent in 1995 as a result of a lack of seeds and chemical inputs. The availability of food continued to decline, caused by the lack of foreign exchange, estimated at US$2.7 billion, needed to meet domestic food needs. The government's efforts towards containing the deteriorating situation included an increase in the quantity of rations for wheat-flour from 1 kg to 7 kg per caput and for vegetable oil from 625 g to 750 g per caput. The increased ration, nevertheless covers less than 50 percent of the required food energy needs.

In *Saudi Arabia,* the support price of wheat has been reduced from riyals (SRIs) 2 000 to SRIs1 500 (US$400) per tonne to reduce the government-sponsored subsidy on wheat. The production of 2.5 million tonnes in 1995 is still slightly above domestic requirements of 1.8 million tonnes. Government policy aims at further reduction of subsidies on wheat, to bring the production more in line with domestic demand. At the same time, the production of vegetables, high-value crops and meat is encouraged.

Cereal production in the *Syrian Arab Republic* rose by 8 percent in 1995. The production of wheat was 4.0 million tonnes, some 13 percent higher than in 1994, while barley production increased by 15 percent.

Issues affecting regional food security
The Near East and North Africa region is traditionally a large net importer of food. The gap between food imports and production, which stood close to 5 million tonnes in 1960-61, stands at more than 20 million tonnes in 1995-96. Of

the countries in the region, only Saudi Arabia and, more recently, the Syrian Arab Republic are exporters of wheat. Four countries – Turkey, Iran, Saudi Arabia and the Syrian Arab Republic – maintain most of the regional stocks of wheat with a stocks-to-use ratio of about 25 to 30 percent compared with about 8 to 10 percent in North Africa.

A major increase in food calorie intake took place in the 1970s, except for in some countries such as Afghanistan and Yemen, thus bringing the region's daily calorie intake well above the average of developing countries as a whole. Although food self-sufficiency was historically a strategic objective of the development plans in many countries of the region, most of the increase in daily calorie intake was achieved through increasing food imports. Indeed, agricultural growth failed to achieve self-sufficiency or even keep pace with the increase in population. The accrual of oil earnings to the region was reflected in domestic subsidies to the consumer and led to rapid increases in food consumption during the 1970s and 1980s. Changing patterns towards high nutritional value items also contributed to a rise in food consumption, which was increasingly met through food imports.

The economic performance of most countries in the region followed the cyclical fluctuations of oil revenue earnings. The collapse of oil prices in the early 1980s, and their steady decline thereafter, was an external shock which required a revision of major policies to remove the structural imbalances in the economies of the region. This was especially pertinent in the case of food security policies, which were characterized by consumer subsidies entailing heavy public expenditure in most countries of the region. However, as expansionary fiscal policies (including unsustainable consumer subsidy policies) continued, economic strains resulted in an increasing slow-down of economic growth. Most of the countries of the region experienced a decline in per caput income, budgetary deficits and other disequilibria.

By the late 1980s or early 1990s, many of the countries, such as Egypt, Jordan, Turkey, Morocco, Algeria and Yemen, entered into structural adjustment programmes with the Bretton Woods institutions. In other countries of the region, economic reform programmes are now also being adopted, a cornerstone of which is the removal of structural imbalances in the economy to gear it towards more efficient use of resources. Major objectives of the reforms in agriculture are increasing domestic production and

removing the general consumer food subsidies. Although a step in the right direction in a long-term perspective, price liberalization and the phasing out of consumer subsidies in the last few years have had a bad effect on the population, especially the low-income groups, contributing to poverty and precarious food security in many countries of the region. This has created the need for special programmes and measures to protect poor farmers, consumers and vulnerable populations, and these have imposed further budgetary burdens.

A substantial proportion of the population of the Near East and North Africa region live in the rural areas and depend on agriculture for their livelihood. Increasing agricultural production therefore remains important not only for increasing food security but for poverty alleviation. Within this context, the lack of availability of adequate supplies of water in the region is a major limiting factor on the growth of agriculture and, consequently, has implications for food security. Over 50 percent of the region's agricultural production is realized from irrigated agriculture. With rapid growth in population and greater urbanization and industrialization, the pressure on the agricultual sector is bound to increase further. In the long run, land reform and water policies will determine the performance of the agricultural sector in the region. Demand management reform in the water sector is the key to a more efficient performance of agriculture in the region and, therefore, to greater food security.

In general, agriculture is bound to remain the key factor determining economic and food security prospects for many countries in the region. Especially for the 14 low-income food-deficit countries in the region, it is through agricultural development that the issues of food import dependence, meeting the growing food needs of urban populations and improving incomes and food security, particularly of poor rural populations, will be more effectively tackled. Exploiting the region's untapped potential and sustaining the quantity and quality of productive resources, however, represent formidable challenges in several countries constrained by harsh natural and climatic conditions, where soil erosion, desertification, waterlogging and salinity have already reached alarming proportions.

PALESTINIAN TERRITORIES
Economic review

The current transitional phase in the Palestinian Territories (PT), from occupation to self-rule, comes at a time of slow growth of the economy caused by various structural and political problems which evolved over the last 30 years. Income growth has stagnated, infrastructure and social services are heavily taxed and, although the agricultural sector produces a marketable surplus, trade remains constrained by limitations on market access for Palestinian producers. At the same time, the natural resource base is deteriorating at a rapid pace and the economic plight is further affected by the frequent closure of the borders with Israel. The visible economic gains brought about by the peace process are still uncertain because political and economic issues remain to be settled and this, it seems, will take time.

A mixture of asymmetric integration in the region and a weak regulatory framework explains much of the uneven pattern of development in PT over the past three decades. The economy has seen periods of growth and decline which were the result of its atypical political circumstances in the Arab world and Israel.

With restrictions on trade and production, much of the pattern of economic growth after 1967 in the Palestinian economy can be explained by the rise and fall of labour export from PT. Economic growth in PT became closely tied to the cyclical economic fluctuations related to oil earnings, much as in the other Arab countries of the region, and the pattern of development in Israel.

The major cause of the rapid economic growth after 1967 in the Palestinian economy was the increased economic integration of the newly occupied territories with Israel, in terms of the availability of employment in, and a surge of imports from, Israel, although exports, especially of competitive products remained restricted by Israel. The number of Palestinians working in Israel increased from virtually none to 75 000 in 1979. The economic upswing in the Arab region, caused by the rise in oil earnings in the first half of the 1970s, led to further labour export which became the major foreign exchange earner to PT through the remittances of expatriate labour. A boom in investment, although primarily in the construction sector, led to an average annual GDP growth rate of 8.5 percent from 1970 to 1979. During this period, the per caput income surpassed that of Jordan and Egypt.

The 1980s ushered in an era of lower oil earnings to the region as a whole and, consequently, an overall economic slow-down. The decline in demand for Palestinian labour and lower growth in the trade and services sectors, combined with the decline in remittances, led to recession in the PT economy as well. From 1980 to 1987, annual GDP growth averaged 3.6 percent in the West Bank and around 1.6 percent in the Gaza Strip. The development of infrastructure, institutions and social services, which was already restricted because of the occupation, suffered further as a result of the economic recession. At the same time, high inflation in Israel had a spill-over effect on the Palestinian economy, affecting the low-income groups in particular. The start of the intifada movement towards the late 1980s led to frequent strikes and closure of the borders with Israel, contributing to stricter restrictions on Palestinian labour movements and economic controls on PT. In 1991, the crisis in the Persian Gulf further exacerbated the situation as a result of the drastic reduction in the Palestinian expatriate labour employed in the Persian Gulf countries, especially in Kuwait, and the closure of the border by Israel for labour movement.

The peace process brings both challenges and opportunities for PT. With full autonomy already in place, Palestinian development efforts are entering a new phase, as a consequence of both the historic Interim Agreement on the West Bank and the Gaza Strip in 1993 and the progress made after the Cairo Agreement in 1994. Since then, an agreement for a joint effort towards economic development has been concluded between the Palestinian Authority, the Government of Israel, the donors supported by the World Bank and UN. Considerable financial assistance is expected to flow in from the international donors in the coming years. The major challenge faced by the authorities is how to use the expected financial capital inflow as a vehicle to remove the structural imbalances in the economy and lay the foundation for sustainable development in the long term.

More specifically, key policy issues to be addressed include a reduction in the traditional dependence on outside sources of employment for the PT labour force by harnessing domestic production opportunities. The trade regime, characterized by a large trade gap, remains heavily dependent on employment opportunities in Israel. What is required is to broaden the production base, diversify markets and liberalize trade with both the Arab countries and Israel to establish an enabling environment consistent

with an export-oriented growth strategy that is conducive to greater economic integration. At the same time, the provision of public infrastructure and services is required not only to improve living conditions but also to support private-sector investment activities and to avoid further environmental degradation.

Role of agriculture

Historically, agriculture has played a more dominant role in the overall economy of PT than in the economies of its neighbours, Jordan or Israel. During the period of economic growth from 1968 to 1974, the share of GDP averaged 37 percent in the West Bank and 32 percent in the Gaza Strip, declining to around 27 and 23 percent, respectively, during the 1975-1986 period as a result of stringent restrictions on trade, control over access to land and water by Israeli authorities and the shifts of labour from low-return agriculture to high-return sectors, especially services.

During the last few years of the 1980s, the agricultural sector regained some of its importance, as is evident from the increase in its share in the overall economy to its historical levels. A good olive crop in the West Bank and a citrus crop in the Gaza Strip remained the major contributors to the growth of GDP. This resurgence was instrumental not only in providing employment opportunities for workers returning from abroad and those previously employed in Israel (which, together, represented a high 40 percent of the labour force in the peak year of 1987) but also in contributing to the Palestinian economy during the recessionary economic climate within the region over this period.

The agricultural sector continues to be an important source of employment to the PT population of 1.7 million. Rural areas contain 70 percent of the overall population. The share of employment in agriculture is 26 percent of the labour force in the West Bank and 19 percent in the Gaza Strip. A distinctive characteristic of this structure is that women are, by far, the major source of labour because male labour has migrated to the cities, Israel or elsewhere.

Agricultural resource use

Agriculture in the West Bank is primarily rain-fed, encompassing 95 percent of the cultivated areas; the remaining 5 percent is devoted to permanent irrigation. Out of about 156 000 ha, about 7 800 ha are under irrigated agriculture. The areas within the Jordan Valley (3 500 ha)

and Tulkarem (2 600 ha) are by far the leading districts in irrigated agriculture. In the rain-fed areas, most of the traditional crops are grown within a low-risk, low-input and low-technology environment. Olives, grapes and almonds constitute 60 percent and wheat and barley 35 percent of the total cultivated area. Of the irrigated areas, 60 percent is used for vegetables and fruits, 25 percent for citrus and 12 percent for bananas. Compared with the practices prevalent in the areas of rain-fed agriculture, those used in irrigated agricultural areas are more advanced in terms of adopting modern technology, especially in the case of protected crops, which are produced under greenhouses with high and low tunnels and using the drip irrigation system.

In the Gaza Strip, the total area devoted to agriculture reached a peak in 1968 (18 200 ha). In the last ten years it dropped to 16 500 ha primarily because of urban encroachments.

At present, 65 percent of the area is irrigated. Historically, citrus has been the dominant crop in the Gaza Strip and consumes about half of the water used for agriculture. The remaining irrigated area is devoted to vegetables and multiple cropping. The non-irrigated area is used to grow fruit-trees, grapes and almonds. Almost half of the farms are less than 1 ha and only 11 percent are more than 4.6 ha.

In the West Bank, there are marketable surpluses in vegetables (11.4 percent), citrus (35 percent), grapes (81 percent) and pickled olives (84 percent). Agricultural production, however, has been either stagnant or declining in the West Bank during the last five years. In the Gaza Strip, a shift in the cropping pattern has contributed to an increase in the production of vegetables from 138 000 tonnes in 1989-90 to 201 000 tonnes in 1991-92; although citrus production has declined from 197 000 to 110 000 tonnes over the same period. Increasing salinity, overpumping of water and lack of market access have lowered the rates of return on citrus fruit and led to a substitution from citrus plants to vegetable production.

Water and agriculture

Water is crucial for the future of agriculture in the West Bank and the Gaza Strip. The annual renewable water sources, which are mainly groundwater from aquifers shared with Israel, are about 850 million m^3 in the West Bank and 80 million m^3 in the Gaza Strip. Demand for water exceeds the available supply. In the Gaza Strip,

groundwater sources are being depleted at an alarming rate. With the current rate of extraction exceeding the maximum sustainable yield, increasing the supply of water in the Gaza Strip is a major issue. Inappropriate cropping patterns and free access to water in the past have contributed to a lowering of the water-table beyond the minimum sustainable level. In many cases this has made further pumping uneconomic. In the West Bank, availability of additional water is constrained by limits set by Israeli authorities and the overall scarcity which leads to increasing economic opportunity costs associated with pumpinq additional units of water.

Water is underpriced in the agricultural sector and overpriced for domestic use. In the long term, this pricing pattern is expected to put pressure on agriculture to release some water for the domestic sector where it fetches a higher price.

The lack of an appropriate pricing structure for water is the major factor limiting the productivity of the agricultural sector in PT. The price of water varies within farming zones in the West Bank. The farmer with ownership rights for spring water in the Jordan Valley and the Nablus area, pays only US$0.045 per cubic metre, while the cost (rent) to the farmer without ownership rights to water is $0.080 per cubic metre.

In the Jordan Valley irrigation water from a well costs on average US$0.076 per cubic metre, which is almost equal to the price for spring water for the farmer with ownership rights in the same area. On the other hand, water pumped from a deep well costs $0.18 per cubic metre in the Nablus area. As the costs of pumping have increased in the Nablus area, the responsiveness of the farmers to switching to modern irrigation technology has increased. This is in contrast to the Jericho area where the cost of water is low and there is no incentive to adopt the more costly drip irrigation system.

According to a recent study, the marginal value of water in the production of different crops in the Jordan Valley ranges from US$0.33 per cubic metre for citrus to a high $1.87 to $2.90 per cubic metre for potatoes, tomatoes and peppers grown under greenhouses. In general, the returns on water are higher for vegetables raised under greenhouses. The differential between the marginal value of water in the Jordan Valley and the price currently charged, in general, indicates a hidden gain or rent associated with the current price of water. This rent or gain is more evident

**NEAR EAST
AND NORTH AFRICA**

for farmers with ownership rights, in particular for spring water (although water extraction volumes are limited by policies enforced by Israel).

The current water policies in PT depict a clear case of economic, institutional and environmental failure. The economic failure is evident in that the average price of water is very low compared with the marginal value of water for crops such as tomatoes, cucumbers and other very high value crops, sending misleading signals to farmers as to the true scarcity value of water and leading to incentives for rent seeking. The results are overuse of water, a decline in the water-table and a corresponding increase in pumping costs. Over the years this has eroded the profitability of many farming activities while at the same time undermining the sustainability of agriculture.

Institutional failure results when property rights are not well defined and enforced. In the West Bank, restrictions from Israel on the extraction of water that are well below its sustainable limits have limited the potential growth of the agricultural sector. The most important factor in the relaxation of past policies, however, will be that it is concomitant with a pricing structure that reflects the opportunity cost of water in the area to ensure efficient and sustainable use. This is particularly important since the removal of similar restrictions on well-digging in the Gaza Strip with the advent of self-rule has already led to the number of wells increasing rapidly in the last two years, which has resulted in approximately 40 million m^3 of pumping over the maximum sustainable limits every year. Although the availability of additional water has resulted in an increase in the production of high-value crops in the short term, the rapid depletion of groundwater resources is not sustainable in the long term. There is an urgent need to revise the pricing structure in the Gaza Strip to reflect the economic cost of use and the long-term or intragenerational depletion cost.

As regards the environmental implications of water policies, the need remains to tax (or enact a user charge on) water polluters to ensure minimal environmental degradation and long-term sustainable development. Water quality in the Gaza Strip has already deteriorated as a result of the decline in the water-table and the corresponding sea water intrusion; increased salinization; excessive use of fertilizers and pesticides; and uncontrolled discharge of sewage water into the soil and the natural drainage system. These factors have affected the productivity of the

**NEAR EAST
AND NORTH AFRICA**

agricultural sector and, if they are not corrected soon, irreversible damage to the natural resources, such as land and water, will lead to an immeasurably high cost to society.

The cornerstone of a future environmental strategy is a combination of supply enhancement and demand management policies. The supply of water can be augmented through water harvesting, treatment of wastewater, desalinization, cloud seeding, artificial recharge of aquifers and rehabilitation of the wells. However, in view of the overall scarcity of water in the region, these need to be complemented by policies that rationalize water demand and improve water-use efficiency. The most important of the demand management policies is appropriate pricing of water which so that it covers at least the operation and maintenance costs in the short term while moving towards full cost pricing in the long term. This will lead to water conservation technologies that are technically feasible, economically viable, socially acceptable and environmentally benign.

Trade and market access
Agricultural trade assumed a significant role in the Palestinian economy during the period of economic boom. Agricultural exports from the West Bank (US$82 million) and the Gaza Strip (US$55 million) comprised 40 percent and 28 percent, respectively, of overall exports in 1981. This share declined in successive years, however. In 1990 the combined exports accounted for only $58 million, representing only 30 percent of the total. Commodity imports in agriculture were (and are) entirely from Israel, including those of wheat, sugar, rice and a host of other commodities. All inputs used in agriculture (seeds, fertilizer, pesticide and water equipment, etc.) were imported from Israel. A slow restructuring of the domestic production pattern (both within the sector and between the sectors), a weak institutional framework governing trade in PT and restrictions on marketing during the occupation reduced the competitiveness of PT agricultural exports over the years. Accompanying this was a shift in the demand for Palestinian agriculture exports caused by the changing domestic economic and political situation in Israel, Jordan and other Arab countries.

Among the major constraints currently facing PT are the limited range and quality of products available for export, the lack of information about external market opportunities,

the disrepair of physical infrastructure and ineffective and weak institutional infrastructure for investment and trade promotion. Frequent border closures, resulting in limitations on the free movement of agricultural produce, also adversely affect agricultural trade with Israel.

With surplus production of many agricultural crops, the extent of economic integration with Israel remains a foremost issue. Following the Cairo Agreement of 1994, the Israeli market could be a very lucrative one for PT agricultural produce. The restrictions on exports of agricultural products from PT to Israel are now being relaxed. The Cairo Agreement provides for free movement of agricultural produce between PT and Israel except for five products (tomatoes, eggplants, cucumbers, eggs and white chicken meat), which will remain subject to quotas until 1997.

The basis of a future economic growth strategy for the West Bank and the Gaza Strip remains market access and the development of agricultural trade. These will require increasing productivity to compete in both the regional and the global markets and a trade regime supported by appropriate tariffs (low and uniform) together with an effective institutional and regulatory framework.

Institutional framework
The Palestinian economy is constrained by ineffective public policy structures, including an inadequate taxing system and weak legal and administrative frameworks with poor implementation capacity. This represents a major obstacle for the formulation and implementation of sound developmental policies and for addressing the pressing problems faced by PT in the areas of land and water management, agricultural and rural development, trade and marketing. In addition, in the absence of an effective financial services sector, especially of medium-term credit institutions, the private sector relies mostly on informal credit sources. Indeed, the institutional support provided to the sector is limited and fragmentary.

Official responsibility for support and development of the agricultural sector rests with the departments of agriculture which operate out of Nablus, Jericho and Gaza. The budgets of the departments have been cut drastically in recent years and all are grossly understaffed. In addition, with no domestic research programme for support, the extension services are limited. A number of NGOs have taken over to fill the gap. While their efforts have definitely been helpful they have been limited by lack of resources.

Assistance programmes

The agricultural sector of the West Bank and the Gaza Strip, as well as various water management proposals, have attracted considerable support from the international donor community and NGOs during the past two decades or so.

The United Nations Development Programme (UNDP) has provided support to agriculture through about eight separate projects, most of them involving some kind of training of farmers. The largest project has been the construction of a citrus processing plant in the Gaza Strip in cooperation with the Government of Italy at a cost of about US$12 million. Assistance for the development of a vegetable packing and grading plant has been provided to the Beit Lahia Cooperative in the Gaza Strip. Numerous domestic water supply projects throughout the West Bank and the Gaza Strip have also been supported by UNDP as a high priority over the past 15 years.

UNDP also plans to focus its future assistance to agriculture by again combining upstream support aimed at providing start-up cost and technical advice to the newly created Ministry of Agriculture with downstream intervention, specifically direct support to the farmers to meet their urgent needs.

The World Bank-led Emergency Assistance Programme (EAP) for PT identified areas of priority investments and technical assistance to PT over the three years 1994 to 1996. A total budget of US$1.2 billion, of which 41 percent is earmarked for the development of the Gaza Strip, includes a programme of public investment ($600 million), private sector support ($300 million), start-up expenditure ($225 million) and technical assistance ($75 million).

A US$26-million programme of assistance for the agricultural sector includes support to the Palestinian Authority, programmes for shifts in the production pattern, maintainance of essential support services and building the market infrastructure. In addition, $25 million is earmarked for NGOs and private-sector initiatives to maintain existing support services and to promote on-farm investment. A sum of $1.3 million is envisaged for technical assistance in the area of capacity building, water, fishing and agricultural statistics.

FAO is providing technical assistance in developing and supporting the Agricultural Planning and Policy Department of the Ministry of Agriculture within the Palestinian Authority, in the area of agricultural planning and policy analysis. Support has been requested to formulate an

**NEAR EAST
AND NORTH AFRICA**

analytical framework for decision-making supporting the economic policy framework in areas such as agricultural price policy, natural resource management, trade policy, rural finance and credit policies, input distribution, the role of government and the private sector and capacity building in agricultural planning, policy analysis and statistics.

REGIONAL REVIEW
II. Developed country regions

CENTRAL AND EASTERN EUROPE AND THE COMMONWEALTH OF INDEPENDENT STATES

CENTRAL AND EASTERN EUROPE: SUBREGIONAL OVERVIEW
Improving economic trends and agricultural performance

Market-oriented progress further strengthened in the Central and Eastern Europe subregion in 1995 with some of the countries approaching a post-transition stage in their general economic and agricultural modernization. Measured by real GDP growth, Central and Eastern Europe [30] stood out as the area with the most rapid economic development (over 5 percent) in Europe in 1995 showing an acceleration over the preceding year (4 percent). The average still covered wide variations within the subregion, ranging from falling outputs in Croatia and The Former Yugoslav Republic of Macedonia (where GDP fell by 1.5 and 3 percent, respectively) to rapid growth in Albania and Poland (at 13 and 7 percent, respectively). Stabilization policies were rewarded with sharply declining inflation rates (except in Hungary) and by a remarkable tripling of net capital inflows (to US$31 billion) into the subregion compared with the previous year. In five small economies (among others Croatia, the Czech Republic and Slovenia), inflation rates could be measured in single digits, between 4 and 9 percent. Unemployment levels, a field of general concern in CEEC, increased at a slower average rate. Indeed, employment started to expand in five countries including Albania and Poland.

Such developments created good general prospects for a further improvement in 1996 even if the positive economic performance did not seem to be evenly distributed among countries of the subregion. There were still countries struggling with very high

[30] For the purposes of this subregional overview, the Central and Eastern European countries (CEEC) includes the following countries: Albania, Bosnia and Herzegovina, Bulgaria, the Czech Republic, Croatia, Hungary, Poland, Romania, Slovakia, Slovenia, The Former Yugoslav Republic of Macedonia and Yugoslavia.

unemployment rates. Moreover, nearly 90 percent of the capital inflow benefited just three countries, the Czech Republic, Hungary and Poland. Overall, it was the more developed member countries of the Central European Free Trade Agreement (CEFTA)[31] which formed a core group of economies with rapid economic growth of 5 to 7 percent (except for Hungary with 2 percent) and dynamic structural development. There was also accelerated growth in Romania (6 percent) and Bulgaria, at a slower rate (3 percent), in 1995.

While the recovery in CEEC was based mainly on the revival of industry (and, to a far lesser degree, on the service sector), the agrofood sector also did better than in the previous year. Very probably, 1995 marked the first year in the transition period in which the aggregate agricultural output of CEEC achieved positive growth. This relied on two principal components: first, the grain output of the subregion attained growth of around 3 percent, caused mainly by a good wheat harvest in 1995; and, second, in livestock production the subregion as a whole succeeded in halting the declining trend and, in a few countries, output in some of the livestock branches began to regain previous levels.

The upswing in total grain production of the subregion was, above all, based on considerably improved harvests in Poland and Romania with increases of about 15 and 6 percent, respectively, and there were slight increases also in the Czech Republic and Slovakia. This easily compensated for decreases in a few countries, such as Hungary and Bulgaria. The state of livestock production offered an improving, although still strongly varying, picture. In most countries, the pig and poultry sectors led the recovery with increasing stock numbers and growing output. In Hungary and Poland, cattle stocks were also rebuilding, although the dairy sector seemed to continue the declining trend throughout most of the subregion (except for the Czech Republic).

Provisional figures suggest that the increase of agricultural output relied in part on productivity improvements. In Poland, the significant upswing in cereal production was attained through improved yields on a decreased harvested area for the principal cereal types. In Romania also, higher yields boosted wheat output while maize production expanded mainly

---

[31] **CEFTA includes the Czech Republic, Hungary, Poland, Slovakia and Slovenia.**

because of an extension of the area sown to this crop. Nevertheless, yields recorded in the main grain-producer countries in 1995 were still lagging behind their prereform results. As compared to 1987-89, wheat yields per hectare in 1995 were still 2 and 17 percent lower in Poland and Hungary, respectively. Maize yields were 10, 25 and 35 percent lower in Poland, Bulgaria and Hungary, respectively, than in 1987-89. By the mid-1990s, corresponding productivity levels in the European Union (EU) were superior with maize yields being twice as high and wheat yields about one-third higher than the CEEC average. With reduced inputs and still weak investment activities in CEEC agriculture, major improvements could not yet be expected in most subsectors in 1995.

Producer prices in most cases improved more slowly than the general price rise. In the Czech Republic, for instance, farm prices increased by over 7 percent and overall consumer prices by more than 9 percent in 1995 (in the preceding year they increased by 5 and 10 percent, respectively). In Hungary in 1995, agricultural producer prices rose by just 15 percent compared with an increase of 28 percent in consumer prices. The generally depressed state of domestic food markets certainly continued to play a role in this. However, the weak negotiating position of agricultural producers, relying on their new, in part fragmented, farm structures and having only a small share in processing and marketing activities, might have played a greater role. Such conditions (with Poland as an exception) still left farmers at a disadvantage in the price formation process *vis-à-vis* the superior market power of highly concentrated procurement and processing enterprises.

Nevertheless, after the severe but inevitable adjustments of the preceding years within the agricultural price system, producer prices fluctuated less dramatically in several countries. Trends in the development of terms of trade for agricultural producers were still mostly negative, even though some positive modifications started to emerge in a few countries at a more advanced stage of economic restructuring. Thus, for example, the terms of trade index for Polish farmers improved by 4 percent in 1995 over 1994. Obviously, this less unfavourable trend in price relations for producers was in part a result of their more flexible output response. Furthermore, the more active policy of

price stabilization pursued by governments (including the introduction of guaranteed minimum prices for a varying number of products from country to country) also played an important role.

Domestic food demand continued to be slack throughout the subregion with livestock products being in weak or even further decreasing demand. Compared with prereform levels, food expenditure still took a greatly increased share of total household expenditure. In 1994 this share averaged about 31 percent for the CEFTA countries (with Hungary showing a further increase in 1995) as compared to 22 percent in the EU. Moreover, in Bulgaria and Romania, the shares were substantially higher, at 48 and 60 percent, respectively.

In several countries, shifts in demand patterns were characterized by a further weakening of interest in products in the medium price range and an increasing demand for cheap (mainly non-livestock) products. Some increase in demand for (often imported) processed products in the high price range could also be observed, however, with these products accounting for just a small portion of overall food consumption. After the introduction of a severe stabilization scheme affecting real incomes, food retail sales fell by about one-fifth in Hungary in 1995. In some countries, including the Czech Republic and Hungary, food retail prices showed a more rapid increase than the general price rise in 1995.

Led by Poland and Hungary, the principal agricultural exporters of the subregion, trends of expanding agricultural trade continued in 1995. Agricultural and food exports from Poland and Hungary rose by 20 and 25 percent, respectively. Romania succeeded in reducing its agricultural trade deficit, while a few nations increased their net exports. In Hungary, this was achieved on the basis of a fourfold growth of wheat exports supported by an 8 percent import tariff surcharge on all imports and by a strong devaluation of the national currency. The Czech Republic, Poland and Slovakia, however, showed continuing deficits in their agricultural and food trade.

In 1994-95, the subregion of CEEC as a whole seems to have returned to an expansionary path in its agricultural trade, particularly in exports. Countries with important production and export potential appeared to be ready to use the opportunities given to them by the

**CENTRAL
AND EASTERN EUROPE**

World Trade Organization (WTO) agreement. In addition to new WTO tariff rates, tariff surcharges appeared in several countries including Bulgaria, Romania and Slovakia. In Hungary and Slovakia, however, they were intended only for short-term application. Slovenia abolished its import surcharge on agrofood products simultaneously with the tariff adjustments required by the WTO agreement for 1995. In order to safeguard domestic market stability, some countries introduced export restrictions and/or even export bans for grain in the face of rapidly increasing prices on international markets. Overall, the level of state intervention in international trade in agricultural and food products did not seem to be declining in the subregion in 1995.

A remarkable development of the year was, however, the renewed expansion of intraregional trade and of trade between the CEEC and Commonwealth of Independent States (CIS) regions in agricultural and food products. Poland more than doubled its agrofood trade (in US dollar terms) with the other CEFTA countries, mainly as a result of threefold imports from those countries. Hungary expanded its exports to the CEFTA area by almost one-half. Both Poland and Hungary stepped up their agrofood deliveries to the CIS region by more than one-third with Poland being the main supplier to that area. The two countries' combined exports of agricultural and food products to CIS countries amounted to more than US$1.5 billion in 1995, marking an expansion of 37 percent over 1994. Within total agrofood exports from Hungary, the combined Eastern European share was already slightly higher than the EU share as a result of this most recent reorientation of trade in 1995.

Such changes appeared to shift regional patterns of agrofood trade towards a new balance in the whole of Eastern Europe, marking the beginning of a process whereby traditional intraregional trade could regain its importance under market-oriented conditions. The new CEFTA agricultural agreement was expected to render a further positive impact as from 1996.

Continuing lack of harmony in the process of structural reforms
Privatization of land, including state farms, progressed further in the subregion in 1995, with the exception of Slovakia (where several policy changes led to a slow-

down in the privatization of state enterprises and a new law reversed the system of land privatization by vouchers started in 1993). Nevertheless, this key process within the transition strategy seemed to be drawing towards an end in most countries. As a result, a highly varying farm structure was emerging, with privatized large-scale farms retaining an important position in some countries, including the Czech Republic and Hungary. The extent of privatization in the up- and downstream sectors varied greatly, with attractive food industry and retail trade companies taking the lead in being privatized.

Nevertheless, in most CEEC countries, the structural state of agriculture and that of the up- and downstream sectors were rarely the same. Monopolistic positions, of state-owned or privatized companies, still prevailed in many downstream branches. This continued to have a negative effect on both the bargaining position of agricultural producers and on consumers' economic interest, and the 1995 changes in price relations seemed to exacerbate the effect. With economic activities recovering in several countries, producer prices were increasing less and food consumer prices more rapidly than the average price rise (with the exception of Poland). For instance, in Hungary, where the general price rise amounted to 28 percent, producer prices increased by 15 percent and food consumer prices by 29 percent in 1995. Thus (with the exception of Poland), highly concentrated downstream companies seemed to benefit most from the recent changes in price relations. Weak competition on the retail market and the lack of organic connections among segments of the domestic market were becoming more obvious in the separated national markets of CEEC. The negotiating weakness of emerging professional organizations of agricultural producers was clearly also contributing to this situation.

The new privatized and, in some countries, fragmented farm structure, should have been given more flexibility by an operational land market and leasing schemes which would be essential for more factor mobility and for financing agricultural operations. Progress was, however, still limited in all CEEC countries in 1995. Positive developments, such as the increasing number of leasing arrangements in some cases, have not yet brought dramatic improvements. The main

difficulties included delayed sharing out of land titles, an incomplete legal framework for the transfer and lease of land property and various restrictions imposed on the emerging national land markets.

Even though the fragmentation of agricultural operations was mitigated by the use of leasing arrangements in Hungary, no legal provisions covered leasing or the legal position of partners. In the same country, reinstated land property was subject to a sales ban for five years and legislation prevented cooperatives and other legal entities and individuals from owning land. In Albania, the sale of farmland was bound to a prerogative option in favour of specifically defined groups of buyers. In some countries, a considerable proportion of the new owners of reinstated land property were urban residents (e.g. 43 and 80 percent in Romania and Bulgaria, respectively). This emphasized the need for operational land markets to be established. Land property was accepted by banks as collateral in very few cases.

The capital scarcity and financing problem of agriculture, thus, could not receive much help from the land market. In line with privatization and the restructuring of national banking sectors, some progress was made in creating specialized banking and credit institutions for the agrofood sector in a few countries. Subsidized credit was available (but not sufficient) in several countries, including Poland, Slovenia and Hungary. Such credits were allocated to farmers in exchange for delivery commitments in Romania. In Hungary, the cooperative rural banking network expanded and channelled state development funds to farmers and small rural enterprises. In the Czech Republic, a state support and guarantee fund contributed much to the flow of subsidized and guaranteed credit to agriculture. A similar institution financially assisted small and medium-sized enterprises in food processing.

In spite of this progress, a comprehensive and sound financing system for agricultural and related operations has not yet been created in any of the CEEC countries. Many factors contributed to this situation, including the poor profitability and low internal accumulation in agriculture as well as debt problems within the sector. The restricting effect of macroeconomic stabilization and foreign capital favouring primarily retail and

processing branches was not helpful in this respect either. As a sign of some relief, however, in countries with the highest increase in agricultural output and/or exports, the financial situation of farming organizations showed an improvement for the first time in 1995.

Having been at the centre of interest ever since the transition process began, the creation of market institutions made further considerable progress in several countries during 1994-95. In the Czech Republic, a good example was the establishment of 15 regional cooperatives for the marketing of milk to processors, resulting in improved milk producer prices. In the grain and pork sectors of Poland the new diversity of marketing channels allowed individual bargaining for farmers. In Hungary, the 1995 amendment of the law concerning market regulation provided for considerably more participation by commodity boards (called product councils) in the development and implementation of official market policy. In various CEEC countries both producers and consumers have by now had their first positive (or sometimes difficult) experiences of the available (or lacking) market institutions. This has resulted in a more flexible approach to entrepreneurial decisions and an improved awareness of market conditions throughout the whole vertical chain.

The main lesson of agricultural market developments in 1995 appeared to be the recognition of the need for more market transparency and more market integration both domestically and internationally. In Albania, where there is a somewhat fragmented farm structure, a free and simple system of weekly price information was established throughout the country in 1994. During the following year this was recognized as an accelerator of agricultural development. On the other hand, lack or non-use of export market information could cost higher profit losses for a subsector than the total amount of state subsidies paid to its producers during a whole year. Such a situation arose for grain producers in Hungary, a major grain-exporting country in the subregion, in 1995.

Development of private small-scale farming
By the mid-1990s, the progress of private family or peasant farming offered a rather unbalanced picture as a result of agricultural restructuring in most countries of

the subregion. As a result of the enormous efforts of farmers, however, private small-scale farming had developed into a significant economic and social factor of the agrofood sector. In terms of its share in land and labour use, local food supply, commercial production and agricultural GDP, this sector acquired an important place in most CEEC countries. In Slovenia and Poland, where private farming remained important throughout the communist period, small-scale private farming used four-fifths of agricultural land and contributed 80 and 89 percent, respectively, of gross agricultural output in 1994. The corresponding figures in Bulgaria and Hungary reached about 40 percent for land use and 81 and 49 percent, respectively, for agricultural output. According to national sources, in Poland, Bulgaria and Hungary, 90, 79 and 33 percent, respectively, of total agricultural labour was engaged in small-scale agricultural activities in 1994-95.

After six years of transition, however, private small-scale farmers continued to face many insufficiencies in their own resources and in their economic and institutional framework; sometimes, for example, they had to operate in a controversial political and social climate. In spite of varying national conditions, the principal difficulties of private farming remained very similar across the subregion and included land fragmentation (particularly in Albania Bulgaria and Romania with farm sizes of 1 to 2 ha), inadequate land legislation, unclear property rights, scarce capital and credit supplies, underdeveloped and often monopolized up- and downstream relations and scarce market information. Behind the farmgate, farmers still had to face a deficit in knowledge of management, marketing and small-scale sustainable production techniques. They also indicated unwillingness to cooperate among themselves. New extension services, however, gained increasing appreciation from private farmers, particularly in Slovenia, Poland and Hungary.

By the mid-1990s, the concept of private family or peasant farming seemed to be more accepted in countries such as Poland, Slovenia and Romania than in Hungary or Slovakia. In a few countries with important traditions in this type of farming, including Poland and Slovenia, the development of such enterprises and their institutional framework appeared to be more dynamic and complete. Even in these

**CENTRAL
AND EASTERN EUROPE**

countries, however, farmers were struggling with severe structural problems stemming in part from small farm size, of an average 8 ha in Slovenia and Poland. In addition, an increasing share of small-scale farms were operated part-time and were thus economically more stable, while a significant number operated at the subsistence level (particularly in Albania and Romania) and/or in the informal economy.

Fundamentally, many of the problems faced by private farmers in most countries stemmed from the lack of a clear and committed long-term policy concept for private family or peasant farming, particularly for young farmers. In some cases inconsistent policy measures towards small-scale farmers (for example, the withdrawal of some forms of support in Hungary) further complicated the situation.

The persistence of many of the problems of transition in this sector was also related to the absence or low level of genuine cooperation among individual farmers. Many of them could not overcome the psychological barrier to voluntary cooperation and association in the related up- and downstream activities, which were essential in times of scarce (financial, technological, managerial and often moral) resources in order to pave the way for the structural adjustment that was inevitable for small farms in order to improve their competitiveness. Nevertheless, relying on their modest resources and on ample experience gained from western Europe, emerging organizations of private farmers were already making increasing efforts in this direction. They were attaining some success in arranging for more producers' cooperation in marketing in a few countries including Albania, Bulgaria and the Czech Republic. For a better international coordination of their activities, several national small farmers' associations established the Central European Council of Farmers in 1995.

Development of human resources, i.e. adult training in modern, environmentally sound techniques and business aspects, appeared to be an urgent task for development policies aimed at the small-scale sector. As experience from western Europe has shown, the long-term solution is the establishment of national systems for the vocational training and installation of young farmers with the necessary expertise to manage their family-type enterprises. Special attention should be paid to establishing young farmers' associations.

Increasing orientation of agricultural policies towards the EU policy model

The declared objective of most CEEC countries to join the EU (five CEEC countries had expressed such a desire by January 1996) dominated the modifications introduced to their agricultural and trade policies in 1995. This was the case even for the WTO member countries among them, which also had to proceed to the first stage of implementation of the Uruguay Round agreement on agriculture. Several of these countries actually increased tariff protection. State support to agricultural producers and to the domestic market seemed to be stabilizing in Hungary, Poland and Romania, but the already modest budgetary provisions for this purpose could not be increased in real terms. In line with its different policy priorities, the Czech Republic reduced its 1995 budget for agricultural market regulation. Nevertheless, the general trend for the more advanced CEEC countries became to align their agricultural policies, policy institutions and mechanisms more closely with those of the EU.

Policy-makers attempted to strike a balance between market orientation and minimum protection for domestic markets, while the need for the two principal groups of agricultural policy mechanisms, i.e. market regulation and structural policies, to follow harmonized objectives and to be complementary became even more evident. Both types of policies need to be active simultaneously and consistently. Minimum market protection must be provisional, targeted and predictable in order that transitory market protection operates only long enough for structural measures to become active. The effect of the latter, in turn, is expected to reduce the necessity of providing renewed market protection in the future.

Part of the 1995 policy experience was thus the continuation of state intervention in the agricultural markets of the subregion. Apart from refining further the mechanisms for market support, credit facilitation, export stimulation and import protection, export restrictions and bans also appeared in several countries. In Croatia, price policies applied floor prices in order to protect the producer prices of key agricultural products. As a consequence, domestic agricultural prices were protected by tariffs and special levies in 1995 and a 1 percent surcharge was imposed on all imports. While

state expenditure on market regulation was reduced by over 50 percent in the Czech Republic, ad hoc application of licences (particularly for export) appeared in 1995. In Romania, input subsidization increased and minimum price guarantees prevailed for wheat and milk. For the latter, and for bread, consumer prices were also regulated by the state. The corresponding trade policy was characterized by a high level of import protection with sharply increased tariffs on wheat and dairy products in 1995. In Hungary's three-stage market regulation system, the number of directly controlled product markets had increased by 1995 to include wheat, maize, milk, pork and beef. Export subsidies amounted to about 50 percent of all agricultural support in 1995.

In the same year, the Czech Republic and Hungary subjected grain exports to licensing and to a virtual export ban in the latter country later in the year in order to maintain domestic market stability.

In the meantime, however, additional agreements concluded under CEFTA in 1995 aimed at eliminating some of the existing trade barriers as from 1996. Policy-makers' recognition of the long-term damages of permanent market protection strengthened slowly. The use of scarce budgetary resources for price guarantees and export subsidies can be rational only to the extent that it helps to implement structural development measures for the improved viability of a certain subsector. Likewise, import protection measures can only be justifiable if simultaneous efforts are undertaken to improve the international competitiveness of the protected subsector and its products. In the long term, however, protectionism decreases competitiveness rather than improving it, because it acts as a disincentive to the export of production from the protected subsector, increases food prices and results in the misallocation of resources.

The unfavourable agricultural trade balance of CEEC countries as a whole with the EU and developments on their domestic retail markets for food emphasized the urgent need for specific policies to improve the international competitiveness of the agrofood sector in CEEC countries. This was seen as a major prerequisite for their successful accession and operation within an enlarged EU market at the beginning of the next century.

The necessity for improving competitiveness in the CEEC agrofood sector

By the mid-1990s some CEEC countries had successfully reoriented their agrofood exports to western European markets. This was regarded as a necessary and positive step on the adjustment path towards establishing international market conditions. Nevertheless, the new trade orientation made the eastern agrofood sectors more dependent on both general economic trends and on specific requirements of markets in western Europe and this produced a special challenge in terms of international competitiveness for the CEEC nations.

The principal exporter countries of the subregion were trying to benefit further from their earlier comparative advantage in agrofood exports. There seemed to be little recognition of the fact, however, that the meaning and content of comparative advantage in agrofood production and trade had undergone substantive changes in Europe during recent decades. In the past, agrofood production and trade were related primarily to natural (geographic, climatic, soil, etc.) conditions and national production traditions. By the 1990s, comparative advantage within the agrofood sector had largely become a knowledge- and technology-specific factor of competitiveness. It was related more strongly to the adaptation of modern production techniques and knowledge (including high-level technical, ecological, management and marketing skills throughout the food chain) and less to natural conditions.

This explains why some western European countries with less favourable physical conditions for agriculture were showing a more successful output and market performance than CEEC countries with better natural conditions and long traditions of food production and trade. In recent years, repeated underuse of EU import quotas for CEEC countries was a case in point. Long years of weak investment activity and particularly the lack of high-technology investments left CEEC agriculture at a great disadvantage in the competition with western suppliers. This manifested itself in the continuing high share of unprocessed products in their exports and in the expanding share of western value added food products in CEEC domestic markets. In CEEC agrofood exports to the EU, grain, livestock, meat, fruits and vegetables occupied a share of well over 50 percent

**CENTRAL
AND EASTERN EUROPE**

in 1994-95. In Hungary, for instance, the export share of these products increased to 67 percent, while the import share of value added food products amounted to 72 percent in 1995. Such proportions demonstrated well the structural weakness of CEEC agrofood trade.

To improve their competitiveness (on both domestic and external markets), agrofood enterprises of the subregion require primarily qualitative upgrading of their operations rather than a development in terms of increasing output. The enlarged EU market is bound to be competitive regarding the qualitative attributes of products and services. Moreover, the interpretation of produce and food quality is undergoing rapid changes on the European market particularly because of an increasing inclusion of consumer health and sustainability aspects into the concept of quality (e.g. concern about healthy nutrition practices, chemical residuals, the ethics of animal husbandry, organic production and environmental protection).

Being closely related to the quality aspect of competitiveness, the problem of human capital and resource development appears to be a factor of key importance for the subregion. A further substantial reduction of the agricultural labour force is seen as necessary for CEEC as a whole if it is to arrive at levels of labour productivity comparable with those of the EU. The remaining labour force within a rather varied farm structure would require substantial retraining in sustainable production techniques, farm management, marketing and general business subjects. This will involve the implementation of specific training programmes with the cooperation of relevant national and international institutions and organizations.

A special feature of post-transition agricultural development is expected to be the continuing presence of a great number of large-scale farms in some countries, at least in the short to medium term (for example, in Hungary there are more than 2 000 enterprises with an average land area of between 1 100 and 1 700 ha). This raises the special challenge of developing and improving farm management systems for large agricultural enterprises under the conditions of a market-oriented economy. In the meantime, the issue of long-term viability of such enterprises seems to remain an open question, related to the specific technical nature of each subsector.

**CENTRAL
AND EASTERN EUROPE**

Obviously, the improved international competitiveness of the CEEC agrofood sector depends on new investments. In its present transitional state and given its scarce resources, however, the agrofood sector of the subregion would benefit more from investment in qualitative improvement and the substantive development of human resources than from investments for rapid output growth and export expansion.

CENTRAL
AND EASTERN EUROPE

COMMONWEALTH OF INDEPENDENT STATES: SUBREGIONAL OVERVIEW
Economic performance and policies

Most Commonwealth of Independent States (CIS) countries[32] have experienced negative growth rates of real GDP since the beginning of the transition process in the early 1990s, and the average yearly decline remained above 10 percent between 1991 and 1994. The downfall started to decelerate in 1995, when the weighted average GDP declined by 5 percent in real terms and, according to European Bank of Reconstruction and Development (EBRD) projections, 1996 should be the first year of positive growth for the subregion as a whole. Real output is expected to increase for the first time since 1990 in the Russian Federation, Georgia, Kazakstan and Kyrgyzstan, while positive growth had already been recorded in 1995 in Armenia and the Republic of Moldova. However, further output contraction (albeit at a considerably slower pace than in recent years) is still expected in some countries, including Belarus and Ukraine. Real GDP in the CIS countries as a whole in 1995 was just 53 percent of its 1989 level, and the projected 1996 recovery would only bring it to 54 percent. It must be stressed, however, that official figures overstate the decrease in output, since they do not cover the growth of activity in the informal sector, which has been substantial in the CIS.

Progress in macroeconomic stabilization has been more significant than output recovery. In 1992 registered consumer price inflation was at four-digit levels in virtually all 12 countries of the subregion. This number had shrunk to seven in 1994 and to two countries (Tajikistan and Turkmenistan) in 1995, although Belarus, the Russian Federation, Ukraine and Uzbekistan still retained inflation levels above 100 percent. Projections for 1996 show further progress, since inflation is expected to be controlled at under 100 percent in all countries except Tajikistan and Turkmenistan. A key role in the drop in inflation has been played by tight fiscal and monetary policies endorsed by the International Monetary Fund (IMF), as the large fiscal deficits associated with the deep recession have been cut down through expenditure reduction, in part linked to the reform process (reductions of enterprise and consumer subsidies). In

[32] The CIS comprises all the countries of the former USSR, except the Baltic states, i.e. Armenia, Azerbaijan, Belarus, Georgia, Kazakstan, Kyrgyzstan, the Republic of Moldova, the Russian Federation, Tajikistan, Turkmenistan, Ukraine and Uzbekistan.

addition, price liberalization was for the most part undertaken in the early stages of transition and its inflationary effect is fading.

Price liberalization is the area of reform where progress has been most uniform and substantial throughout the CIS. Virtually all countries have liberalized most prices, although, in general, control has been retained on energy and utility prices, and have largely phased out state procurement at non-market prices. Progress in other areas of the transition process has been less uniform. The private-sector share of GDP in mid-1995 ranged from 15 percent in Belarus, Tajikistan and Turkmenistan to 55 percent in the Russian Federation. Between these extremes were Armenia (45 percent), Kyrgyzstan and Ukraine (35 percent), Georgia and Uzbekistan (30 percent) and Azerbaijan and Kazakstan (25 percent). The privatization of small-scale enterprises has been comprehensive in the Russian Federation and Kyrgyzstan, and substantial numbers of small-scale enterprises have been privatized in most other countries, while privatization of large- and medium-scale enterprises is generally less advanced. Almost all countries have achieved some liberalization of trade, the exchange rate regime and interest rates. Progress has been slow in other areas of banking reform, however, and in the development of non-banking financial institutions, as well as in the areas of competition policy and the establishment of an adequate set of legal rules on investment.

Recent developments include the implementation of the government mass privatization programme, based on vouchers, in Ukraine; further progress of government privatization programmes in the Russian Federation and Kyrgyzstan; and progress towards cost-recovery levels of energy prices in the Russian Federation, Uzbekistan and Ukraine. The 1994 agreement on the creation of a free trade zone among CIS countries has so far made only limited progress in the creation of a custom union among the Russian Federation, Belarus and Kazakstan.

Recent performance of the agricultural sector
The decline of agricultural output, which has affected the subregion since the beginning of transition, continued in 1994 and 1995. The sector has been hit by the demise of former support policies, demand

CENTRAL AND EASTERN EUROPE

decline linked to real income reduction, the difficulties of the farm-restructuring and enterprise-privatization processes and the disruption of trade among the republics of the former USSR. In 1994, according to official statistics, only Armenia and Turkmenistan avoided lower agricultural output, in 1995 the only two countries to experience output growth were Armenia and Moldova. In the Russian Federation agricultural GDP declined between 1991 and 1995, albeit generally at a slower pace than the rest of the economy.

As for sectoral trends in the major food-producing countries,[33] both total cereal and total wheat production declined in the Russian Federation between 1993 and 1995 because of yield and, to a lesser extent, area reductions. Similar trends, although more marked, were recorded in Kazakstan, while in Ukraine output has recovered in 1995 after a sharp contraction in 1994. Given normal growing conditions, projected 1996 output is expected to exceed 1995 levels in all three countries, with significant recoveries in Kazakstan and the Russian Federation, largely because of yield increases. The three countries have experienced virtually continuous decline in all aggregates of animal husbandry between 1991 and 1995. The cumulative 1991-95 drop of inventories has varied between 21 and 45 percent for swine, sheep and goats and poultry, but has been more moderate for cattle, especially cows. These trends have been amplified by productivity declines and have resulted in cumulative output reductions generally about 20 to 30 percent for milk, 30 to 55 percent for eggs and 40 percent for meat.

The severe crisis of the livestock sector has been a common feature of the transition process in all CIS countries; the sector had benefited, more than crops have, from significant state support and the impact of the elimination of producer and consumer subsidies has therefore been serious. Furthermore, income changes have had negative effects on demand. In the four major food-producing countries, annual per caput food consumption in 1995 was generally one-third lower than its 1990 level for livestock products and between 49 and 64 percent lower for sugar; the consumption of cereals and potatoes was, conversely, generally close to or above 1990 levels.

According to the Organisation for Economic Co-operation for Development (OECD)[34] trade in bulk

[33] These are the Russian Federation, Kazakstan, Ukraine and Belarus.
[34] OECD. 1996. *Agricultural policies, markets and trade in the Central and Eastern European countries (CEECs), selected New Independent States (NIS) of the former Soviet Union, Mongolia and China, 1994 and 1995.* Paris.

**CENTRAL
AND EASTERN EUROPE**

agricultural commodities among the CIS countries has continued its declining trend in 1995, following a general pattern of trade decline among the republics of the former USSR. Most official trade still occurs through bilateral agreements,[35] although there is a continuous decline in the quantities established by such agreements and in their fulfilment, and an increasing importance of individual, unofficial trade flows and of direct food supply agreements among single provinces.

Political pressure to restrict imports because of concern over increasing food imports in the Russian Federation – about one-third of all imports in 1995 were foodstuffs and processed food products – resulted in higher import taxes on foodstuffs, with a maximum tariff of 30 percent on most items.

Farm restructuring

The present structure of farms in the CIS is the result of a historical evolution of the land-tenure system, in which there was virtually no private property, and of a process of reform that, as a consequence, in most cases has been centred on the distribution of formal ownership rights to farm workers, rather than on the restitution of land to previous owners. In the Russian Federation the process of farm restructuring has occurred in two major initial stages: a distribution of underused state and collective farmland, on the basis of heritable lifetime tenure, was implemented in 1990; and a general distribution of entitlements to farm and non-farm assets of state and collective farms to their workers was undertaken in 1991. Such assets were claimed as shares in the large farms reorganized as joint-stock farms or collective enterprises or they could be withdrawn for independent farming, leased or sold to other farmers.

A variety of approaches have been followed in farm restructuring throughout the subregion, from Armenia's comprehensive land reform programme, which allocated land according to family size and resulted in a pattern of agricultural ownership and farming based on very small holdings, to Tajikistan's complete lack of reform to date. The Russian Federation approach has been adopted in most countries, although in Belarus a 1993 Supreme Soviet decision nullified the 1991 law on reorganization, while Kazakstan restricted reform to state farms.

[35] The reduction in trade has been associated with the general downturn of activity, although in the initial stages of transition export restrictions, the loss of confidence in the rouble and the deterioration in the rouble payment mechanism have also played a role. The latter two factors have also led to the creation of an extensive network of bilateral trade agreements regarding intergovernmental or interenterprise barter. See World Bank. 1992. *Trade and payments arrangements for states of the former USSR.* Studies of Economies in Transformation, Paper No. 2. Washington, DC.

**CENTRAL
AND EASTERN EUROPE**

At present there are four types of farms in the major food-producing CIS countries: large farms, most of which are reorganized farms in the Russian Federation and Ukraine, occupied between 88 and 96 percent of land in the four countries in 1995; individual farms, resulting either from the distribution of underused land or from withdrawal from large farms, held between 1 and 5 percent of land; garden plots owned by urban residents have increasingly been devoted to food production; and household plots, to which all workers and employees of large farms were already entitled under the Soviet system, occupy about 10 percent of land in Belarus and Ukraine and far smaller percentages in Kazakstan and the Russian Federation. The share of household plots in production is however much larger and has increased virtually constantly in all four countries, representing in 1995 the bulk of production of potatoes, fruits and vegetables and between 30 and 70 percent of production of main livestock products, partly as a result of the increasing use of payment in kind or through unofficial transfers from the large farms. Although they are private, household plots are closely linked to the structure of large farms, on which they depend for inputs and support services, and their increasing importance can be interpreted partly as a shift to subsistence production within such farms.

A number of factors have contributed to orient the farming system towards the maintenance of large enterprises (albeit reorganized) rather than towards the development of individual medium-sized farms. Legal obstacles have played a crucial part, for instance, in the Russian Federation, Ukraine and Kazakstan, land shares are still not linked to physically identified plots and, throughout the CIS, the definition of rules regarding both freedom of withdrawal and land transactions has been extremely controversial and uncertain in many countries. The legal framework has generally provided security of land use and heritability to cultivators, but transferability, which is an essential feature of private property, is limited to various degrees. As for rules of withdrawal, in some cases there have been attempts to introduce a requirement of unanimity of consent from all shareholders.

There are however also economic reasons for the perpetuation of a farm structure based on large farms. The near absence of private agricultural credit markets,

which is in turn partly linked to the incomplete definition of individual property rights to land, creates a capital constraint on the establishment of individual farms; the lack of a private and/or public supply of agricultural support services, which have traditionally been provided by large farms, further discourages individual farming; and the recessive and unstable economic environment makes individual farming risky. In addition, the large farms have traditionally dispensed a range of social services, such as medical care and schooling, and farmers may have chosen not to withdraw their land shares in order to avoid the risk of loosing such services.

The extent to which the issue of property rights on land is unresolved and controversial is revealed by recent legislative developments in the Russian Federation and Ukraine (as well as in Belarus and Moldova). Although the new Russian Constitution, adopted in December 1993, removed the constitutional bar to the purchase and sale of agricultural land, and although a new Civil Code providing enlarged freedom in land transactions was adopted in 1994, the complete legal framework needed to implement the theoretical rights to purchase and sale has not yet been developed. The Civil Code was to go into force only after the approval of a new Russian Federation Land Code. A draft Land Code has been discussed since 1994 and a 1996 version passed by the State Duma and opposed by President Yeltsin would introduce severe limitations to land transactions. In the meantime, many provincial governments adopted their own legislation and, although a 1995 Presidential Decree established some provisional norms along the non-restrictive lines of the new Civil Code, it appeared that this would not overrule regional laws. In Ukraine a draft law, establishing that the allocation of land shares in large farms should be completed by the end of 1995 and lifting restrictions on land leasing and sales, was rejected by the Supreme Rada in November 1995.[36]

Upstream and downstream sectors
The sharp deterioration of the terms of trade between agricultural producers and input suppliers which has taken place since transition began has caused dramatic decreases in usage, sales and production of inputs. Between 1991 and 1995 tractor production decreased

[36] See OECD, op. cit., footnote 34, p. 221; Agra Europe. 1996. *East Europe.* London.

CENTRAL AND EASTERN EUROPE

by a factor of 18 in Kazakstan and by a factor of 8 to 9 in the Russian Federation and Ukraine, while the reduction of mineral fertilizer and compound feed production has generally been less dramatic; between 1994 and 1995 machinery production declined in the three countries, while mineral fertilizer production has since recovered in Kazakstan and the Russian Federation.

In the Russian Federation the government resisted farmers' requests to reintroduce state controls on input prices, but in 1994 it created a machinery leasing programme – in practice a time-repayment plan – intended to support the agricultural machinery producers as well as farmers. A large share of the inputs acquired by farms in 1995 were supplied through such plans, for which allocations were established by the federal Ministry of Agriculture, the regional authorities and a former government agency, reorganized as a joint-stock company, which acted as the sole distributor to farmers, who could pay in cash or through delivery of grains to the state. Agricultural input provision, thus, seems to have occurred in 1995 along lines which bear many similarities with pretransition methods, including the link between input supply and state procurement. In Ukraine the state also still distributed inputs as part of advance payments for procurement in 1995. Indeed, state provision of inputs remains tied to state procurement in most CIS countries. Emerging alternative arrangements are still based on input-for-crop barter, with international agribusiness companies (in Ukraine and the Russian Federation) or with local machinery rental stations.

In the agroprocessing sector, the CIS countries have inherited a structure characterized by the existence of local monopolies, because under central planning each district was to have only one or two processing firms and the transportation infrastructure was built accordingly. Such monopolistic positions are reinforced by other factors, such as, in the case of the Russian Federation, legal restrictions on movements of produce, intended to ensure local food procurement, and the poor state of the transport infrastructure and its insecurity caused by criminality. This has rendered the privatization of food processing enterprises a contentious issue, as farmers' requests to have some control over the privatized enterprises was frustrated in

both the Russian and Ukrainian privatization programmes since farms did not have the resources to compete with other bidders. In the Russian Federation complaints about the privatization of the food processing industry induced President Yeltsin to issue a decree in 1994 requiring the State Committee on Management of State Property to re-examine privatization. In Ukraine, in 1995 the Rada adopted a law establishing that agrofood processing enterprises should reorganize as open joint-stock companies with 51 percent of their shares to be given free of charge to their suppliers and failure to comply implying a return to state ownership. The law was vetoed by the president, represented in a slightly modified version in 1996 and vetoed again.

State procurement

The share of total produce bought up by the traditional procurement agencies, including payments in kind for workers and barter of produce for inputs, fell in recent years throughout the CIS at the expense of private marketing channels. The share of produce that bypasses the state channels varies greatly from state to state and tends to be greatest in those countries where reforms are relatively more advanced or in countries where central management has been eroded by civil strife (Georgia and Tajikistan) and least in countries where centralized control continues to be important. Procurement tends to absorb the bulk of production which requires industrial processing or specialized storage, because there tends to be a considerable degree of state control on such downstream activities, and to have a very limited role for produce which can be marketed directly.[37]

As a percentage of production, state procurement of grains, vegetables, potatoes and livestock declined sharply between 1991 and 1995 in Kazakstan, the Russian Federation and Ukraine. In 1995 state purchases absorbed virtually all production of fibre flax in all four major food-producing countries and a high proportion of sugar beet in Ukraine and Belarus. At the opposite end of the spectrum, the role of procurement is generally minimal for potatoes and vegetables. State procurement of grains was still around 30 percent of officially reported production in Belarus in 1995, 17 percent in the Russian Federation, 15 percent in

[37] FAO. 1995. *Preliminary assessment of 1995 foodcrop production and 1995/96 cereal import requirements in the CIS.* Rome, FAO.

Ukraine and 8 percent in Kazakstan. For livestock products, the state still absorbs 35 to 54 percent of production in the Russian Federation and lower percentages in Ukraine and, especially, Kazakstan.

The decline of the role of state purchases is caused by several factors. Low prices and long delays in payments because of the agencies' lack of funding are at the origin of farmers' unwillingness to deliver their product to the state agencies. As a result, most of the state procurement agencies are unable to meet their purchasing targets; this was the case in 1995 in both the Russian Federation and Ukraine, where a presidential decree has abolished the system for all agricultural products except grain.

Subsidies, price and credit policy

In the former USSR, state support to agriculture was based essentially on the price and subsidies mechanism and on credit policy. Procurement prices consisted of a base price plus bonuses based on quantity, quality and the financial needs of farms. Weak state and collective farms received price bonuses in an effort to improve their financial position; such differential price bonuses were the most significant category of agricultural subsidies in the 1980s. Farm inputs were subsidized, and consumer subsidies, usually paid to the processing industries, kept consumer prices down. Credit was allocated to state-owned enterprises by the government banking system. Concessional interest rates and periodic loan forgiveness effectively transferred income to selected groups and enterprises and state-allocated credit was widely used to bail out inefficient and high-cost producers. As state and collective farms rapidly accumulated debt in the 1970s and 1980s, debt rescheduling and debt forgiveness became frequent practices.

With transition, producer and consumer subsidies were mostly cut or eliminated and farmers faced rising production costs and depressed output prices because of low demand. Monopoly positions in the inputs supplying industry and widespread control of basic food prices in the early stages of transition exacerbated the price-cost squeeze.

Government attempts to introduce new support mechanisms for agriculture are at the basis of the establishment of agencies which are supposed to offer

contracts at guaranteed prices to support producers in the Russian Federation, Kazakstan and Ukraine. However, the Russian Federal Foodstuffs Corporation and the Kazak Commodity Credit Corporation differ fundamentally from similar agencies in the west in that they are also entrusted with state procurement. Furthermore, production credit is generally tied to guaranteed deliveries.

In the context of a continuing crisis in the agricultural sector, the old support mechanism through credit has not been entirely abandoned; in 1995 the Russian Federation resorted to agrofood sector debt rescheduling and debt write-off, the latter amounting to more than all the explicit support for agriculture provided in the same year's budget. In Ukraine the main subsidies to agriculture took the form of negative interest rates and non-enforcement of repayment terms. However, the sector was taxed by a combination of low procurement prices and delayed payments coupled with high inflation and restriction of imports, which actually offset subsidies.

The development of a private agricultural credit market which may reduce agricultural sector dependence on state credit and its demands on state budgets is a very important and unresolved issue in the CIS. Credit supply is rationed economywide because of accumulated debts, general economic decline and insufficient international financing. In the case of agriculture, the incomplete definition of private property rights on land hampers the development of a land market and of a rural credit market based on the use of land as collateral. In addition there are complex problems of reform of the financial institutions since, for instance, the heritage of the former USSR is a system where deposit mobilization in rural areas through the savings bank and lending to agriculture through Agroprombank were in practice separated and interests paid on deposits were low and inflexible, so that the banking system did not fulfil a role of financial resources reallocation in rural areas.

AGRICULTURAL AND ECONOMIC REFORMS IN BELARUS AND THE REPUBLIC OF MOLDOVA

The Republic of Moldova and Belarus are new countries, formed in 1991 from the splintered Union of Soviet Socialist Republics (USSR). Economic reform in Moldova, although troubled, has generally been more resolute than in Belarus. While Moldova continues to receive support from the international financing agencies (the International Monetary Fund [IMF], the World Bank and the European Bank for Reconstruction and Development [EBRD]), loan disbursements to Belarus from these agencies were suspended early in 1996. Both countries have faced the demise of the Soviet rouble and old planning relations with Russia and the shock of greatly increased prices of raw materials purchased from the Russian Federation and other republics.

Macroeconomic setting

Moldova adopted a stabilization programme relatively early among the countries of the former USSR. In 1995 GDP was at only 40 percent of its 1990 level but in the same year moderate positive growth was recorded for the first time (at 2 percent according to EBRD). Agricultural production also grew, by 5 percent. Since mid-1994 monthly inflation has been in the low single digits and in 1995 it was the lowest in the Commonwealth of Indendent States (CIS). The national currency introduced in November 1993, the leu, became convertible on current account transactions in July 1995. The money supply is extremely tight, however, and barter so prevalent that much of the economy has been referred to as "demonitized".

Belarus was one of the last countries of the former USSR to introduce reforms and adopt a stabilization programme, and inflation has been among the highest in the CIS. Not until October 1994 did Belarus make the Belarussian rouble its sole currency. Delay in initiating a reform programme allowed Belarus to delay contraction, but real GDP dropped by 20 percent in 1994 and by 14 percent in 1995. The prospects for positive economic growth are further away in the future than for Moldova.

By December 1995, prices in Belarus had increased 8.1 times over the previous year, compared with a CIS average of 3.5 times. In late 1995 and early 1996

monthly inflation was officially low, but international economics agencies questioned the methodology of its measurement. They also considered the fiscal policy in Belarus to be unsustainable, since it matched revenue shortfalls with temporary freezes and the accumulation of arrears. Most central bank credit continues to be directed and subsidized, perpetuating the expectation of continual credit bailouts.

IMF stopped granting credits to Belarus in September 1995. The reasons for this involved the central bank's reimposition of exchange controls and its reluctance to let the rouble depreciate (a "crawling peg" has since been adopted) or to create excessive credit for agriculture. In early 1996, the World Bank suspended payment of a US$37 million loan because of inadequate progress in privatization.

The human costs of austerity
In both *Moldova* and *Belarus* the costs of austerity in terms of human suffering have been significant. As in many other transition economies, unemployment in both Moldova and Belarus is officially low, but official statistics probably underestimate actual unemployment. In Moldova, where official unemployment was only 2 percent in 1995, a survey using broader criteria set the figure at 11 percent (excluding Transdnestria). For those working, arrears in wage payments are a perennial problem. Statistics showing the average decline in consumption (discussed below) do not reflect the larger decline among the growing segment of the population who are officially poor.

Soviet agricultural subsidies and Moldova's and Belarus' specialization and trade within the former USSR
Adjustments in Belarus and Moldova to the break-up of the former USSR have to be examined within the context of the complex pattern of subsidies to agricultural production and consumption which characterized Soviet interrepublic trade. These subsidies emanated from Moscow and were largely eliminated in 1992. For the former USSR as a whole, budget subsidies for agriculture in the late 1980s were roughly 10 percent of GDP. Exact measures of the benefit of Soviet-era subsidies to agriculture in Moldova and Belarus are not available, but those paid to Belarus

BOX 12
BELARUS

With a territory of 280 000 km^2, Belarus is the sixth largest of the 15 former USSR republics.

Some 80 percent of Belarus' population of 10 million is by nationality Belarussian and most of the rest are Russian or Ukrainian. Over 80 percent of the population speaks Russian fluently. Except for the western region, which was annexed from Poland after the Second World War, the collectivization of agriculture was completed in the early 1930s. Belarus' per caput gross social product (GSP) was among the highest of the 15 Soviet republics. Of the former USSR republics, it has been the most active in seeking economic integration with the Russian Federation, and in May 1996 Belarus ratified an agreement with the Russian Federation to form a new economic and political union, the Community of Sovereign Republics (CSR).

Belarus has few natural resources except for peat, potash and its strategic location which allows it to contain the rail, road and pipeline routes connecting the Russian Federation to central and western Europe. The population is one-third rural and two-thirds urban. The country's industry depends heavily on imported raw materials and semi-manufactured goods; 90 percent of energy needs are imported from the Russian Federation.

Before the breakup of the former USSR, agriculture accounted for 21 percent of the republic's GSP, against an average of 16 percent for the USSR. Some 30 percent of the labour force was directly employed in agriculture.

Winters in Belarus are fairly short and summers long, moist and cool. The vegetative period lasts from 175 days in the northeast to 205 days in the southwest, and average yearly rainfall varies from 700 mm in the north to 500 mm in the south. Three-quarters of the territory of the country is classified as agricultural land and two-thirds of that is arable. The remainder is evenly divided between meadowland and pasture.

Historically, Belarus has specialized in flax and potato production. Although feeding efficiency was inferior to that of western Europe, Belarus was known in the former USSR for relatively high-performance dairy cattle and pigs. Most grain is spring grain, with only a small quantity of winter wheat and maize. Rye is particularly suited to Belarus. A relatively high, but diminishing, share (40 percent) of sown land is devoted to fodder crops, including maize for silage.

BOX 13
THE REPUBLIC OF MOLDOVA

With a territory of 33 700 km², Moldova is the second smallest of the former USSR republics and its 4 million inhabitants make it also the most densely populated. Moldova shares a common culture and language with Romania to the west; approximately 65 percent of the population are ethnic Romanian, one-half of whom do not speak Russian fluently. Slavs, about one-quarter of the population, are concentrated in the capital city, Chisinau (formerly Kishinev), and Transdnestria, which is a sliver of land between Ukraine and the Dniester river containing one-quarter of Moldova's territory. Since 1992, Transdnestria has sought unsuccessfully to secede from Moldova. As part of Bessarabia, present-day Moldova was part of the Russian Empire from 1812 until 1918, but (except for Transdnestria) was independent or part of Romania until annexed by the USSR after the Second World War. Collectivization of agriculture was not completed until 1950, and many people still remember the small freeholds which previously characterized agriculture in Moldova.

Soils are predominantly rich chernezem and chestnut. Rainfall varies from an average 550 mm annually in the north to 375 mm in the south, and the country is subject to frequent drought. Of 2.1 million ha of arable land, 100 000 ha are irrigated. Conditions are suitable for a diverse variety of long-season crops and about one-fifth of the arable land is in permanent orchards and vineyards – Moldova's most notable specialization is fruit, including table and wine grapes. About three-quarters of arable land is sown to grains, including equal areas to winter wheat and maize and about 10 percent each to pulses and winter barley. Other crops include sugar beet, sunflower and tobacco. Only 12 percent of Moldova's agricultural land is meadowland or pasture. Moldova's northern region had some of the best dairy yields in the former USSR. Pigs are important throughout Moldova as are sheep, especially in the south.

Moldova's per caput GSP was the lowest of the former USSR's European republics. Including labourers in private plots, 47 percent of the population was directly engaged in agricultural production, the highest such share in the European USSR. The share of agriculture in GSP was the highest in the former USSR (27 percent against an average of 16 percent). One-half of industry is involved with the processing of livestock products, vegetables, fruits and wine. Moldova was and is totally dependent on the Russian Federation for energy resources.

appear to have been larger than those to Moldova because of the greater capital intensity of production and the greater relative specialization in highly subsidized livestock in Belarus. Moldova's agriculture is less capital-intensive and its exports were concentrated more in unsubsidized horticultural products, sugar and oilseeds.

Both Belarus and Moldova participated in the USSR interrepublic grain and livestock trade complex as net exporters of subsidized livestock products and net importers of subsidized grain. During 1986-1990, Belarus imported one-third of its average annual grain consumption of over 10 million tonnes. Of this, about 2.2 million tonnes was foreign grain imported with foreign exchange centrally allocated by Moscow. Moldova was dependent on imports from other former USSR republics for approximately 20 percent of its grain consumption. In 1990, Belarus exported 19 percent of its meat, 25 percent of its milk and 4 percent of its egg production to the other former USSR republics. For Moldova the figures were 25, 8 and 16 percent, respectively.

Consumption of livestock products sold at controlled state retail prices was highly subsidized by Moscow. For example, price specialists calculated that the average budget subsidy for beef in 1989 was approximately 250 percent and, for milk, 100 percent. (That is, the retail price of beef, which was nearly uniform across the entire former USSR, was 3.5 times the average cost to the Soviet state of production and trade.) For pork it was about 100 percent. On this basis, subsidies for retail prices of foods produced from crops (e.g. wheat bread, sunflower and sugar) were generally negative. The latter, which are exported by Moldova, were taxed at the rates of 5 and 35 percent. For Belarus, except for milk, the budget subsidies expressed in this manner were somewhat larger than in Moldova; the beef subsidy was 264 percent compared with 234 percent in Moldova, milk was 67 percent compared with 70 percent and pork, 120 percent compared with 91 percent.

Consumption of domestically produced feed grains was subsidized by the monopolistic Soviet state grain procurement system. This system acquired grain at differentiated zonal prices which extracted land rent from low-cost grain producers.

Among crops, Belarus delivered mainly flax and potatoes to other republics, while importing from them significant quantities of vegetables, fruit, sugar and vegetable oil, as well as milling wheat and feed grains. Among major agricultural commodities, Moldova imported feed grains and milling wheat. In 1990, Moldova exported (almost entirely to the former USSR) 20 to 25 percent of its fresh and processed vegetables and fruit, including approximately 80 percent of both canned vegetables and fruit. Moldova also exported to the former USSR about one-third of its sugar production and one-half of its vegetable oil production. Tobacco was another important export.

The structure of input use suggests that since 1991 increases in energy and other agricultural inputs imported from the Russian Federation have hurt Belarus' agriculture more than Moldova's. In the late 1980s, the share of capital per agricultural worker in Belarus was one-third higher than in Moldova. The expenditure on electricity per farm worker was two-thirds higher and the rate of application of mineral fertilizer per sown hectare (266 kg in 1986-90) was approximately double the Moldovan level.

Food price liberalization and budget support
Both Moldova and Belarus inherited the macroeconomic imbalance and repressed inflation which played a large role in the demise of the former USSR.

The Russian Federation's price liberalization in early 1992 forced *Moldova* to liberalize most prices in 1992. The republic delayed completely freeing food prices until June 1994, however, when the last budgetary subsidies for milk and the cheapest types of bread were eliminated. This was accompanied by increases in direct assistance to the poor.

A comparison of prices for a number of food items in Chisinau's retail stores and collective farm markets at the end of December 1995 and beginning of 1996 indicates that retail prices were the same in both, i.e. that prices in retail stores mostly cleared demand.

As of late 1995, the international economics agencies questioned whether *Belarus* had really freed retail food prices. There had been several administrative increases of both farm and retail prices, including substantial increases (by factors of 10 to 20) in August 1994. The

CENTRAL AND EASTERN EUROPE

latter occurred only after it was increasingly apparent that subsidized food products were being exported through shuttle trade to the Russian Federation. Officially, all retail food prices were freed by December 1994, but in the same month the central government issued Decree No. 249 which urged regional governments to regulate trade and food processing margins. Pressure from IMF led to a formal repeal but the practice is thought to continue to be widespread.

A survey of reported prices in Mensk retail stores and collective farm markets in December 1995 indicated a congruency of prices in both channels for most goods. Eggs were an exception; their price was 80 percent higher in the market than in city stores.

Post-reform adjustments in consumption, agricultural production and trade

Domestic livestock consumption and trade. Prior to reform, average per caput meat consumption in the USSR, at more than 60 kg on a comparable basis, was higher than in some countries in western Europe where income levels were several times higher.[38] With price liberalization, income decline and the reduction or elimination of subsidies throughout the economies in transition, consumers have substituted other foods, including potatoes and bread products, for livestock products. Moldova's 1995 per caput consumption of all livestock products (as officially measured) declined to approximately half the 1990 levels. The decline in consumption in Belarus was less; 27 percent for meat, 17 percent for milk products and 7 percent for eggs.

Livestock production and trade. Moldova's and Belarus' livestock exports went mainly to the Russian Federation, where per caput consumption of meat and dairy products each dropped by approximately one-third between 1990 and 1995.[39]

In 1994, Moldova's official meat exports to the CIS (mainly the Russian Federation and Azerbaijan) were only 38 percent of 1990 exports, while Belarus' exports were down to only 26 percent of the 1990 level. In dairy products, Moldova exported 4 percent of the 1990 level and Belarus only 17 percent.

Reflecting the drop in domestic and export demand, Moldova's 1995 meat, milk and egg production were respectively 53, 51 and 60 percent lower than in 1990.

[38] The World Health Organization has observed that norms for livestock consumption in the former USSR and Eastern Europe were in excess of recommendations for western Europe and not justified by differences in climate. See United Nations Children's Fund (UNICEF)/UN. 1994. *Crisis in mortality, health and nutrition.* Economies in Transition Studies, Regional Monitoring Report No. 2. Florence, Italy.

[39] According to household budget data, Russian per caput vegetable oil, fruit and vegetable consumption increased on average in 1995 over 1994, especially for higher-income people, constituting a movement towards western-type diets.

In Belarus the decline in meat production was similar (46 percent) with milk and egg production falling somewhat less (32 and 7 percent, respectively).

The actual decline in value added in livestock production is not as high because, previously, large amounts of feed were imported by both countries. From average annual imports of over 2 million tonnes in the second half of the 1980s, Belarus' net grain imports dropped to an average of 1.5 million tonnes in the two marketing years 1992-93 and 1993-94, and to less than 800 000 tonnes in 1994-95 and 1995-96. Moldova's net grain imports dropped from just under 600 000 tonnes per year to an average of less than 500 000 tonnes from 1992-93 to 1994-95; most of these imports were on concessionary terms connected with the 1992 and 1994 droughts. Moldova had estimated net grain exports from its 1995 grain crop of 110 000 to 230 000 tonnes.[40]

There are indications in Moldova and Belarus, as in other former USSR countries, that the cumulative contraction of livestock supply and better grain harvests in 1995 and 1996 are finally improving the profitability of livestock raising.[41] In January 1996 swine and poultry numbers in Moldova rose compared with the previous year. Egg production rose by 14 percent in Moldova and stabilized in Belarus, compared with 1995. In both countries (as elsewhere in the CIS) there has been a recent rise in egg production, reflecting poultry's more efficient conversion of feed.

Input adjustment and grain production. Crop production in most of the former USSR has proved to be more profitable during the transition than has livestock production. This is in spite of the increase in prices of energy, fertilizer, other chemicals and equipment used in production, and is in large part caused by farms' ability to get by with fewer purchased inputs, which, in turn, reflects the wastage and inefficient use of many inputs that used to occur, particularly in grain production. The reduction is especially apparent in the use of mineral fertilizer. In Moldova, for example, in 1995 the mineral fertilizer application (active ingredient) was 9 kg per hectare of sown area, only 6 percent of the level for 1989-91. Fertilizer use per sown hectare has also fallen significantly in Belarus; to 39 kg of nitrogen, 52 kg of potash (both less than half their

[40] Estimates of USDA, Economic Research Service.
[41] Belarussian calculations indicate that the farm price parity ratio fell each year to a level equal to two-thirds of the 1986 ratio, but rose in 1995 to a level equal to 78 percent of the 1986 relation. Organisation for Economic Co-operation and Development (OECD). 1995. *Review of agricultural policy and trade developments in Belarus.* AGR/EW/EG (95) 40. Paris.

1990 levels) and 12 kg of phosphate (less than one-fifth of the previous level).

Changes in crop area and production. Given *Moldova's* reduced imports of wheat from the former USSR, the area planted to winter wheat have increased since 1989 from 287 000 ha in 1990 to approximately 400 000 ha for the 1996 harvest. The areas planted to vegetables and sugar beet have remained approximately stable, while sunflower areas have increased and the areas under fruit orchards and vineyards have continued an upward trend that started in the early 1980s. Officially reported production of all these crops has fallen to between two-thirds and three-quarters of 1986-90 levels, reflecting drought, possibly reduced fertilizer use and possibly changes in reporting methods related to privatization.

In *Belarus* total sown area declined by 4 percent during 1991-95 compared with the previous five years. The area sown to feed crops declined by 5 percent and grain area has shifted towards wheat. The area sown to vegetables and potatoes has increased somewhat and shifted drastically to private production. Sugar-beet area had declined during the late 1980s and early 1990s, but it began increasing in 1992; rape area doubled in 1994. Labour-intensive flax area (at its peak of 340 000 ha in 1956) fell 50 percent from 149 000 ha in 1990 to 96 000 ha in 1994, but increased to an estimated 102 000 ha in 1995.

Agricultural trade. Moldova has continued to export vegetable oil and sugar to the CIS, although at lower levels than before. These are products for which CIS prices had been lower than world prices; some of them, including sunflower seeds, are now being exported to non-CIS countries. Moldova has retained much of its export to the CIS of canned and fresh fruits, including grapes, and of quality wines. Belarus continued to export flax and small quantities of potatoes to the CIS.

In 1994, both Moldova and Belarus were small-scale net exporters of livestock products to, and net importers of plant products from, the non-CIS countries. For Moldova, net exports of livestock products were about US$12 million and crop imports, $11 million. Belarus had net exports of livestock products to the non-CIS of about $9 million and net imports of crop products of

$11 million. Both countries have received western grain through the use of commodity credits.

The World Bank has commissioned a study of the changing costs of production of various agricultural products in Moldova and Belarus with a view to seeing how unsubsidized agriculture can compete in export markets.[42] According to this study, in Belarus the only crop with undisputed high potential for export is flax, followed possibly by rapeseed. Beef and perhaps dairy products have the potential to become major efficient exports if feeding efficiency is improved. On the other hand, Belarus appears to be a relatively high-cost producer of grain, sugar beet, pork and poultry products.

Moldova's export possibilities are considered more diverse. Sugar-beet production costs are low, as are those for winter wheat and maize. In 1995 Moldova exported grain and, given its low costs, is seen as being a future regular exporter of grain. Moldova's costs of sunflower seed and oil are also a fraction of the world price. Exports of horticultural products, including wine, depend in part on investment to improve varieties and processing and packaging to world levels. The same is true of Moldova's livestock products.

The prospects for future trade in both countries also depend on the trade regimes they establish. Moldova has applied to join the World Trade Organization (WTO), and sought to keep tariffs below 20 percent. Belarus recently raised tariffs on some products to bring them into line with those of the Russian Federation, which has a customs union with Belarus.

Procurement price and credit. Marketing through state channels has been reduced for many commodities, to a greater extent in Moldova than in Belarus, where in 1995 30 percent of grain, nearly 90 percent of sugar beet, 70 percent of meat and almost 60 percent of milk production were still sold to state organs. The degree to which state purchases still dominate agricultural transactions is an important indicator of reform. The Soviet-era state procurement system from which Moldova and Belarus are evolving involved complex direct subsidy and cross-price subsidization which discouraged the development of alternative unsubsidized private business and marketing channels. Subsidized inputs were available as quid pro quo for

[42] World Bank. 1996. *Agricultural trade and trade policy: a multi-country analysis, Moldova Technical Report*; World Bank. 1995. *Agricultural trade and trade policy: a multi-country analysis, Belarus Technical Report.* Washington, DC.

marketing through state procurement organizations. Traditionally, even when farms could legally sell products produced "above plan", retail subsidies were only available to products marketed within state channels.

In *Belarus* the procurement system has continued to be used to implement subsidies, including soft credit. Core to state intervention is the idea of farm price parity, according to which farm prices should increase by the same percentage as farm input prices. Adherence to this idea, however, impedes restructuring.[43] Belarus' formal policy commitment to this idea was so strong that during 1994, the government linked procurement prices to an index of inputs and increased them almost weekly.

The mechanisms used to try to obtain parity have ranged from preferential allocation of imported Russian fuel to budget subsidies for agriculture amounting to 22 percent of budget expenditures in 1992 and 7.2 percent in 1995. An extrabudgetary agricultural support fund with its own extrabudget share of value added tax (VAT) revenues was created in 1995. Recent interventions in agriculture have mostly involved directed low-interest soft credits. Typically, these funds have been tied to participation in seasonal input purchase and state procurement. Subsidized credits continued into 1995 and (despite IMF proscriptions) into the 1996 planting season.

By contrast, in *Moldova* directed credit for 1996 seasonal inputs originated in auction (at nominal rates of about 20 percent annually) from the central bank and was made available to farm supply organs and farms on commercial terms, where nominal rates were approximately 3.5 percent monthly in March 1996. The inflation rate was then approximately 2 percent monthly. In late 1995, the Government of Moldova relented under domestic pressure and also made some direct loans to agriculture.

Transformation and privatization in agriculture
Of the CIS countries Belarus has the highest share of employment in state enterprises (agricultural and other) at 64.1 percent while Moldova has one of the lowest at 38.9 percent. In most Belarus joint-stock companies the majority of stock is owned by the state. Belarus drew up plans in 1995 for converting agricultural processing

[43] See the criticism of application of the idea of price parity in Russian agricultural policy in FAO. 1993. *The State of Food and Agriculture 1993.* p. 193-195. Rome.

enterprises into joint-stock companies, to be owned by state and collective farms. Although Moldova's progress in privatization has been slower than its progress in stabilization, it is faster than it is in Belarus.[44] Among all enterprises, the percentage of private or "mixed" ("transformed enterprises" in which the state continues to own part of the stock) increased from 34 percent in 1994 to 62 percent in 1995. Moldova accelerated its privatization process in 1995 along the lines of the Czech model, using patrimonial bonds or vouchers distributed to the population. These were used to purchase over 2 200 large, small and medium-sized enterprises; most of them being purchased in 1995. There have been some cash sales and the next stage of privatization is expected to rely more on this type of transaction.

In 1989, *Belarus* had approximately 900 state and 1 600 collective farms, each with about 450 workers and an average cultivated area of 2 100 ha. As of mid-1995, 14 percent of state farms and 31 percent of collective farms had gone through a preliminary valuation of assets and nominal share division among workers and members according to their past work contribution. Belarus had 3 000 individual private farms on 1 January 1996, the same number as the previous year. The average size is 21 ha, their total area of 62 100 ha is 0.6 percent of total agricultural land area. The number of farms is forecast to increase to only 5 100 by the year 2000.

In 1990 *Moldova* had between about 1 000 and 1 100 state and collective farms and other "interfarm" crop or livestock enterprises. By early 1996, state and collective farms in the process of reformulating their legal structure had created 160 joint-stock companies (80 of them in 1995), 194 agricultural production cooperatives (63 in 1995) and 146 associations of individual peasant farms (79 new in 1995). Shares in 660 state enterprises, which are to be privatized free of charge, were distributed to approximately 850 000 people (including pensioners and service workers). As of 1 December 1995, individuals on 422 (64 percent) of these farms had received (undivided) property shares and 28 percent of these shareholders have received actual certificates. Under Moldovan law, individuals or individuals with family members are free to apply to the farm and local authorities to receive actual land plots

_____

[44] It is difficult for various reasons, including the practice of "privatizing by merely changing the signs", to measure and compare privatization through statistical measures. Much must be judged by attitude as, for instance, by the fact that Belarus has retained the names state and collective farm.

and, as of 1 January 1996, 48 000 applicants (half of those who had applied) had received actual physical land plots.

Moldova was slower initially than a number of former USSR republics in starting peasant farms; it had only five at the end of 1991,[45] although in 1995 the number of individual peasant farms registered in the republic grew by 2 100, to 16 100. Moldova's individual farms average only 1.6 ha. Together, registered and unregistered (of which there are approximately 30 000) individual farms cover a reported 58 000 ha of land; three-quarters of which is ploughed land, with the remaining one-quarter shared almost equally between fruit orchards and vineyards. The area covered by peasant farms is equal to 2 percent of the total agricultural area.

Private plot agriculture in Moldova and Belarus

Owners of "subsidiary" plots retain their membership or employment in the collective or state farm or its successor. Even before current reforms, both Moldova and Belarus had substantial areas covered by the private plots of rural people. Together with the far more numerous but smaller suburban gardens and "orchards" of city dwellers, Moldova had about 200 000 ha in such arrangements – about 11.5 percent of total arable land (or 7.8 percent of all agricultural land). Belarus had approximately 609 000 ha in such holdings, accounting for some 10 percent of arable land. These were relatively high percentages, compared with 3.5 percent for the Russian Federation, 7.5 percent for Ukraine and only 2.6 percent for the former USSR as a whole.

In Belarus, the area of agricultural land used privately in "subsidiary activities of the population" has more than doubled in recent years. Moldova's first stage of agrarian reform raised the limit on family holdings from 0.2 ha to 0.3 ha, and up to 0.75 ha for very large families. The area covered by such plots increased to 325 000 ha in 1995. This, together with the area of individual farms, was approximately 18 percent of Moldova's arable land.

Private crop and livestock production is increasing in Belarus, particularly as a share of total agriculture, but is still concentrated in expanded, traditional "subsidiary" plots.

---

[45] By comparison, Belarus had over 700 peasant farms and the Russian Federation had 50 000. Armenia, whose policy was to decollectivize early, created 165 000 individual farms by the end of 1991, each averaging a little over 1 ha.

Lessons and long-term objectives from Moldova's and Belarus' comparative experiences

Stabilization. Recent economic performances in the region seem to confirm the importance of stabilization as a prerequisite for recovery. By 1995, 15 transitional economies which had successfully reduced inflation to less than 50 percent per year experienced positive economic growth.[46] The reform experiences of Moldova, where a stabilization programme has proved successful, and Belarus, where success is questioned, show some of the factors that determine the political ability to bear the hardships of austerity:

- Austerity has proved easier to undertake in countries such as Moldova or the Baltic republics which have fewer cultural and historical ties with the Russian Federation and the Soviet economic system and want to move away from them.
- Rural people accept more readily the reduction of state economic support for agriculture if there appears to be no alternative, because the state is weak, the level of development low or the share of agriculture too large for the rest of the economy to support. (This situation arises in Moldova, Georgia, Armenia and Albania.)
- Austerity programmes have also proved easier where agriculture has a varied range of labour-intensive commodities and where urban people have close family ties with the countryside. In Moldova, this has helped provide a food and employment safety net, reducing the urban lobby for intervention to promote food and job security.
- The same applies where there is less need for credit from outside. Belarus' capital-to-labour ratio is one-third higher than Moldova's, the Russian Federation's is one-quarter higher than Belarus'. Indeed, agricultural input industries can create another lobby for soft credit and other subsidies which limit restructuring.

Agricultural finance. This remains perhaps the most critical problem for agriculture in stabilized economies in transition. Evidence suggests that in the transitional economies, hard budget constraints curtail the abuses of soft credit and promote needed adjustments in resource allocation, even among firms that remain state owned.[47] Still, without the development of a finance

[46] S. Fischer, *et. al.* 1996. Stabilization and growth in transition economies: the early experience. *Journal of Economic Perspectives*, 10(2): 45-66.
[47] J.C. Brada. 1996. Privatization is transition – or is it? *Journal of Economic Perspectives*, 10(2): 80.

system, long-term growth is not possible. In Moldova, for example, there is no long-term credit for investment in new grape plantings suitable for quality wine production. In spite of the reduction in inflation, the risk of credit default was reflected in a spread between the central bank rediscount rate and commercial bank short-term lending rates approaching 100 percent.

The inadequacy of agricultural financing reflects to a large extent the absence of property rights that afford sufficient collateral, as well as the absence of bankruptcy laws. Establishment of these may help, but there is the danger that legislation does not suffice and austerity will end, its benefits wasted, unless other steps are taken. Observers of Central and Eastern Europe note that, after a long experience of mass credit default and forgiveness, it takes a long "drought" of credit to cause borrowers to invest voluntarily in reputations for credit worthiness.[48] Alternatives to traditional agricultural banks need to be investigated, such as the revolving funds managed by small groups of borrowers which reinforce repayment among themselves.

Privatization. Property "transformation" has consisted simply in "changing the signs" on enterprises which continue a codependent relationship with the state. On the other hand, evidence from several Central and Eastern European countries indicates that hard budget constraints force even state-owned firms to respond to market incentives.[49] These facts suggest that privatization may be considered the ultimate goal of the transition process rather than an immediate objective.

Moldova, as a country with relatively favourable conditions, presents some of the surviving complexities of privatization of farming. As in other former USSR countries, including Belarus, rural workers in Moldova have a formal right to withdraw from the state or collective farm with a share of land and capital assets. Much attention has been focused on the legal prohibition of land markets as a reason for not implementing this right more fully. Land markets could facilitate farm restructuring by allowing the assimilation of land tracts, collateral for loans and reduction of risk through the ability to sell the land if the farmer's attempt to establish a private farm does not succeed. However, in Moldova polls show declining support for private ownership of land and in spring 1996 the

[48] A. Rapaczynski. 1996. The roles of the state and the market in establishing property rights. *Journal of Economic Perspectives*, 10(2): 102.
[49] Brada, op. cit., footnote 47.

parliament rejected a proposal to shorten the present moratorium (until 1 January 2001) on the sale and mortgage of land.

There are various reasons for the less than full support of private property in agriculture and these will probably diminish as prospects for agricultural profits increase and the present evolutionary developments continue. A very apparent fear of rural people is that they have few options for the disposal of their land shares and might be forced to surrender them with little benefit. The remarkable expansion of the size of family subsidiary plots and livestock inventories among farm workers occurs within a traditional set of rights and responsibilities between workers and the farm, which provides machinery services, feed, marketing and credit. In time, and with economic growth and improved profitability of agricultural production, small farm entrepreneurship developed within this framework will increase the market for the asset shares of those who opt out. Development of full property, registration and markets for garden plots may gradually re-establish social expectations with regard to the security of property in farmland.

Economic relations with the Russian Federation. In 1992 and 1993 the Russian Federation's programme of price liberalization and stabilization forced an end to the prior economic relationships with Belarus, Moldova and other former USSR republics. This in turn forced first Moldova and then Belarus to liberalize prices and adopt stabilization programmes. The Russian Federation is now pursuing new economic relations with former USSR countries within several frameworks: a revised CIS; a customs union with Belarus (and also with Kazakstan and Kyrgystan); and a special Community of Sovereign States with Belarus, formed in May 1996. For successful reform throughout the former USSR, the most promising outcome would be for reforms in the Russian Federation to continue and to be transmitted to the other republics. Macroeconomic discipline would continue and there could be mutual agreements for state institutions to guarantee economic rights and establish market infrastructure to ease customs procedures or eliminate tariffs, establish common commercial codes, reduce transportation bottlenecks and provide market information systems.

A significant backward step would be the reintroduction of orders and bilateral clearing as an attempt to create markets for goods in various industries that have not yet fully restructured and are not yet competitive at world prices. The attractiveness of bilateral clearing with state orders to support it grows out of the collapsed demand for inferior production. It also stems from the absence of normal financing for supportable production, and restricted access to alternative Western markets. For example, Belarus exported 4 million tonnes of mineral fertilizer, worth approximately US$260 million in 1994 (only potash exports from Canada and the United States exceeded this amount), but encountered charges of dumping in western Europe. Western cooperation, tutelage and guidance leading to full World Trade Organization status are needed.

UNITED STATES

THE 1996 UNITED STATES FARM ACT INCREASES MARKET ORIENTATION

The Federal Agriculture Improvement and Reform (FAIR) Act of 1996, which was made law in April 1996, is a sea change in United States agricultural policy. After 63 years, it ends the United States' agricultural support policy orientation established during the "New Deal" era by the Agricultural Adjustment Act of 1933. After a seven-year declining phase-out of government income support payments that will continue until 2002, direct support payments to United States farmers are scheduled to end. If this radical shift in farm policy is fully implemented and maintained, it will have major implications on United States farmers and, through them, on the world at large.

The new law completes the decoupling of production decisions from programme payments. Decoupling began in the 1985 farm law with the freezing of individual farm payment yields used to calculate deficiency payments, and continued in the 1990 farm law with the introduction of the so-called normal flex acres, which reduced the land area on which payment was to be made by 15 percent and allowed planting flexibility on these non-payment acres. Decoupling gives the FAIR Act the potential to affect the structure and performance of United States agriculture.

The FAIR Act departs from past policies by abolishing target prices and deficiency payments, thereby removing the link between income support payments and farm prices and eliminating the income-stabilizing feature of farm programmes implemented in the 1970s. Federal payments to crop producers and farm landowners under the new law will be somewhat lower than over the last decade. With the acreage reduction programmes (ARPs) eliminated, farmers will have far greater flexibility in making production decisions and the freedom to plant any crop, except for fruits and vegetables, on base acres. As a result, producers will become more reliant on the market as a guide for production decisions. Producers and landowners are also likely to experience greater farm income variability because FAIR Act payments are fixed amounts and not related to the level of market prices.

UNITED STATES

Pressure for reform

Developments from within the agricultural sector and forces from the general economy had both generated pressures for fundamental change in United States agricultural policy. Many farmers and policy-makers felt that the planting restrictions implemented during the 1980s were particularly limiting. Indeed, programme plantings were based on historical plantings dating back to the 1970s. Production technology and markets have changed in the meantime. The fact that the area eligible for programme payments was decided on the basis of the lesser of current plantings and a moving average of historical plantings had created an incentive for farmers to maintain historical production patterns. Farmers wanted increased planting flexibility, although farm legislation in 1990 had begun to address these concerns. In addition, many argued that the annual acreage reduction programmes, which put United States farmland out of production, provided an incentive for foreign competitors to expand production, thus reducing United States agricultural exports.

Apart from agriculture, increased concern for reducing the federal budget deficit strengthened pressures for reform. Farm programme costs were high and benefits were concentrated both geographically and among large-scale producers. Federal commodity programme outlays were highly variable – ranging from US$7 billion in fiscal year 1995 to a record $26 billion in fiscal year 1986.

The 1995-96 market setting also contributed to the reform effort. High commodity prices weakened the case for price and income support programmes and there were calls for reduced government intervention to free producers from government regulations and allow them to produce to meet the demands of the marketplace.

United States farm programmes altered

United States agricultural law encompasses a wide range of issues related to agriculture. Only the major changes related to production agriculture are discussed here.[50] The FAIR Act fundamentally changed United States agricultural programmes for the so-called "contract crops" (wheat, maize, grain, sorghum, barley, oats, rice and upland cotton). Support to dairy production was phased down, while support for

[50] The provisions of the FAIR Act are summarized and compared with previous law in E. Young and D.A. Shields. 1996. 1996 FAIR Act frames farm policy for seven years. *Agricultural Outlook Supplement*, Economic Research Service, United States Department of Agriculture (USDA), April 1996.

peanuts was reduced and the authority for setting marketing allotments (producer marketing quotas above which penalties apply) for sugar was repealed. Trade and food aid programmes were reoriented towards greater market development, with increased emphasis on high-value and value-added products for export. The FAIR Act extends many conservation and environmental programmes; in particular, the Conservation Reserve Programme is reauthorized.

Deficiency payments replaced by decoupled contract payments. The FAIR Act replaces the deficiency payment programme that was in place since the early 1970s with a new programme of decoupled payments for seven years. To receive payments and be eligible for loans on contract commodities, a producer must enter into a production flexibility contract for the period 1996-2002. The contract requires that the participating producer complies with existing conservation, wetland and planting flexibility provisions and keeps the land in agricultural uses. Cumulative outlays for FAIR Act contract payments for fiscal 1996-2002 are fixed at slightly over US$36 billion (Figure 11). Payment levels are allocated among contract commodities according to percentages specified in the FAIR Act (e.g. maize 46.2 percent, wheat 26.3 percent, upland cotton 11.6 percent, rice 8.5 percent, other feed grains 7.4 percent).

At the same time, planting flexibility increases. Under previous legislation, a producer's payments were reduced if more than 15 percent of the farm's base area for a crop was planted to other crops or if more than the total permitted area was planted. Farmers were often required to leave a portion of their cropland uncultivated under ARP as a condition for receipt of deficiency payments. Under the FAIR Act, ARPs are eliminated and participating producers are permitted to plant all of their contract area plus additional area to any crop (with limitations on fruits and vegetables) with no loss in payments, as long as they do not violate conservation and wetland provisions.

The FAIR Act retains a modified form of non-recourse commodity loans, the major government price support instrument. Farmers may receive a loan from the government at a designated rate per unit of production (loan rate) by pledging and storing a quantity of a commodity as collateral. The loan rates for most crops

Figure 11

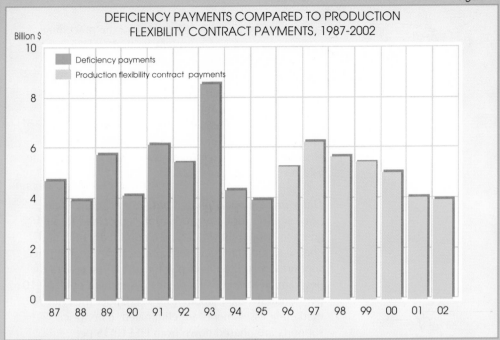

DEFICIENCY PAYMENTS COMPARED TO PRODUCTION FLEXIBILITY CONTRACT PAYMENTS, 1987-2002

Note: Production flexibility contract payments have been adjusted for deficiency payments owed to farmers and repayments owed by farmers to the government for the previous farm programme.

UNITED STATES

continue to be based on 85 percent of the preceding five-year average of farm prices, excluding high- and low-price years. However, maximum loan rates are specified in the new law at the 1995 level for most crops. Marketing loan provisions, which allow repayment of loans at the lower of the loan rate or market prices, are retained, thus continuing some income protection for the contract commodities and ensuring that no government-owned stocks accumulate as a result of forfeited loans.

Dairy price support phased out. In the United States, price support for dairy production is provided through government purchases of butter, non-fat dry milk and cheese to maintain fluid milk prices at designated price support levels. Producers pay for part of the cost of the programme through a marketing assessment of US$0.10 per hundredweight (about 45.4 kg). Under the FAIR Act, marketing assessments are eliminated; dairy price supports are phased down from US$10.35 per hundredweight in 1996 to $9.90 per hundredweight in 1999 and the programme ends on 1 January 2000. In 2000 a recourse loan programme starts, in which loans for butter, non-fat dry milk and cheese must be repaid with interest at loan rates equivalent to $9.90 per hundredweight of milk, to assist processors in the management of dairy product inventories.

The United States has a system of federal milk marketing orders, which are regulations issued by the Secretary of Agriculture specifying minimum prices and conditions under which milk can be bought and sold within a specified area. The orders classify and fix minimum prices according to the products in which milk is used. The 1996 FAIR Act consolidates the 33 federal milk marketing orders into between ten and 14 orders.

The Dairy Export Incentive Program (DEIP) is extended until 2002 and expanded to include market development activities. The Secretary of Agriculture is directed to use DEIP to the maximum extent permitted under the GATT Uruguay Round agreement.

Sugar programme modified. The sugar programme operates without net cost to the federal government. Sugar prices are supported through non-recourse loans offered to sugar processors. The raw cane sugar loan

UNITED STATES

rate is still frozen. Under the FAIR Act, the refined beet sugar loan rate is also frozen at its 1995 level. Non-recourse loans[51] are available only when the tariff-rate quota on sugar imports is at or exceeds 1.5 million short tons (i.e. slightly less than 1.4 million tonnes). The loans become recourse, that is the borrower must repay with cash and cannot choose to repay with the commodity, when the tariff-rate quota is less than 1.5 million short tons. Marketing assessments are paid on all processed sugar. The assessments were increased by 25 percent under the FAIR Act. Under previous legislation, USDA had authority to implement domestic sugar marketing allotments, but this authority has been repealed.

Major trade provisions made more specific. Trade and food aid programmes are reoriented towards greater market development with increased emphasis on expanding high-value and value-added product exports. Annual Export Enhancement Program (EEP) expenditures are capped (Figure 12). In addition, total EEP funding during fiscal 1996-99 is more than US$1.6 billion below the maximum levels permitted under the Uruguay Round agreement. During the 1995/96 crop year, however, the United States made only limited use of EEP because world prices were high and spending was well below the levels allowed under the Uruguay Round agreement. As long as markets remain tight, the United States is likely to continue to make limited use of EEP.

The Market Promotion Program[52] is renamed the Market Access Program and its funding authority is capped at an annual US$90 million for fiscal 1996-2002. The bill authorizes PL (public law) 480, Title I (long-term concessional sales) agreements with private entities in addition to foreign governments. Other major changes to PL 480 broaden the range of commodities available for PL 480 programming, provide greater programme flexibility and improve the operational and administrative aspects of the Market Promotion Program. The Food Security Commodity Reserve, which was formerly know as the Food Security Wheat Reserve, is expanded to include a total of 4 million tonnes of rice, maize and sorghum, in addition to wheat, all of which can be used to meet humanitarian food aid needs.

[51] Farmers or processors may pledge a quantity of a commodity as collateral and obtain a loan from the Commodity Credit Corporation (CCC). The borrower may repay the loan with cash or forfeit the commodity to CCC (the government has no alternative but to accept the commodity as payment).

[52] The government provides funds for export market promotion. Participating organizations include non-profit agricultural trade organizations, regional trade groups and private companies.

Figure 12

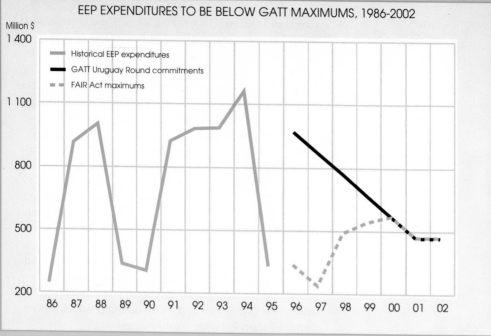

EEP EXPENDITURES TO BE BELOW GATT MAXIMUMS, 1986-2002

UNITED STATES

Major conservation provisions. The FAIR Act addresses
a wide range of environmental and conservation
programmes. Many of these programmes were
simplified to make them more consistent and workable.
The primary conservation programme is the voluntary
Conservation Reserve Program (CRP), under which
producers submit bids to retire environmentally
sensitive cropland from production for ten to 15 years.
Producers receive annual rental payments for retiring
the land and maintaining specified conservation
practices. Under the FAIR Act, the maximum CRP area
is capped at 36.4 million acres (14.7 million ha), the
current level of enrolment. Farmers can remove less
environmentally sensitive land from the programme
prior to expiry of the contract if it has been enrolled for
at least five years. Programme land in expiring contracts
or in contracts terminated prior to expiry is eligible to
be enrolled in production flexibility contracts on
leaving CRP. New land can be enrolled in CRP to
replace the land in expired contracts or early
termination or current land can be re-enrolled at
contract expiry.

General impacts of the new legislation

The FAIR Act accelerates trends of the previous two
major farm acts towards greater market orientation and
reduced government influence in United States
agriculture. The trend towards fewer but larger farms is
expected to continue. The sector will remain highly
competitive, with successful producers requiring strong
technical and managerial skills. The reduced role of
government programmes will make farmers more
vulnerable to supply and demand shocks, so such
alternative marketing arrangements as marketing
contracts and integrated ownership are likely to be used
more to manage price and production risks. The
following focuses on four areas of potential impacts and
concludes with a discussion of the effects on net farm
income.

CRP. The amount of cropland enrolled in CRP will play
a significant role in determining the impacts of the FAIR
Act on United States agriculture. In 1995 almost 100
million ha of cropland were planted to contract crops
and soybeans. About 2 million ha were left uncultivated
under ARP, compared with about 14.7 million ha left

UNITED STATES

uncultivated under CRP. CRP thus represents a significant source of potential cropland in the United States.

USDA has authority under the FAIR Act to establish targets for the level of CRP enrolment and the composition of the land enrolled. Farmers will decide whether they want to keep land in CRP or to farm it and receive FAIR Act contract payments on eligible land. There is, therefore, considerable uncertainty regarding future CRP enrolment. Prior to the enactment of the FAIR Act, many analysts expected enrolment to decline from 1995's 14.7 million ha to between 10 and 12 million ha by 2002. The provisions of the FAIR Act suggest similar levels of total enrolment, but the composition by crop of the enrolled area could change depending on the environmental criteria selected for enrolling new land and extending previous contracts.

Contract commodities and soybeans. With the removal of ARPs and planting constraints, the FAIR Act increases farmers' planting flexibility. Production patterns are likely to shift at the farm level and regionally to take advantage of regional differences in the comparative benefits of producing specific crops. The impacts of the programme will vary from region to region reflecting the mix of agricultural products produced, the degree of diversification and the production alternatives used. In the past, programme constraints may have inhibited such shifts.

In aggregate, however, under the FAIR Act the national level of cropland planted to most of the major field crops will be similar to the levels that would have occurred under previous legislation, with planted area increasing by 2 to 4 million ha over the next ten years from 99.4 million ha in 1995. Under previous legislation, the role of government programmes was already declining and government payments were largely decoupled from producer planting decisions at the margin. The 15 percent normal planting flexibility was sufficient in aggregate to attain crop and commodity supply response equilibrium. Aggregate planting levels for wheat, feed grains and soybeans are therefore expected to be similar under the FAIR Act to what they were before – changes in plantings for these crops will largely be related to overall changes in the size of CRP.

UNITED STATES

Plantings for rice and cotton, however, will change under the FAIR Act. Rice production is expected to decline in regions such as southwestern Louisiana and Texas where production costs are high, primarily reflecting the elimination of the 50 percent planting requirement to receive payments under previous legislation and increased planting flexibility. The upland cotton area could become slightly higher. If previous legislation had continued, upland cotton would have been the only crop expected to be required to leave land uncultivated under ARP. The elimination of ARPs would free additional land for production. Furthermore, cotton has been the only crop over the past five years to have seen a net gain in area planted caused by the planting flexibility provision of the 1990 Farm Act, which suggests favourable market returns compared with other crops. Some cotton area could, however, move to other crops, thus offsetting much of the potential for increased cotton plantings, as producers use the additional planting flexibility under the FAIR Act to guard against production and income variability.

Dairy. The FAIR Act modified the dairy price support and federal orders programmes by phasing out price support and consolidating milk marketing orders. The rate of growth in milk production is expected to slow in response to the lower prices and reduced net returns to dairy farming. The consolidation of milk marketing orders may have regional price implications. Impacts on other parts of the livestock sector are expected to be minimal as feed costs under the FAIR Act are expected to be similar to those under previous legislation.

Sugar. Elimination of the authority for sugar marketing allotments may create opportunities for more efficient sugar producers to increase production. Any expansion, however, is likely to be constrained by the possibility of recourse loans being triggered if the tariff-rate quota on sugar imports falls below 1.5 million short tons. The most likely scenario is for the United States to remain a sugar importer with total production at similar levels to those expected under previous legislation. The expansion of sugar-beet production in certain regions is likely to be offset by declines in sugar-cane production. Again this is primarily a continuation of trends that were occurring under past legislation.

UNITED STATES

Export markets. The FAIR Act should make United States agriculture more competitive in world markets. Even if prices drop to support levels, marketing loan provisions, whereby borrowers are allowed to repay non-recourse loans on the basis of the world market price when that price is below the loan rate, will help ensure that there is marketing rather than accumulation of government-owned stocks. Against a backdrop of strong global economic growth and liberalized trade under the Uruguay Round agreement, the FAIR Act will allow producers to respond to market signals. Export Enhancement Program (EEP) expenditures add little to exports when prices are high, so reduced EEP spending under the FAIR Act will mean only minimal reductions in United States exports of wheat and barley while prices remain high. Elimination of authority for ARPs and suspension of the Farmer Owned Reserve mean that the United States will not restrict supplies available to the marketplace to support market prices. Greater planting flexibility will permit faster adjustments in United States production in response to changing world market conditions. Reorienting trade programmes towards market development may also enhance their effectiveness.

Farm income implications. Farm incomes are expected to be somewhat higher under the FAIR Act than under a continuation of previous agricultural legislation. This largely reflects higher government payments to farmers under the act, as production flexibility contract payments exceed projected deficiency payments that held under previous farm legislation. Furthermore, changes in the timing of payments to farmers provide an additional boost to farm income in the first year of the programme – pushing 1996 net incomes up by over US$4 billion. Dairy sector receipts should be lower under the FAIR Act after 1996 as a result of reduced support, with the elimination of the dairy assessment partly offsetting the lower support. Net rents to non-operator landlords should be higher under the FAIR Act as higher government payments increase land values.

The effects of market risk on net farm income will increase, with incomes becoming more variable as farmers place greater reliance on the market for revenue. Net farm income is more variable under the FAIR Act because government payments are no longer

linked to market prices. Loan rates, which remain but at relatively low levels, continue to provide some income protection.

Farmers will continue to face the pressures of moving to a market economy under the new farm legislation. They will need improved skills to operate in this arena of greater income volatility with less government support to mitigate downturns in income. When making production, marketing and financial decisions, farmers will need to pay increased attention to risk management in order to deal effectively with year-to-year fluctuations in income. Many farmers will need to refine or develop new skills in the use of savings and investments, the use of futures and options markets, forward contracting and other marketing arrangements.

Conclusions

The Federal Agriculture Reform and Improvement Act of 1996 furthers the market orientation of the United States agricultural sector in a number of ways. First, it completes the decoupling of farmers' production decisions for major crops from government payments by widening planting flexibility to cover the entire farm (except for limitations on planting fruits and vegetables). Second, it eliminates annual supply control programmes by ending the acreage reduction programmes. Third, government payment rates are no longer inversely related to the level of prices that farmers receive.

Aggregate crop production is expected to increase over time in response to growing domestic and international market conditions and trends. The FAIR Act should improve United States agriculture's ability to compete in world markets. Under the act, United States market prices should reach levels at which exports will adjust to prevent stock buildups.

While the Act will end direct support to United States farmers by 2002, it still remains to be seen whether the government will have the political will to implement the new policy even during periods of adverse production or marketing conditions.

PART III

FOOD SECURITY: SOME MACROECONOMIC DIMENSIONS

FOOD SECURITY: SOME MACROECONOMIC DIMENSIONS[1]

INTRODUCTION

The year is 1996. The subject is food security, which is defined as the access for all people at all times to enough food for an active, healthy life.[2] FAO has planned and prepared a World Food Summit for 13 to 17 November 1996 in Rome with the slogan "Food for All". The International Food Policy Research Institute (IFPRI) organized a ministerial conference on the same subject in June 1995; over the past few years, the world's attention has been focused on

_____

[1] This chapter was commissioned by FAO from external authors to explore some macroeconomic issues related to food security from an alternative perspective in order to broaden, deepen and enrich the debate on this very important subject. This was done in the awareness that professional economists have strong and honest differences in their interpretations and assessments of facts and information related to many issues, including those relating to food security. FAO welcomes the contribution to the debate without taking any official position on its content.

[2] FAO. 1983. *Report of the Committee on World Food Security, 8th Session.* Document CL83/10. Rome. The definition was endorsed at the International Conference on Nutrition in 1992 and, with minor variations of wording, it is now in widespread use among those dealing with poverty and food security issues.

the myriad issues surrounding food security in its many dimensions. A plethora of papers, monographs, reports and articles have explored, described and analysed the multiple facets of food security.

Indeed, FAO in preparing for the World Food Summit has published three volumes containing 15 papers on subjects related to food security ranging from the ethics of food security to investment for food security (Box 14). In addition, a policy statement and plan of action for adoption by heads of state and governments or their representatives at the Summit have been drafted, taking into account the views of governmental and non-governmental participants in the preparatory process.

Much of this work on food security has in fact been concerned mainly with food insecurity and has until relatively recently focused on the adequacy (or inadequacy) of food production to meet the nutritional needs of a growing population at the global or regional level. While production is of course important, and efforts to increase it need to continue with renewed vigour, it is only part of the picture; farmers do not grow food for altruistic reasons, but to feed themselves and their families through either production or sales, and in most developing countries the majority of the population is directly or indirectly dependent on agriculture. Furthermore, consumers (including many farmers) purchase food and in the absence of sufficient purchasing power they are unable to exert effective demand for food. In this special chapter, the question of food security is examined from a macroeconomic perspective.

The story starts rather unconventionally with a look at the economic development of Europe over the last five to six decades in order to understand what constitutes food security and provide a basis for understanding the problems of food insecurity (much as the medical profession studies health as a means of understanding disease). After a brief review of the conditions, mainly in Europe, in the aftermath of the Second World War, from which postwar thinking about food security evolved in the developed and developing countries as well as in the transition economies of Central and Eastern Europe and the former USSR, the chapter goes on to compare the food supply projections of FAO, IFPRI and the World Bank and concludes that, while there is no room for complacency and investment and technological progress must continue, sustainable food production, even for a growing population, is not the major issue. The question of effective demand for food is. In other words, the issue at stake is can people afford to buy the food that is available, and to purchase enough to ensure an adequate diet?

The chapter then moves on to a discussion of the critical role of governments in choosing the appropriate combinations of monetary, fiscal, trade, investment and social policies to create an economic environment that is conducive to the attainment of food security. Although no individual government can control international economic conditions and the economies of many countries are too small to be able even to influence those conditions, each government is responsible for determining its

BOX 14
**WORLD FOOD
SUMMIT: TECHNICAL
BACKGROUND
DOCUMENTS**

Synthesis of the Technical Background Documents

Volume 1

1. **Food, agriculture and food security: developments since the World Food Conference and prospects**
2. **Success stories in food security**
3. **Socio-political and economic environment for food security**
4. **Food requirements and population growth**
5. **Food security and nutrition**

Volume 2

6. **Lessons from the green revolution: towards a new green revolution**
7. **Food production: the critical role of water**
8. **Food for consumers: marketing, processing and distribution**
9. **Role of research in global food security and agricultural development**
10. **Investment in agriculture: evolution and prospects**
11. **Food production and environmental impact**

Volume 3

12. **Food and international trade**
13. **Food security and food assistance**
14. **Assessement of feasible progress in food security**
15. **Technical atlas**

domestic policies in the light of those conditions. The various policy responses of government and the international community required to deal with short-term fluctuations and long-term trends are then explored. The chapter examines a range of issues that affect a country's ability to achieve food security, including: the domestic macroeconomic and trade policies; food reserve stocking; the domestic generation of foreign exchange; foreign exchange and balance of payments support for food security from international agencies;

the role and use of futures markets for stabilization; and the importance of debt reduction for the severely indebted low-income countries. Factors and policies affecting overall economic growth and their differential effects on the urban and rural economies are explored in order to examine food insecurity in both urban and rural areas, and what can be done in policy terms to increase food security.

Although sound economic policies are necessary for the achievement of food security, they are not easy to implement in the absence of real political consensus. In the final analysis, food security in any country is the responsibility, and must be under the authority, of the national government in conjunction with local authorities working with concerned groups and individuals within society. The international community and international agencies can assist, but cannot substitute for the actions and political will (which reflects both the scope and the limits of political action) to achieve food security within the country itself.

WHAT IS FOOD SECURITY?

The desire to achieve some level of food security is as old as humankind itself. Until the last decade or so, the debate in most countries worldwide focused largely on the adequacy of food production to meet domestic needs, with a concomitant national policy emphasis on self-sufficiency in the supply of agricultural products. This focus, especially in the developed countries, has to be seen in the context of the Second World War and its aftermath, which had a profound effect on the minds of governments and societies. Throughout western, Central and Eastern Europe, for example, the years of the Second World War saw real food shortages caused not only by the disruption of agricultural production, but also (and for some countries this was much more important) by supply requisitioning and disruption of international trade and internal marketing arrangements. The early post-war years were characterized by economic reconstruction and tight exchange controls to conserve scarce foreign exchange reserves and these restricted the ability to feed the population through agricultural and food imports, although the existence of "currency zones" (such as the sterling area and the rouble zone) and the Marshall Plan enlarged the trading possibilities beyond national boundaries. Food rationing and price controls for both urban and rural consumers were used to ensure an equitable allocation of the food available during the war, and these were phased out over several years after the war's end. At the same time, policy measures to encourage the expansion of agricultural production on a long-term basis rather than to meet the immediate crisis needs were introduced and the emerging welfare states cast wide safety nets to protect the vulnerable sections of the population, including the poor, the sick, the elderly, the unemployed, the mentally and physically disabled and children.

The circumstances that produced these agricultural and food policy responses were characterized by a period of reconstruction and rehabilitation for countries that were already industrially advanced with relatively small and declining agricultural sectors and low population growth rates. While special incentives were provided to agriculture, this was not done at the expense of industry. In western Europe, for the 15 countries that now constitute the European Union (EU), the annual growth rates of agricultural and industrial production for the years 1948 to 1958 were 3.5 percent and 7.3 percent respectively, while average population growth was 0.7 percent per annum. Exports grew at about 9 percent per annum compared with 6 percent for imports.

After the period of reconstruction, industrial and agricultural output growth rates slowed, but the volume of trade, including agricultural and food products, soared, with imports and exports growing, and continuing to grow, at an annual rate of about 11 percent.[3] The relative decline of the importance of the agricultural sector in terms of the economy as a whole meant that although the budgetary costs of agricultural support remained high in absolute terms, they decreased as a proportion of national expenditure.

The outcome of the post-war agricultural policies (and not just in the countries covered by the Common Agricultural Policy [CAP] of the EU because all countries made similar efforts to increase agricultural production) has been high levels of self-sufficiency in agricultural production – of well over 100 percent in many temperate-zone products, although this does not mean that each country is more than 100 percent self-sufficient in every product. The EU is a substantial importer and exporter of agricultural and food products with the rest of the world, even though a large proportion of its trade is intra-EU, and it has made an important contribution to increasing world food supplies.

Given this record, it might seem inappropriate to question whether the EU can be said to have achieved food security and in what sense it may or may not have done so. These questions are important, however, because the mindset that laid so much stress on agricultural self-sufficiency in the light of the wartime experiences has only recently begun to change in western Europe, and the transition economies of Central and Eastern Europe now have to face similar questions as they reorient their agricultural and food policies. So it is important that food security be defined clearly.

Food security has been defined as the access for all people at all times to enough food for an active, healthy life.

---

[3] An overview of the development of world and regional trade can be found in FAO. 1995. Agricultural trade: entering a new era? in *The State of Food and Agriculture 1995*. Rome.

The three key ideas underlying this definition are: the adequacy of food availability (effective supply); the adequacy of food access, i.e. the ability of the individual to acquire sufficient food (effective demand); and the reliablity of both. Food insecurity can, therefore, be a failure of availability, access, reliability or some combination of these factors.

Inherent in this modern concept of food security is an understanding of food producers and consumers as economic agents. Food availability is the supply of food, which depends, *inter alia*, on relative input and output prices as well as on the technological production possibilities. Food access is concerned with the demand for food, which is a function of several variables: the price of the food item in question; the prices of complementary and substitutable items; income; demographic variables; and tastes or preferences.[4] According to Barraclough, to ensure food security, a food system should be characterized by:

- the capacity to produce, store and import sufficient food to meet basic needs for all population groups;
- maximum autonomy and self-determination (without implying self-sufficiency), which reduces vulnerability to international market fluctuations and political pressures;

- reliability, such that seasonal, cyclical and other variations in access to food are minimal;
- sustainability, such that the ecological system is protected and improved over time;
- equity, meaning, as a minimum, dependable access to adequate food for all social groups.[5]

It is worth adding explicitly that a secure food system must be able to deliver inputs and outputs (both those produced and consumed domestically and those traded internationally) where and when they are required.

Within this understanding, is the EU, for example, food secure?

[It] cannot really be claimed that the high levels of self-sufficiency experienced in most branches of EC [European Community] agriculture make a positive contribution to the level of food security enjoyed by the EC's citizens. It is helpful to draw a distinction between self-sufficiency in production and a self-sufficient farming system. The EC's high levels of self-sufficiency in production are often dependent upon heavy use of imported or exportable animal feeds and fuels which are just as susceptible to economic or military blockade as are the foods they produce; and provide no relief for local harvest failure.[6]

So it cannot be agricultural self-

---

[4] For a fuller discussion of the demand for food and the distinction between demand and consumption, see FAO. 1995. Policy reform and the consumer. In *The State of Food and Agriculture 1995*. Rome.

[5] S.L. Barraclough. 1991. *An end to hunger? The social origins of food strategies.* A report prepared for the United Nations Research Institute for Social Development (UNRISD) and the South Commission based on UNRISD research on food systems and society. London and Atlantic Highlands, NJ, USA, Zed Books Ltd in association with UNRISD.

sufficiency that makes the EU food secure, yet food secure it undoubtedly is at the level of the EU itself and of each member state in circumstances short of the cataclysmic. The high post-war levels of economic growth, together with low population growth rates, have resulted in high and growing levels of material prosperity for the majority and the provision of safety nets for the vulnerable. The increasing levels of agricultural productivity and total output, new technologies for food processing and storage, good distribution infrastructure and, critically, an economic system that supplies the goods that consumers wish to purchase have resulted in the availability of a wide range of high-quality and safe foods for domestic consumption and export. In spite of the fact that the policy measures used to implement CAP led to higher consumer prices than would alternative measures, rising consumer incomes and declining real prices of agricultural produce mean that the share of food expenditure in the household budget continues to decline. For all practical purposes, the EU participates in a liberal trading environment on the basis of fully convertible currencies, which, together with strong and stable links with its main trading partners, ensures its ability to import at will. It is this bundle of characteristics that underpins food security in the EU and also in the rest of western Europe as well as such countries as Japan,

Canada, New Zealand, Australia, the Republic of Korea, Taiwan Province of China, Hong Kong and Singapore. In practice, this is also true of the United States, although the size and nature of its resource base and infrastructure are such that of all the developed countries, it is perhaps the least vulnerable to external events.

Nevertheless, there are pockets of food insecurity in even the richest countries because food security at the national level does not mean that every household in the country is food secure. The meshes of the safety net may be too large to prevent some individuals and specific groups of individuals from falling through and government policies in several industrialized countries have tended recently to increase the mesh size. A proportion of the population can be living in absolute, not just relative, poverty. Within countries, the food-insecure poor comprise different sub-groups, differentiated by location, occupational patterns, asset ownership, race, ethnicity, age and gender. Thus, at the household or individual level there may be problems of food insecurity caused by inadequate access to food. The relationship between national and household food security is one of the most important and difficult issues confronting governments in all countries at all levels of wealth and development. It is further complicated by the fact that "having adequate household access to food is *necessary but not sufficient* for ensuring that all household members consume an adequate diet... and consuming an adequate diet is *necessary but not sufficient* for maintaining a healthy nutritional status".[7] A distinction has

[6] A. Swinbank. 1992. The EEC's policies and its food. *Food Policy*, February 1992, p. 53-64.

sometimes been made between chronic and transitory food insecurity at the household level.[8] Chronic food insecurity involves a continuously inadequate diet caused by the persistent inability to acquire food. Transitory food insecurity is a temporary lack of adequate food access for a household, arising from adverse changes in food prices, food production or household incomes. With this perspective, the policy options for reducing food insecurity are seen as depending on whether the case is chronic or transitory. Measures to address chronic food insecurity would include increasing the food supply, focusing on development assistance or income transfers for the poor and helping the poor to obtain knowledge about nutrition and health practices. Transitory food insecurity could be ameliorated by stabilizing

_____

[7] P. Diskin. 1994. *Understanding linkages among food availability, access, consumption and nutrition in Africa: empirical findings and issues from the literature.* Michigan State University International Development Working Paper No. 46. Department of Agricultural Economics/Department of Economics. Michigan State University.
[8] World Bank. 1986. *Poverty and hunger.* World Bank Policy Study. Washington, DC, World Bank. The World Bank seems to have largely dropped this distinction in its recent strategy paper: H.P. Binswanger and P. Landell-Mills. 1995. *The World Bank's strategy for reducing poverty and hunger: a report to the Development Community.* Washington, DC, World Bank. The emphasis is now on short-term and medium-term policy measures for addressing both types of food insecurity. However, some authors have tried to maintain the earlier distinction.

supplies and prices and assisting vulnerable groups with emergency employment programmes, income transfers or food. How useful this distinction is in making policy choices is open to question. For instance, how temporary is "temporary"? Are the unwanted food insecurity effects of structural adjustment and transition programmes temporary or chronic? Do we have to know before we decide how to deal with them?

The answer is "no". The need is for policy measures that address all aspects of food insecurity with a view to providing the vulnerable with safety nets (which can vary over an individual's lifetime and in response to external emergencies) and to creating the conditions that can lead to an eradication of endemic hunger. This requires economic growth. Countries that have seen negative (or stagnant) growth rates of agricultural production and GDP with a growing population have ever-diminishing resources (which were often very small to start with) to share among an increasing number of people. Improving the equitableness of income distribution can only achieve limited results in these circumstances and, as has frequently been seen, will be strongly resisted by the potential losers. So growth is necessary and, against a background of economic growth, experience shows that it is less difficult (although still never easy) to implement measures that increase equity, particularly if the growth is broadly based to include the agricultural sector. Indeed, many if not all of the countries that are now regarded as being food insecure are characterized by an agricultural sector on which a large proportion of the population still depends directly or indirectly for a livelihood, and this was not true of post-war Europe. Increasing agricultural productivity and incomes in such countries therefore increases the effective demand for food and so is at the heart of improving food security. One of the lessons that can be learnt from Europe, however, is the importance of economic policies that at least do not discriminate against agricultural development and growth.

It is clear from the foregoing discussion that the subject of food security in its most complete sense touches on many different technical disciplines, each of which provides a partial illumination of some of the complex issues at stake. This chapter is written from a political economy perspective and focuses on some of the major economic and trade policies that bear on the achievement of food security.

WHAT ARE THE PROSPECTS FOR WORLD FOOD SECURITY?

On a global level, food security for all requires that the supply of food be adequate to meet the total demand for food. While this is a necessary condition for the achievement of food security, it is by no means sufficient. Although currently enough food is supplied globally, it is estimated that in 1990-92 some 839 million people in the developing countries had inadequate access to food, fundamentally because they lacked the ability to purchase or procure enough, that is, they lacked the means to exert effective demand. This figure, unacceptably high though it is, reflects a substantial degree of progress since the beginning of the 1970s; the number has declined in absolute terms from about 917 million and in relative terms from 35 percent of the population of developing countries to 21 percent, mainly as a result of progress in East Asia (including China) and parts of South Asia, such as India and Pakistan. The situation is most serious in Africa where the number of chronically undernourished people in the sub-Saharan countries more than doubled over the period according to FAO estimates.[9] Figure 13 shows the past and projected changes in the number of undernourished people in the developing countries.

What are the medium-term prospects for food supply and demand? FAO, IFPRI and the World

---

[9] FAO. 1996. *Food, agriculture and food security: developments since the World Food Conference and prospects for the future.* World Food Summit technical background document No. 1. Rome.

Bank have all attempted to make projections to the year 2010.[10] Although there are some problems with comparability because of such factors as the differences in base year data, country and commodity coverage and regional definition, indicative comparisons of production, total use and net trade in cereals are possible. The results of the three models are presented in Tables 6 to 9.

It can be seen that there is broad agreement regarding projected annual percentage rates of change in production and total use at the global level and for all developing countries taken as a whole, as well as for some of the developing country regional groupings. The greatest divergences in opinion centre on the former centrally planned economies (CPEs), sub-Saharan Africa, the Near East and North Africa and China (see Box 15 on p. 276 for an alternative view of Chinese trade prospects), as well as on total use (essentially consumption) in Latin America and the Caribbean. The FAO and IFPRI projections for net trade at the level of aggregation of "total developed" and "total developing" countries are very close and substantially lower than those of the World Bank, which foresees a far more rapid growth in world grain trade largely as a result of expanded wheat imports into the Asian countries to meet changing consumer preferences away from rice. The FAO and IFPRI

net trade projections are more variable for the regional groupings, most notably for sub-Saharan Africa, the CPEs and Latin America and the Caribbean.[11]

As in all exercises of this type, the outcomes are critically dependent on the validity of the assumptions made about the exogenous environment, rates of changes in the individual variables, the interaction among the different variables and the accuracy of the baseline data.[12] Nevertheless, all three studies conclude that the growth in global supply will be sufficient to meet the growth in global demand, and all highlight sub-Saharan Africa as an area that should cause particular concern, whatever the deficiencies of the model might be.[13] Although real world grain prices are expected to continue their long-term decline (despite the recent price spike),[14] the rate of increase in the demand for food

_____

[10] The main findings of each are presented and discussed in IFPRI. 1995. *Population and food in the early twenty-first century: meeting future food demand of an increasing population.* Edited by N. Islam. IFPRI Occasional Papers. Washington, DC.

_____

[11] In subsequent model revisions for projections to 2020, IFPRI results for 2010 have been revised most notably for the former CPEs (production and consumption) and for sub-Saharan Africa (net imports), which are now much closer to the FAO projections.
[12] An extensive discussion of methodological issues, population projections and the findings for the main regional groupings can be found in IFPRI, op. cit., footnote 10. Further consideration of the regional issues is available in various numbers of the IFPRI Food, Agriculture and the Environment Discussion Paper Series.
[13] These findings are considered by one reviewer to be unduly pessimistic about the prospects for food security in sub-Saharan Africa. See G.I. Abalu in IFPRI, p. 121-126., op. cit., footnote 10.
[14] This is addressed later in the chapter.

in sub-Saharan Africa is expected to outstrip that of supply, and the ability to meet the increasing demand would therefore depend on the ability of the individual countries to pay for those imports not covered by food aid.

The conclusion that global food supplies can increase fast enough to meet expected demand at constant or even declining real food prices leaves no room for complacency on the supply side. Continuing increases in agricultural output, be they through area expansion (absolutely, through multiple cropping or through reduced fallow periods) or productivity increases, require sustained efforts to improve agricultural technologies and their rate of adaptation and to avoid or reverse environmental degradation so that the output increases are not only sustained but sustainable. In other words, sufficient resources must be

committed to investment in agriculture on a continuous basis if the projected potential output increases at global, regional and country levels are to be realized.

If there is no room for complacency on the supply side, there is even less on the demand side. The projections are not based on meeting basic nutritional needs, but on expected effective demand, i.e. the ability to pay. By the year 2010, it is expected that the absolute numbers of chronically undernourished people in the developing countries will have fallen – estimates vary depending on the assumptions made – to perhaps some 680 million, representing 12 percent of the population of these countries instead of 21 percent as at present. While it is reassuring to be told that the world can in principle produce enough food to meet likely

Figure 13

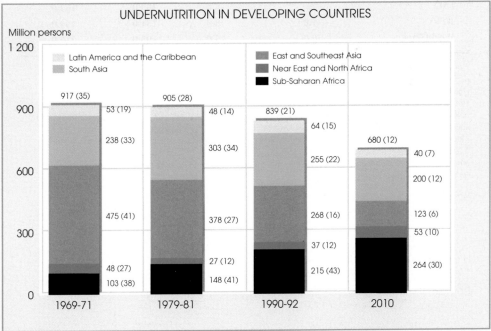

UNDERNUTRITION IN DEVELOPING COUNTRIES

Source: FAO

Note: Figures in brackets are percentages of the total population

TABLE 6

Data for 1989-91 and projections comparisons for all cereals (rice milled): developed countries

	World	Developed countries		
		Former centrally planned economies[1]	Other industrialized[2]	Total
	(... million tonnes ....)			
PRODUCTION				
Actual 1989-91	1 726.5	266.0	597.8	863.8
Projected 2010				
FAO	2 334.0	306.0	710.0	1 016.0
IFPRI	2 405.0	389.0	785.0	1 174.0
World Bank	2 311.0	324.0	733.0	1 058.0
TOTAL USE				
Actual 1989-91	1 729.8	302.1	475.0	777.1
Projected 2010				
FAO	2 334.0	301.0	553.0	854.0
IFPRI	2 406.0	381.0	634.0	1 015.0
World Bank	2 308.0	308.0	540.0	848.0
NET TRADE				
Actual 1989-91	3.6	-37.2	129.7	92.5
Projected 2010				
FAO	...	5.0	157.0	162.0
IFPRI	-1.0	8.0	151.0	159.0
World Bank	0.0	15.0	195.0	210.0

Notes:

... not applicable.

Figures do not add because of rounding.

Stocks are included in projections, so production deducted from total use does not measure net trade.

[1] Includes former East Germany in World Bank data. Former East Germany included in "Other industrialized" in FAO and IFPRI data. (Former East Germany data for 1988-90: production 10.7; total use 12.7; net trade -2.3.)

[2] Includes the Republic of South Africa. Includes Israel in FAO and IFPRI data. (Israel data for 1989-91: production 0.2; total use 2.5; net trade -2.2.)

Source: IFPRI. 1995. *Population and food in the early twenty-first century: meeting future food demand of an increasing population.* Washington, DC.

TABLE 7

Data for 1989-91 and projections comparisons for all cereals (rice milled): developing countries

			Developing countries					
	Sub-Saharan Africa	Near East and North Africa[1]	Asia and the Pacific			Latin America and the Caribbean	Others not allocated by region	Total
			South Asia[1]	China including Taiwan[2]	Others			
	(... million tonnes ....)							
PRODUCTION								
Actual 1989-91	54.7	76.8	202.8	326.8	104.6	97.0	...	862.7
Projected 2010								
FAO	110.0	119.0	292.0	473.0	165.0	159.0	...	1 318.0
IFPRI	86.0	118.0	297.0	426.0	153.0	152.0	...	1 232.0
World Bank	83.0	97.0	282.0	475.0	151.0	144.0	20.0	1 253.0
TOTAL USE								
Actual 1989-91	64.7	114.2	203.3	339.8	119.3	111.4	...	952.7
Projected 2010								
FAO	129.0	191.0	302.0	488.0	185.0	185.0	...	1 480.0
IFPRI	118.0	183.0	307.0	440.0	176.0	165.0	3.0	1 392.0
World Bank	96.0	169.0	312.0	502.0	189.0	172.0	20.0	1 459.0
NET TRADE								
Actual 1989-91	-8.5	-38.4	-3.2	-14.7	-12.7	-11.3	...	-88.8
Projected 2010								
FAO	-19.0	-72.0	-10.0	-15.0	-20.0	-26.0	...	-162.0
IFPRI	-32.0	-65.0	-10.0	-14.0	-23.0	-13.0	-3.0	-161.0
World Bank	-14.0	-73.0	-31.0	-22.0	-37.0	-28.0	-5.0	-210.0

Notes:

... not applicable.

Figures do not add because of rounding.

Stocks are included in projections, so production deducted from total use does not measure net trade.

[1] Afghanistan is in South Asia in World Bank data, Near East in FAO and IFPRI data. (Afghanistan data for 1989-91: production 2.6; total use 2.9; net trade -0.2.)

[2] Taiwan Province is separated from China in World Bank data and is included in "Others" (Asia and the Pacific). (Taiwan data for 1989-91: production 1.9; total use 8.1; net trade -6.1.)

Source: IFPRI. 1995. *Population and food in the early twenty-first century: meeting future food demand of an increasing population.* Washington, DC.

TABLE 8

Annual percentage growth rates of production and total use of all cereals: developed countries

| | World | Developed countries | | |
		Former centrally planned economies[1]	Other industrialized	Total
	(.. million tonnes ....)			
PRODUCTION GROWTH RATES				
Actual 1970-80	2.7	1.4	2.9	2.4
Actual 1980-91	1.6	1.4	0.2	0.6
Projected 1989-91 to 2010				
FAO	1.5 (1.6)	0.7 (0.5)	0.9 (1.1)	0.8 (0.9)
IFPRI	1.7 (1.6)	1.9 (1.5)	1.4 (1.3)	1.6 (1.4)
World Bank	1.5 (1.2)	1.0 (0.2)	1.0 (1.0)	1.0 (0.8)
TOTAL USE GROWTH RATES				
Actual 1970-80	2.5	2.9	0.9	1.6
Actual 1980-91	1.8	0.1	0.6	0.7
Projected 1989-91 to 2010				
FAO	1.5 (1.5)	0.0 (-0.1)	0.8 (0.8)	0.5 (0.4)
IFPRI	1.7 (1.6)	1.2 (0.9)	1.5 (1.3)	1.3 (1.1)
World Bank	1.5 (1.4)	0.1 (-0.4)	0.1 (0.7)	0.4 (0.3)

Notes:
Historical growth rates are ordinary least squares estimates from annual data, which include rice in milled form.
Projected growth rates not in parentheses measure the growth rate from 1989-91 absolute levels to projected levels in 2010, not adjusting for differences in regional definitions or for the different base years.
Projected growth rates in parentheses are measured from the base year actually used by each study (1988-90 for FAO, 1987-89 for IFPRI, 1990 for World Bank) as these data were known at the time the studies were conducted.
[1] Includes former East Germany in World Bank data. Former East Germany included in "Other industrialized" in FAO and IFPRI data.
Source: IFPRI. 1995. *Population and food in the early twenty-first century: meeting future food demand of an increasing population.* Washington, DC.

TABLE 9

Annual percentage growth rates of production and total use of all cereals: developing countries

| | Sub-Saharan Africa | Near East and North Africa[1] | Developing countries | | | Latin America and the Caribbean | Total |
| | | | Asia and the Pacific | | | | |
			South Asia[1]	China including Taiwan[2]	Others		
	(.. million tonnes ....)						
PRODUCTION GROWTH RATES							
Actual 1970-80	1.4	2.8	2.7	4.0	3.0	2.4	3.1
Actual 1980-91	3.4	3.4	2.9	3.0	2.5	0.6	2.7
1989-91 to 2010[3]							
FAO	3.5 (3.4)	2.2 (2.3)	1.8 (1.8)	1.9 (2.0)	2.3 (2.1)	2.5 (2.3)	2.1 (2.1)
IFPRI	2.3 (2.4)	2.2 (2.1)	1.9 (2.2)	1.3 (1.6)	1.9 (1.9)	2.3 (1.8)	1.8 (1.9)
World Bank	2.1 (3.3)	1.2 (1.9)	1.7 (1.6)	1.9 (1.6)	1.9 (1.8)	2.0 (2.1)	1.9 (1.8)
TOTAL USE GROWTH RATES							
Actual 1970-80	2.5	4.5	2.2	4.4	3.2	3.9	3.6
Actual 1980-91	3.1	3.6	3.0	2.6	3.2	1.5	2.8
1989-91 to 2010[3]							
FAO	3.5 (3.4)	2.6 (2.5)	2.0 (1.8)	1.8 (1.9)	2.2 (2.1)	2.6 (2.4)	2.2 (2.2)
IFPRI	3.0 (3.0)	2.4 (2.2)	2.1 (2.3)	1.3 (1.7)	2.0 (2.1)	2.0 (1.7)	1.9 (2.0)
World Bank	2.0 (3.1)	2.0 (2.4)	2.2 (2.0)	2.0 (2.1)	2.3 (2.1)	2.2 (2.5)	2.2 (2.2)

Notes:
Historical growth rates are ordinary least squares estimates from annual data, which include rice in milled form.
Projected growth rates not in parentheses measure the growth rate from 1989-91 absolute levels to projected levels in 2010, not adjusting for differences in regional definitions or for the different base years.
Projected growth rates in parentheses are measured from the base year actually used by each study (1988-90 for FAO, 1987-89 for IFPRI, 1990 for World Bank) as these data were known at the time the studies were conducted.
[1] Afghanistan is in South Asia in World Bank data and in Near East in FAO and IFPRI data.
[2] Taiwan is separated from China in World Bank data and is included in "Others" (Asia and the Pacific).
[3] Projections.
Source: IFPRI. 1995. *Population and food in the early twenty-first century: meeting future food demand of an increasing population.* Washington, DC.

BOX 15
PROSPECTS FOR CHINA'S GRAIN TRADE

Opinions differ about the role China will play in the world grain market. Estimates of China's net grain imports over the next 15 to 30 years range from a forecast of fundamental self-sufficiency to a very unlikely high of 200 million tonnes depending on the assumptions made about several key parameters. A number of sources maintain that China's grain imports could reach 30 to 40 million tonnes, an amount that is less than the former USSR imported in the late 1980s and that would have little effect on the long-term real price of grain. To economize on transport costs and facilities, most of these imports are likely to go to the large cities and coastal region, thus assuring adequate supplies at stable prices.

As a result of policy changes made in 1994, Beijing has delegated responsibility for the grain supply of each province to each provincial government. This means that Beijing has largely lost control of the national grain supply since provinces producing surplus grain can (and do) restrict exports to other provinces until they are certain their own needs have been met. This was one reason for the volatile price situation in 1994; grain did not readily move from the surplus to the deficit areas. Thus the

move to a national market, which seemed assured by the 1993 reforms, has now been delayed, probably for several years and, if China does import enough grain for its large cities and the coastal area, the national market may well be delayed for decades. In recent years, China has procured about 80 million tonnes of grain domestically, although this figure was probably even lower in 1994 and 1995. Consequently, 40 million tonnes is a very large figure relative to the marketed grain in China.

Although 30 to 40 million tonnes of grain imports is a possibility a decade or more into the future (wheat imports are some 11 million tonnes per year), whether the figure will in fact be that high depends on: what China does to encourage domestic grain production in terms of price policy, research, facilitating farm enlargement and ensuring adequate supplies of good-quality fertilizer; the rate at which the demand for livestock products grows; and the country's ability to generate foreign exchange. With regard to pricing policy, it was announced in March 1996 that state grain purchasing prices were to be raised by 20 percent to encourage increased production. New information from surveys in China and satellite pictures suggests that the grain area has been seriously under-reported, which means that the potential for yield increases is far greater than was previously thought. The survey data also suggest strongly that stocks have been substantially underestimated.

In assessing the demand for livestock products there are serious discrepancies in the official data on meat and poultry production from the various sources. The output data for meat and poultry implied a per caput availability of more than 32.5 kg in 1993, while the household survey data put consumption at about half that amount. If per caput consumption was in fact 32.5 kg (which has since increased according to the same data measurement methods to about 38 kg), consumption growth should start to slow down, although there has not yet been any indication of this happening. What is perhaps more disturbing is that, while meat and poultry production is said to have increased substantially since 1985, per caput urban purchases only increased from about 22 kg in 1985 to 24.5 kg in 1993, with rural consumption increasing from 12 kg to 13.3 kg over the same period, according to the household surveys. Over the same period, the output of meat and poultry almost

doubled from 19.3 million tonnes to 38.4 million tonnes, while the population increased by 12 percent. Another data series puts per caput consumption of pork, beef and mutton at 16.75 kg in 1985 and 27.37 kg in 1993, while yet another, on per caput consumption of selected consumer goods, puts per caput consumption of meat and poultry at 16.5 kg for 1985 and 22.6 kg for 1992. All of these figures are in the *Statistical Yearbook of China*.

A major factor affecting future demand for grain is the consumption of meat. There is great uncertainty about how much meat is now being produced and consumed and how much grain is being used to produce meat, milk and poultry. Most of the published projections of future demand for and supply of grain fail to recognize the ambiguities in the data on the production and consumption of livestock products.

The response of the government to rising imports is also critically important.[1] Continued investment in agriculture and agricultural research, appropriate pricing policies

and increased use of imported production technology, such as seed, are ways of boosting domestic supply. However, given that far larger import volumes than have hitherto been experienced seem probable, investment will also be needed in the marketing infrastructure and institutions to cope with the expanded grain trade.

---

[1] S. Rozelle, J. Huang and M. Rosegrant. 1996. Why China will not starve the world. *Choices*, First Quarter 1996.

demand, the probable inability of so many people to exert sufficient effective demand to feed themselves at even minimally adequate levels is deeply disturbing. Experiences in the countries that have made and are continuing to make good progress, even in the face of a difficult international economic environment, show that governments are the key players in implementing domestic and trade policies which can lead to the achievement of national food security and that economic policies are of particular significance.[15]

GOVERNMENTS AND FOOD SECURITY

It is difficult to apply the concept of food security at the global or the regional level where region is defined on a geographical rather than a politico-economic basis. Sub-Saharan Africa has been identified as a region where food insecurity is likely to worsen. What this actually means is that a high proportion of countries in that region are expected to have a worsening food security position. Conversely, some of the regions that are expected to improve overall, or at least not to worsen, include individual countries that might see deterioration. The highest level of aggregation at which the concept can reasonably be made operational is that of the national government (the only realistic – and even then partial – exception to this would be the EU because of its degree of politico-economic cohesion) since the achievement of food security depends on action by those who have the power and the responsibility to act. This does not preclude the necessity for action by external agents, such as donor governments, international agencies, NGOs and multilateral and bilateral lenders, to support developing country governments in the fulfilment of their responsibilities.

Since the early 1980s, policy reforms initiated in many countries have been biased in favour of greater market orientation and a more open economy.[16] There has been a

---

[15] There is a wealth of documentation on this subject at all levels of technicality. FAO produces a wide range of publications on specific aspects and the technical background documents for the World Food Summit 1996 (see Box 14, p. 263) provide extensive coverage of many aspects of food security. Useful overviews are also provided in: World Bank. 1995. *World Development Report 1995.* New York, Oxford University Press; P. Pinstrup-Andersen and R. Pandya-Lorch. 1994. *Alleviating poverty, intensifying agriculture, and effectively managing natural resources.* Food, Agriculture and the Environment Discussion Paper No. 1. Washington, DC, IFPRI. In addition, several background papers for IFPRI's 2020 Vision initiative have been prepared covering a wide range of relevant topics.

---

[16] The main pressures underlying these policy reforms are presented in FAO. 1995. Policy reform and the consumer, in *The State of Food and Agriculture 1995.* Rome.

movement away from the concept of development, including agricultural development, as planned change by public agencies. Indeed, this period has seen a serious questioning of the very role of government – what it should and should not properly do in a market economy. In this context, it is clear that government has a vital role to play if a functioning free-market economy, rather than one that is merely a free-for-all, is to emerge in such a way that the sustained and sustainable economic growth on which long-term national food security depends can occur and that its benefits are distributed equitably.

What then is the role of government and what can governments do that no other body can? Put simply, governments need to govern and this has traditionally been taken to mean securing the borders and protecting the population from both external and internal threat, i.e. keeping the peace without which food security is threatened. It also means ensuring the establishment and enforcement of a legislative and judicial system that defines the rights and obligations of individuals and legal entities, regulates their activities in the public interest and protects their agreed rights. A strong, fair and stable legislative framework is necessary to guide and regulate the individual players in the market and to ensure that they all play by the same set of rules through enforcement of the law so that market activity can contribute to food security for all. Only governments can create the favourable and stable macroeconomic and trade environment that can enable national food security to be realized. For countries in transition, be it from

centrally planned to market economies, because of the implementation of structural adjustment policies or simply as a part of the normal process of economic development, the role of government is especially difficult. Governments need to invest in the infrastructure for progress. Inherent in this must be the recognition that investment in the development of human resources (building human capital of both women and men) and action to alleviate poverty add to, rather than subtract from, a country's growth potential and are essential for ensuring food security for all sections of the community. This type of investment includes the provision of those services and infrastructure that have a large public good component, such as education, health, public utilities and roads, and that cannot therefore be provided adequately by the private sector. In addition, the demands of adjustment or development might in some cases require the government to provide temporarily some of the services that can in principle be supplied by the private sector once the successful implementation of policy reform has allowed its capacities to develop sufficiently. In order to avoid stifling the development of the nascent private sector, any such activities, whether undertaken by governments or other agencies, need to be carefully planned and coordinated.

The achievement of food security on a sustainable basis therefore requires that governments take action on a number of different policy fronts. Trade and macroeconomic policies that permit and foster overall economic growth and increase competitiveness in export markets are needed; they should also correct past distortions that favour one sector of the economy to the detriment of others. Agricultural sector policies should be designed to promote sustained and sustainable sector growth in order to increase both domestic food supply and those agricultural and food exports for which the country has a comparative advantage. Although economic growth is very important for addressing the underlying causes of food insecurity, "economies cannot be expected to grow quickly enough to eliminate the chronic food insecurity of some groups in the near future, even under the best of circumstances. Moreover, long-run economic growth is often slowed by widespread chronic food insecurity. People who lack energy are ill-equipped to take advantage of opportunities for increasing their productivity and output".[17]

Furthermore, gross inequalities of income distribution may prevent the resource-poor from participating in the growth process and certain policy reforms may of themselves have substantial negative impacts on vulnerable groups in society. Special measures may be needed in the short and medium terms to deal with specific cases of food insecurity and to ensure that essential food imports can be financed. Over the long term, some special measures will always be needed, although their nature may change.

It must be re-emphasized that the successful implementation of agricultural and food policies alone cannot achieve a national objective of food security. The elimination of absolute poverty, the root cause of food insecurity, requires action across the board to enable people to escape the cycle of poverty and malnutrition that traps successive generations. Yet the achievement of food security does not have to wait for the eradication of poverty. It is repeatedly stated by international agencies, donor governments, world summits and just about everybody involved in development that the resources and the means to eliminate food insecurity exist, but that the problem is the lack of political will. If governments would only readjust their priorities accordingly, the problem could be solved – although discussion about the time-frame required is studiously avoided. "Success stories" tend to concentrate on the policies that a particular country has implemented without delving too deeply into the socio-political circumstances that enabled it to implement those policies. Rarely is it asked why the political will might be lacking:

> Political will is journalistic shorthand for the overcoming of the conflicting interests, ideological blinkers and structural constraints that usually make it impossible for governments to do what is technically feasible and clearly necessary to solve a serious problem. The term contributes to good journalism, but poor social science. Social scientists have to explain why political will is lacking and what might be done to produce it.[18]

The findings of research on food systems by the United Nations

---

[17] World Bank. 1986. *Poverty and hunger.* A World Bank Policy Study. Washington, DC.

[18] Barraclough, op. cit., footnote 5, p. 266.

Research Institute for Social Development (UNRISD) are unusual in that the question of political will is raised explicitly. They cast doubt on the political possibilities, rather than the strictly technical ones, of rapidly improving food access for the very poor. This applies to industrialized countries who have widely differing levels of social and economic deprivation as well as to countries at other stages of development. Governments are, after all, dependent on the groups to whom they owe their support, and their room for manoeuvre is correspondingly restricted:

> If the problem is really systemic, as the UNRISD team believes, then it can be dealt with effectively only through both fundamental public policy and social change. The latter implies new power relationships among individuals, social classes, groups and nations. Social changes do not come about easily. Convincing political leaders that hunger and poverty are serious and solvable social problems does not bring about political will, although in some circumstances it might help.... In alleviating hunger, politics matters.... How are sufficient political pressures generated to force governments to adopt effective strategies leading to rapid diminution of poverty and hunger? Answers are unique for each time and place. Where social forces have emerged capable of bringing about such policies, however, there have been at least three broad and closely interrelated social processes at work.[19]

The three social processes referred to are identified as: modernization

processes – the social impact of economic growth and technical change; the rapidly increasing availability and dissemination of information, which contributes to social change by changing perceptions and ideologies; and popular participation – the mobilization and organization in a real sense of those previously excluded by lack of control over resources or influence over government. The interactions between political, social, economic and ecological systems and processes as they affect people's access to food – locally, nationally and internationally – are extremely complex and the problems admit of no easy solutions. It follows, and is frequently observed, that there is rarely anything as simple as a technical solution to a complex problem. To take a simple example, assume crop yields can be increased by increasing fertilizer applications, whether fertilizer will in fact be applied depends on many other factors, such as are fertilizer imports regarded as being sufficiently important for the government to guarantee foreign exchange availability on a reliable basis? can the distribution system get the fertilizer to the right place at the right time? do the farmgate prices for output justify its use? can farmers obtain the resources to buy it in the first place? and are some farmers restricted in their access to fertilizer for political or other non-economic reasons?[20] It is important to note that here the issue is not so much

---

[19] Ibid.

[20] As an example, there have been cases where a government agency has restricted, for example, fertilizer supplies to those supporting a particular political party.

the political will to establish state interventions or subsidies to encourage an otherwise uneconomical fertilizer use, but the political will to remove existing distortions or privileges.

There are many technical questions (covering a wide range of professional disciplines) concerning food insecurity that require technical answers. Should fertilizer be applied? In certain agro-ecological circumstances, if yields are to be increased, it should be. However, because the basic problems of food insecurity are not purely technical, the solutions are not purely technical either. So fertilizer will be applied only if the political, social and economic configuration determines that it shall be. The rest of this chapter examines some of the economic questions of food security and the policy implications for the governments concerned.

RELIABILITY AS A COMPONENT OF FOOD SECURITY: SHORT-TERM FLUCTUATIONS AND LONG-TERM TRENDS

It is an accepted legal precept that hard cases make for bad law; it could with equal justice also be said that short-term crises make for bad policy. This chapter was written against the background of a perceived global grain crisis, which is of its nature short-term while nevertheless having serious longer-term impacts on several low-income food-deficit countries (LIFDCs). While reacting to an urgent situation, it is important that the longer-term issues are not ignored.

The reliability component of food security concerns both availability and access and is often confused with stability, although the questions of what stability and for whom are rarely addressed explicitly. Weather and other acts of nature affect the stability of supply; abrupt changes in demand affect the stability of price; and the interaction of macroeconomic and sectoral policies within and across countries can affect both.

Fluctuations on the supply side of cereal production have a disproportionate impact on prices because of the relatively small short-term price elasticity of demand for cereals in the aggregate. A major cause of supply instability is a weather-induced shock such as occurred in the early 1970s, when the 1973 cereal crop fell to 3.5 percent below trend, and again in 1995 when the production fall was 3 percent below trend (the effects of this are still being seen). Adverse weather conditions in North America, northern Europe and major parts of the former USSR, together with failure of the monsoon in South Asia, resulted in the 1973 cereals crop being 3.5 percent below trend. This, given that the United States Government had decided in the late 1960s to stop holding large stocks, together with a number of other factors that occurred simultaneously (such as the first oil price shock and its aftermath, which contributed to increases in the prices of many agricultural inputs, and the change in Soviet policy to import cereals during domestic shortage rather than slaughter livestock herds) caused a sharp and rapid escalation of prices in international cereal markets (Figure 14).

A similar weather-induced phenomenon occurred in 1995, with a drop in global production to 3 percent below trend. World grain prices rose sharply during 1995 and further price increases are possible given the unusually low policy-induced stocks and problematic growing conditions in several producing areas. From January to June 1996, United States wheat export prices were up by about 30 percent from a year before, but importers of United States grain were frequently facing price increases of 50 percent or more caused by the reduction or elimination of the export price subsidy. The United States export price of maize, the leading coarse grain, rose by 46 percent over the same period, and this is reflected in prices paid by importers. Rice prices have also risen markedly, despite significant stocks in India and China. The grain import costs faced by many importing countries have increased even more because key exporters have largely suspended export price subsidies. Exporter supplies are tight and world grain stocks have dropped

to the lowest level since the early 1970s, the stocks-to-use ratios for cereals being only 14 percent.

Current analysis and market information suggest that grain prices are likely to ease only after the 1996 output level is well defined. Serious drought or other indications of a significant production shortfall, however, could lead to higher and even more volatile prices. If crop conditions progress normally, wheat prices are expected to ease noticeably after the northern hemisphere harvest, perhaps in October and November when the expected large out-turn in Canada is known. The coarse grain market is susceptible to even greater short-term volatility as a result of heavy dependence on just one geographic region – the United States cornbelt area.

The grain market phenomenon is thus one of short-term fluctuations involving sharp price rises and less sharp price falls (the price falls are naturally of less concern to the importing countries, although not to the exporting countries whose policies have been designed to mitigate the falls to a greater extent than the rises) around a long-term decline in the trend of real world grain prices. The rate of decline appears to be slowing down, but there is as yet no real evidence that it has bottomed out. Even at its peak, the 1995/96 price spike reflected a lower real price than at any time between 1970 and 1985, and has never exceeded about 45 percent of the real price in 1974 (Figure 14). The commodity markets for the major tropical agricultural export crops also show great price variability around even more steeply declining long-term real prices.

The price impact of the weather-induced supply shocks of 1973 and 1995 on international markets was of longer duration in both instances than it would have been in an open-market, liberal trading environment because many countries, both exporters and importers, have policies that isolate the domestic market from the international market. This isolation means that price signals from the international market do not reach domestic producers or consumers, who therefore do not adjust to international market conditions. In effect, longer-lived instability is exported to the international market by these countries. The adjustment that occurs takes place within the few countries that have relatively open agricultural economies and tends to be large because the adjustment burden is not being shared by all.

Specific examples illustrate the effects of policy on international market stability. The EU, for instance, has long had in place a support policy for wheat producers that maintains a stable producer price, usually well above the international price. This is achieved through a variable levy system that maintains a constant threshold price, and this is the price paid by importers of wheat in the EU. A variable levy or tax based on the difference between the threshold price and the international market price is imposed on EU imports. To dispose of surplus wheat production into the export market, an export restitution is paid to exporters based on the difference between the domestic support or intervention price and the international market price.

In the cases of both the 1973 and 1995 production shortfalls, the

Figure 14

CONSTANT 1990 AND NOMINAL WHEAT EXPORT PRICES 1970-1996
(US dollars per tonne)

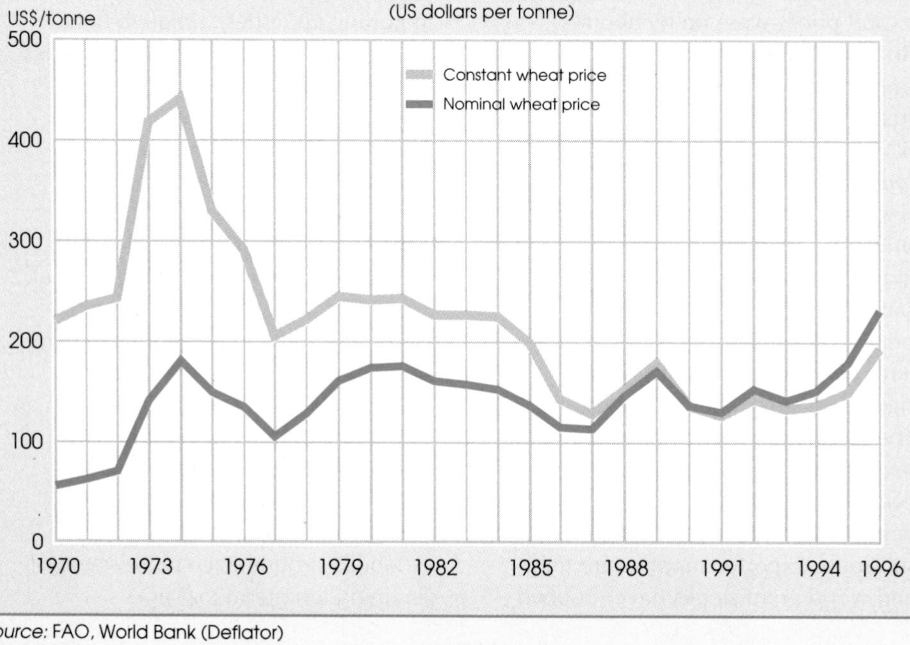

US$/tonne

Constant wheat price
Nominal wheat price

Source: FAO, World Bank (Deflator)

international price for wheat rose above the threshold price and the EU switched from the variable levy and export restitutions to an export tax that maintained the level of the threshold price. Thus, just as EU producers were shielded from having to adjust to the normally lower and fluctuating international price by reducing production, they were also discouraged from adjusting to the higher international price by increasing production because of the export tax. The stabilization of consumer prices also meant that consumers had no incentive to adjust their consumption patterns to changing conditions in world markets. This means that the EU, a major producer of wheat, did not adjust production downwards in response to low international prices and, in fact, exported surpluses into the international market, thereby exacerbating the low prices. In addition, it did not adjust production upwards in response to a higher international price, instead it withheld exports into the international market, thereby exacerbating the international price rise. In the first instance, producers in adjusting exporting countries lost and consumers or governments in importing countries gained, while in the second instance producers in adjusting exporting countries gained and consumers or governments in importing countries lost. The CAP reforms of the early 1990s, including a set-aside provision, have dampened, but not totally negated, the effects described above. South Africa also took measures to stabilize domestic prices by halting grain export contracts in mid-1995. The United States policy reforms have involved a switch to partially and then fully decoupled deficiency payments, but at the same time there was, and still is, the Export Enhancement Program (EEP) (although its use has been suspended during the 1996 price spike). Both the United States and the EU have further dampened producer response to price fluctuations by the use of land set-aside schemes.

Consumers *or* governments are referred to in the above paragraph because a number of wheat-importing countries also shield themselves, this time their consumers, from changes in the international market price, particularly when that price rises precipitously. Such countries, sometimes using a parastatal marketing agency, purchase wheat in the international market at the international market price and sell into the domestic market at a higher price (tax) if the international price is low or at a lower price (subsidy) if the international price is high. So consumers in these importing countries are not forced to adjust to international market conditions, demand either too much or too little and force further adjustments into the international market. This increases the adjustment burden on those countries that do the adjusting.

As Johnson put it:

> Much of the price variability in international market prices is man-made – it is the consequence of policies followed by many governments. In short, national policies that stabilize domestic prices for consumers and producers do so at the cost of international price variability unless the domestic price stability is achieved by holding stocks of sufficient size to create what is in effect a

perfectly elastic supply curve for the relevant food product. But countries other than Canada, India and the United States have not held stocks of such size; consequently almost all national programmes of domestic price stability are achieved by varying imports and exports to make supply equal domestic demand at the predetermined and stable price. In this way, all the potential price effects of domestic demand and supply variations are imposed on the world market.[21]

Nevertheless, changes are occurring in the global environment within which international trade takes place; from the point of view of global and national food security, future strategies need to differ from those of the past. It is also clear that the food security policy responses to the short-term fluctuations and long-term trends need to be different.

There is an underlying concern about the possible disruption of world grain markets in the sense of price spikes caused by massive increases in demand by some of the major importing countries. The countries that are large enough to have the potential to do this are China and India; their size and geographical and agricultural diversity provides some cushioning of weather-induced shocks to domestic grain supply and also gives them export possibilities in good years. A summary of the situation and policies in each is given in Boxes 15,

on p. 276, and 16. Box 17, on p. 290, provides an overview of the changing policies of the United States, the major grain exporter.

Over the past four decades, the United States has been the major intertemporal (interseasonal) stockholder of cereals, with the EU also maintaining significant grain reserves since the late 1970s when it became a net cereal exporter. Canada has at times carried far smaller grain reserves while neither Australia nor Argentina have had the storage capacity to do so. Food reserve stocks in India until very recently have been strictly domestic. The stocks held by both the United States and the EU were the result of agricultural policies that supported the domestic price above market clearing levels, requiring the authorities to purchase and hold stocks until a predetermined market price trigger allowed their release into the market. In addition, the various area set-aside schemes and the conservation reserve programmes, which held land out of cereal production, acted as a further complementary stock of grain, albeit in the form of uncultivated land rather than physical quantities of grain. These so-called policy-induced stocks will be drastically reduced or eliminated as market and trade liberalization occurs. This means that the world will no longer be able to rely on such policy-induced stocks to cushion the price effects of a production shortfall.

Two separate but related issues arise. First, what is likely to be the behaviour of the global cereals market in a more liberal trade and markets environment? Work is under way at FAO and elsewhere on analysing this

---

[21] **D.G. Johnson. 1984. *Alternative approaches to international food reserves.* Paper prepared for the FAO Symposium on World Food Security, Rome, 3 to 7 September 1984. ESC:FS/SYMP/84/5.**

question, but unfortunately only preliminary results are available at the time of writing. Economic theory and an empirical understanding of markets, however, can lead to some informed qualitative speculation. Consider the case of a reduction in world production. Without the cushion of policy-induced stocks to buffer the price rise in response to the production shortfall, the international price rise is likely to be sharper, but with more open economies and liberalized markets there will be greater international market price transmission to more producers and consumers in more countries. This should mean that a larger and quicker supply and demand adjustment will occur in response to the price change, with producers increasing output and consumers shifting consumption in favour of relatively cheaper foodstuffs. Future international market price spikes are therefore likely to be more violent initially, but shorter lived. Following on from this the question arises as to what extent the private sector will assume the stockholding function formerly borne by governments with policy-induced stocks. The private sector would not be expected to carry stocks of a similar magnitude becuase such levels would most probably be unprofitable. Nevertheless, the private sector will hold stocks up to a profitable level and to that extent those stocks would buffer and reduce the magnitude of market price spikes.

This discussion has focused on upward price movements. An examination of Figure 14, p. 284, shows that downward price movements have tended to be far less sharp and deep, reflecting the policies of some of the main grain-producing countries which have been designed to protect their farmers from severe price falls. To the extent that liberalization and policy reform remove or reduce the effects of such policies, the international market would see greater downward price variation than it has in the past. Thus in years of good harvests, price falls would be more pronounced, enabling importing countries to reap the benefits and providing perhaps greater profit incentives for private-sector stocking.

The second issue is that a number of countries may still feel the need to hold some level of food security reserve, as distinct from any working stocks held by private importers and traders. (Countries that do not will bear the full brunt of market instability.) These countries basically have two options; they can hold a physical stock of the commodity or they can hold a foreign currency fund for food security reserve purposes. The main advantage of this second option is that the country does not incur the significant costs of holding the actual commodity and of stock management and that it can earn interest on the hard currency account. However, the use of such a fund during periods of global supply shortfall will exacerbate the price spike. The trade-off for the country involved is the additional import cost caused by the price spike minus what has been earned on the foreign exchange account as compared with the cost of holding the commodity reserve until it is needed.

While a foreign exchange food security fund has both fiscal and monetary implications (e.g. tax revenues or borrowings to establish the fund, a positive balance of

BOX 16
FOOD SECURITY AND TRADE IN INDIA

India has put food security very high on the national agenda. From being a substantial net food importer in the 1970s, it was nearly self-sufficient in grain production from the early 1980s, more than self-sufficient in the 1990s and carries a high level of buffer stocks. The Food Corporation of India (FCI), which was instituted in 1965, is the main agency for the procurement, storage and transport of grains for distribution through the public distribution system and for maintaining the buffer stocks. The procurement and issue prices of food grains are fixed by the government; the issue price does not cover all the economic costs and the difference represents a government subsidy to consumers. The government also subsidizes the carrying costs of the buffer stocks, which amount to about 30 percent of the value of the stocks.

In the past few years, grain output has increased considerably from around 180 million tonnes in 1992/93 to almost 192 million tonnes in 1994/95. Stocks had reached 28.7 million tonnes by March 1995, but transport and storage problems were slowing procurement despite increased output. Nevertheless, most of the wheat coming to market in 1995 was bought by FCI and other public-sector agencies under price support operations, with private traders handling only small quantities of very high-quality grain at prices well in excess of the support prices. By the end of the summer harvest season, stocks had reached between 36 million and 37 million tonnes, but these had been reduced to 29 million tonnes by November 1995. Plans to lower the issue prices of wheat and rice at state-run retail outlets to redress the price increases of previous

payments item and earnings on the fund until it is needed), a physical commodity stock reserve has mainly fiscal implications if purchased locally, but also monetary if acquired through imports. First there is the expense of establishing the stock reserve either through tax revenues or through borrowing. Then there are the maintenance costs associated with the reserve including stock administration, transport, storage, handling and rotation, which need to be financed from the same sources. Finally, distribution and replenishment costs are incurred when the food security reserve is called upon in accordance with the pre-existing rules governing its use. Ideally, the stock would be replenished when prices are low and depleted when high; but, as has been seen, policy reforms that permit substantial price falls have yet to feed through to the international market. The government budget for establishment, operation and years had to be postponed for budgetary reasons, despite the rising costs of carrying ever-increasing stocks. Export restrictions were lifted to allow exports of 2.5 million tonnes of rice and 2 million tonnes of wheat for the year, and there was pressure from the Ministry of Agriculture to have the ceilings abolished to permit greater reliance on exports and imports to manage food grain supplies.

The most important constraints on increasing exports are inadequate storage, transport and port facilities. However, the removal of the public-sector monopoly on key aspects of infrastructure, including the ports, is encouraging new private-sector investment, and the redevelopment of the ports is expected to be finished by 1997. If this is achieved, some experts believe that India could be exporting 3 million tonnes of wheat and 4 million tonnes of rice by 2002 (rice stocks are currently running at 16 million tonnes). This would make it a major player in the small world rice market, where its prices are competitive. In the wheat market, however, it is less price competitive.

There seems to be a strong consensus among the different political parties for continuing with the economic liberalization process while supporting agricultural development and giving high priority to food security. India therefore seems likely to engage more in international trade in grain markets in the future and will perhaps at some point decide to reduce its very large and expensive buffer stocks in favour of a greater reliance on imports. If so, India might play an even greater part in world markets once the port capacity has been modernized and expanded.

management of the physical commodity food security reserve has an opportunity cost over and above the monetary cost for either government or the private sector. This opportunity cost may be great or small, depending on the alternative uses that might have been made of the funds. Given the shortage of both capital and recurrent budgetary funds in developing countries, the opportunity cost if properly calculated is likely to be very high.

The issue of food security stocking, either as a physical commodity or liquid reserves, nationally or multilaterally through the various fund facilities available, is highly complex in economic terms. When the non-economic factors are included, together with the country-specific conditions for both economic and non-economic factors, it is obvious that each country needs to address the question from its own perspective and to repeat the exercise as the important

BOX 17

FOOD AID AND FOOD TRADE:
THE 1996 UNITED STATES FARM BILL

The United States Government has traditionally carried a significant quantity of grain stocks, largely as a result of the operation of its domestic farm programmes. These stocks have played an important role in promoting price stability in world grain markets. The United States also has a long history of providing food aid to developing countries as well as export credit programmes for commercial exports of grains and other agricultural commodities.

The recent heightened concern about world food security finds the United States with low grain stocks, which limits its flexibility to respond. National concern about balancing the federal budget is also reducing the response possibilities, especially for food aid and related expenditures. Therefore the United States is emphasizing its efforts to increase commercial grain supplies rather than responding with food aid.

It appears that the United States is strongly committed to ensuring that its grain will continue to be available to meet export demand, without any of the restrictions related to tight grain supplies. Importers have been assured that the United States will not restrict exports. Authorization has been provided for the release of up to 1.5 million tonnes out of the 3.8 million tonnes currently in the Food Security Wheat Reserve to meet obligations for emergency humanitarian food assistance needs. Domestic programmes have been adjusted to encourage increased crop output in 1996.

Export programmes in 1996

The United States export programmes include food assistance under Public Law 480 (PL 480) and credit programmes for commercial exports. Funding is specified for commodity exports under PL 480 Titles I, II and III:

• Title I funding for the United States fiscal year (FY) 1996 (which ends on 30 September) is US$316 million. The programme offers long-term loans at highly concessional terms to specified developing countries.
• Title II funding for FY 1996 is US$821 million. This programme provides food aid on a grant basis through the World Food Programme and various NGOs and under bilateral agreements.
• Title III funding for FY 1996 is US$50 million. This programme offers food commodities on a grant basis in conjunction with a specific set of long-term development activities by the recipient country.

Export credit guarantees are provided to assist in financing commercial exports of United States agricultural commodities. The GSM 102 Programme provides credit guarantees for financing terms of six to 36 months (US$5 billion for FY 1996), while the GSM 103 Programme can provide guarantees for loans with terms of three to ten years ($500 million for FY 1996).

Recent agricultural legislation

The new legislation, the Federal Agriculture Improvement and Reform Act of 1996, makes several changes that may affect United States exports in the future. The following items appear to be the most relevant:[1]

• *Planting and production flexibility.* Producers who had participated or had certified area in the wheat, feed grains, cotton and rice programmes for at least one of the last five crop years may sign a Production Flexibility Contract authorized under the new legislation. The contract will cover seven crop years, from 1996 to 2002, and will allow producers to continue receiving payments, at a declining level, with flexibility on contract area to grow any commodity except fruit or vegetables.

• *Conservation Reserve Program (CRP).* **CRP is re-authorized to the year 2002, with up to 14.7 million ha enrolled at any one time. Except for lands that are of high environmental value, the Agriculture Secretary is to allow participants to terminate any contract entered into prior to 1 January 1995 on written notice, provided that the contract has been in effect for at least five years. The Secretary maintains discretionary authority to conduct future "early-outs" and sign-ups of lands that meet enrolment eligibility criteria.**

• *Agricultural trade programmes.* **PL 480 Title I is amended to authorize**

---

¹ For a more detailed analysis of the act, see "The United States 1996 Farm Act increases market orientation" on p. 246.

agreements with private entities in addition to foreign governments. The repayment terms are modified to eliminate the minimum repayment period of ten years and to reduce the maximum grace period from seven to five years. Title II changes increase the maximum level of funding that can be provided as overseas administrative support for eligible organizations from US$13.5 million to $28.0 million and adds intergovernmental organizations such as the World Food Programme to the list of organizations eligible to receive the funds. Other changes under PL 480 include an amendment to broaden the range of commodities available for inclusion under the programme and extending authority to enter into new PL 480 agreements to the year 2002. Up to 15 percent of the funds available for any PL 480 title can be used to carry out any other title and up to 50 percent of Title III funds can be used for Title II.

• *Export guarantee programmes.* **Annual programme levels for GSM 102 and 103 are mandated at US$5.5 billion to 2002 and flexibility is allowed as to how much is available for each programme. A new short-term credit guarantee programme is authorized for**

credit periods of not more than 180 days.

• *Export Enhancement Program (EEP).* **The changes limit EEP to US$350 million for FY 1996, $250 million for FY 1997, $500 million for FY 1998, $550 million for FY 1999, $579 million for FY 2000 and $478 million each for FY 2001 and FY 2002.**

• **A new** *Food Security Commodity Reserve* **is established to replace the Food Security Wheat Reserve. Commodities authorized for the 4-million-tonne reserve include maize, grain sorghum and rice in addition to wheat. Authority for replenishment of the reserve is extended to 2002.**

variables change. In determining government policy with regard to food security stocking, governments need to take account of private-sector activity in grain trading and storage and to decide what the respective roles of the public and private sectors should be.

No single small country is able to do anything about the world market. The question therefore is which policy measures, in addition to the trade-related economic policies discussed in the next section, can governments in low-income, food-importing countries introduce to ensure reliability of food availability and access, both in response to short-term fluctuations and over the longer term? IFPRI, for example, has suggested four sets of measures:

> Many developing countries have found that strategies to keep grain affordable to consumers, such as holding large public grain stocks or setting ceiling prices, are unsustainably expensive. There are, however, things they can do:
> - hold small grain stocks to provide some insurance against price spikes;
> - use foreign exchange insurance or special credit arrangements, such as the International Monetary Fund's Compensatory Finance Facility [sic], to finance needed imports;
> - use world futures and options markets to hedge against future price increases;
> - invest in transportation, communication, and agricultural research to ensure competitive rural markets and enhance the capacity of farmers to respond to changing prices.[22]

The first point, food stocks, has been addressed in this section. The last is covered in the next section in the context of trade-related economic policies. Points two and three are each given a section of their own because balance of payments support and the use of futures markets are increasingly being suggested by some international agencies and development experts as having vital roles to play in the achievement of food security in developing countries; however, as the following analysis suggests, both have very limited scope for assisting the poorest food-importing countries. Of far greater significance for more than 30 low-income countries is the external debt burden. While this is primarily a long-term concern it clearly has implications for the ability to respond to short-term food price shocks and a section of this Special Chapter is devoted to examining the consequences for food security of high levels of debt.

---

[22] **P. Pinstrup-Andersen and J.L. Garrett. 1996.** *Rising food prices and falling grain stocks: short-run blips or new trends?* **2020 Brief No. 30. Washington, DC, IFPRI.**

TRADE-RELATED ECONOMIC POLICIES

A country's trade-related economic policies influence food security indirectly through their effect on the growth of the economy as a whole and of particular economic sectors. They also have a more direct impact on food security and nutrition status by affecting such factors as rural and urban household incomes, the ability to import food to meet domestic shortfalls and demand for food items not produced locally and the earning of foreign exchange to finance the varying share of food imports in total imports:

> The expansion of agricultural trade has helped provide greater quantity, wider variety and better quality food to increasing numbers of people at lower prices. Agricultural trade is also a generator of income and welfare for the millions of people who are directly or indirectly involved in it. At the national level, for many countries, it is a major source of the foreign exchange that is necessary to finance imports and development; while for many others, domestic food security is closely related to the country's capacity to finance food imports.... Agricultural trade policy has long reflected the widely held belief that, because of its importance and vulnerability, the agricultural sector could not be exposed to the full rigours of international competition without incurring unacceptable political, social and economic consequences. This view has led to high and widespread protection of the sector.[23]

It has been argued that the instability in commodity markets that has apparently resulted from agricultural border protection has in its turn led to further pressures for protection. Whether or not this is true, many developing countries have nevertheless implemented economic policies that have been biased against the production of tradable goods in general and exports in particular, as well as against agricultural products. Taxation of the agricultural sector has been high in several countries. A major research study by the World Bank covering 18 countries over a 25-year period found that: "The indirect tax on agriculture from industrial protection and macroeconomic policies was about 22 percent on average... nearly three times the direct tax from agricultural pricing policies (about 8 percent). The total (direct plus indirect) was thus 30 percent."[24] The overall effect has been an average income transfer out of agriculture of 46 percent of agricultural GDP, ranging from 2 percent for the countries that protected agriculture to 140 percent for the heaviest taxers. In such countries, investment in food production has therefore been suboptimal and agricultural growth has been stifled, as has economic growth as a whole. Trade-related economic policy reforms and the

---

[23] FAO, op. cit., footnote 3, p. 265.

[24] **The results of this survey are published in five volumes in the World Bank's.** *The Political economy of agricultural pricing policy.* **Baltimore, MD, USA and London, Johns Hopkins University Press. A summary of the major policy findings is given in M. Schiff and A. Valdés. 1992.** *The plundering of agriculture in developing countries.* **Washington, DC, World Bank.**

ongoing structural adjustment programmes should lead towards correction of the long-standing anti-agriculture bias, if the reforms are carried out with real commitment and consistency. "The adjustment in Africa displays several weaknesses. From the evidence of recent policy actions, African governments have yet to display a real commitment to policy reform. Macroeconomic imbalances continue to characterize many economies, even those... that have been engaged in adjustment for more than a decade. Governments continue to interfere in markets."[25] The same authors stress the critical role of exchange rate policy in stimulating growth and reducing poverty through the correction of economic disequilibria.

The maintenance of overvalued exchange rates is of particular significance as they impose a tax on exports and subsidize imports. This tool has been used at high cost to stabilize and hold down domestic food prices for urban consumers at the expense of the domestic producers of import-competing and exportable agricultural products, often in the face of severe domestic inflation which has been poorly controlled or exacerbated by economic policy measures. In the long term, therefore, the effects are damaging for food security as: structural changes in the tastes and preferences of urban consumers that

do not take account of real international prices, as well as increasing urban incomes, exert pressure to maintain and increase food imports; the ability to pay for those imports has been reduced by depressing the expansion of agricultural and food exports which, for many low-income countries, are the main source of export earnings; the benefits of long-term falling real cereal prices have not been realizable in the face of high domestic inflation; and greater exchange rate overvaluation is related to lower GDP growth. Correcting overvalued exchange rates, which increases the domestic price of tradable food items, and controlling inflation, which slows down the rate of increase in domestic food prices and reduces the cost of stabilization measures, should therefore be put high on the policy reform agenda, and kept there. Rather than delay painful macroeconomic adjustment, which needs to allow for balanced sectoral growth by removing the biases against agriculture, governments may be better advised to implement compensatory interventions aimed at the groups most vulnerable to rises in the prices of tradable foods.

As noted earlier, there appears to be a long-term shift in the terms of trade away from the traditional agricultural export crops in favour of food crops. Thus, over time, a country's comparative advantage will change. Trade and macroeconomic policies, as well as sectoral pricing policies, need to permit the agricultural sector to respond to changes in comparative advantage patterns by reallocation of resources. However, in anticipation of these changes, governments need to

[25] L. Demery and L. Squire. 1996. Macroeconomic adjustment and poverty in Africa: an emerging picture. *The World Bank Research Observer*, 11(1): 39-59. The authors review evidence from six African countries using data from detailed household surveys.

invest in the long-term development of agriculture and the rural economy.

The implementation of appropriate trade and macroeconomic policies is critical for another important aspect of food security; the ability to finance the importation of food that is not produced domestically or is not produced in sufficient quantities, both when there are short-term price fluctuations and in order to meet the ongoing import needs reliably.

The sharp grain price rises of 1995-96 have increased the import bills of several countries. Many of the countries in Africa face significant problems with grain imports, especially in East Africa. Also, grain import requirements in North Africa are much higher than usual because of short crops in Morocco and Tunisia, although the normally high caloric intake levels in the area probably offer some flexibility in short-term use rates. Only a few Asian countries appear to be facing serious import problems, but the volume of grain could be substantial. The most significant problems are considered to be in Bangladesh and Afghanistan. Several countries in Latin America and the Caribbean are having difficulties with the higher prices of grain imports as grain output has recovered only slowly from the previous year's drought.

While increasing food aid is often the response to this type of situation, such a solution does not appear to be feasible at least in 1996/97. The overall level of food aid has been declining recently and was expected to be lower this year. Higher prices can be expected to reduce further the quantity of food aid, as most aid allocations are planned and budgeted in value terms. It is to be hoped that the lower food aid availabilities result in careful use of what funds there are in order that the needs of the most severely affected countries and regions can be met, although this would leave a significant number of other developing countries, which are generally in a marginal position with respect to financing grain import requirements, to search for alternative methods of finance in a period of higher prices.

The long-term issue concerns the ability of export earnings to keep pace with food import bills. The relatively rapid decline in real prices of agricultural export commodities has been exacerbated by increased supplies of such commodities in several low-income countries. If one small country increases its exports, it will not affect the world price, but if a large number do, the effect will be to depress prices further and faster. Commodity agreements have had very little success in supporting world prices and are unlikely to yield substantial benefits to the exporting countries in the aggregate. Schiff and Valdés suggest that for "the few export products where developing countries have market power, appropriate export taxes or quotas should be imposed".[26] However, it might not prove easy to settle the levels for such taxes or quotas because the appropriate tax or quota in one country depends on the levels set by other countries exporting the same commodity. Furthermore, the ability of exporting countries to set taxes and quotas will depend on the countervailing power by the importing countries or corporations.

---

[26] Schiff and Valdés, op. cit., footnote 24.

There are a number of policy issues that governments can address to the end of financing food imports. For example, there are long-term measures that can be taken to increase a country's export earning capability over time and to increase domestic food production and reduce production, processing and marketing costs. To this end, governments can implement non-distorting measures to increase the export earnings capability of the agricultural and food sector. This should not imply the promotion of export crops at the expense of food crops, nor the promotion of food exports at the expense of food security. The question is one of improving exportability, which must take account of international market demand and is closely linked to improving domestic food availability, which is an important aspect of food security. The reason for this is that for potential exportability to be realizable by large numbers of farmers of different types exploiting different agro-ecological conditions, the internal domestic marketing system must be able to deliver inputs and outputs whenever and wherever they are needed to minimize production and marketing costs and meet market demand on competitive terms.

Policy measures to improve domestic and export marketing should therefore address the needs for hard and soft infrastructure: an adequate agricultural and food research and extension base; improved processing, preservation and storage techniques and facilities; food standards for domestic and imported products, as well as quality control and grading to meet international requirements; information on production, domestic markets, nutrition and international markets; adding value in-country to the basic commodity or producing high-value commodities, such as fruit and flowers, including new product development; export promotion; export credit guarantees; and export insurance.

Where available and appropriate, governments could also take steps to make the maximum use of such programmes as the EU's STABEX scheme and Sectoral Import Programme[27] and the increased availability of foreign exchange assistance (as opposed to balance of payments assistance) could be explored. There might also be possibilities for short-term assistance for financing commercial imports under the General Agreement on Tariffs and Trade/World Trade Organization (GATT/WTO) Decision on Measures Concerning the Possible Negative Effects of the Reform Programme on Least-developed and Net Food Importing Countries, although the position is not yet clear.

---

[27] **The purpose of the EU's Sectoral Import Programme is to provide foreign exchange for the purchase of certain high-priority imports, such as fertilizer, agrochemicals, machinery and spare parts for agricultural processing and fishing equipment. The equivalent amount in local currency must be forthcoming and the scheme is open to private-sector agents as well as government agencies.**

THE USE OF FUTURES AND OPTIONS MARKETS

Market participants in the developed countries make extensive use of futures markets to hedge against short-term price and revenue risk, whereas the developing countries, perhaps with the exception of large-scale traders in international markets, have made relatively little use of these markets. Global changes in agricultural policy, the trend towards freer world trade in agricultural commodities and the emergence of sophisticated financial instruments to manage risk have led some organizations, such as the World Bank and IFPRI, to believe that the use of such instruments could play a useful stabilization role in the developing countries, thereby enhancing a country's ability to achieve food security. However, as the following investigation suggests, a very much more cautious approach is in order, not least because the use of futures and options markets does not necessarily enable prices to be stabilized and never allows them to be stabilized from one season to the next. Any positive effect on food security, therefore, is likely to be felt only indirectly through reduced trading and, hence, balance of payments risks.

The use of futures markets to reduce risk associated with cash price movements in agricultural commodity markets is a long-established practice dating back to 1865 in the United States.[28] Their ease of use has caused futures markets to expand dramatically to include numerous and varied markets throughout the world. In the early 1970s, almost 13 million, principally agricultural, futures contracts were traded in the United

States. By the early 1990s, the number of contracts (futures and futures market options) had increased to over 421 million, of which 17 percent (over 70 million) related to agricultural markets. This growth in trading resulted mainly from the introduction of futures markets for a wide range of commodities and financial instruments and from the initiation in 1982 of options contracts, including for agricultural commodities.

The use of futures markets to reduce short-term price risk for grains and oilseeds, livestock and meat, and food and fibre crops such as coffee, cocoa, sugar and cotton has become commonplace for United States processors, food manufacturers, commodity traders, and to a lesser extent producers. Although precise data are not available, the volume of trading in United States agricultural futures markets by foreign traders and processors has increased substantially in recent decades. Futures markets for agricultural commodities already exist or are under development in several other countries, but none of them approaches the size, liquidity and range of instruments offered by the Chicago Board of Trade (CBOT),

---

[28] The function and use of futures markets, including the distinction between hedging and speculation and the different uses made of them by producers, traders, processors and speculators, is the subject of a large literature. A good introductory explanation of futures markets for agricultural commodities can be found in D.M.G. Newbery and J.E. Stiglitz. 1981. *The theory of commodity price stabilization: a study in the economics of risk.* Oxford, UK, Clarendon Press.

which is consequently a reference point for much of the world trading in futures markets for agricultural commodities. In spite of the data deficiencies, the use of futures markets by traders and processors in domestic markets (as opposed to international trading) is probably far more pronounced in developed than in developing countries and, in general, producers use futures markets far less than traders and processors do (in developing countries producers hardly use futures markets at all). Several suggestions have been advanced to explain why the developing countries, with a few notable exceptions, have made so little use of futures and options markets for hedging purposes.

The transaction costs of hedging may be too high. Hedging may be conducted by means of futures contract markets and futures options markets. In both cases, buyers and sellers incur a brokerage or commission fee for execution of the transaction. Fees vary depending on the type and amount of service rendered, but in liquid, competitive markets with a substantial volume of trading such costs are not prohibitive.

While a futures market contract is binding and obligatory for buyers and sellers, a futures option provides the right but not the obligation to buy or sell the underlying futures contract at a specified price and time. Option buyers pay option sellers a premium much as insurance buyers pay a premium to an insurance company. The costs (intrinsic value and time value) of options are substantial and in developing countries that are short of credit or hard currency may be considered prohibitive.

Futures contracts may specify grades or delivery location that make hedging unattractive in developing countries. Futures contracts contain specific terms with respect to class and grade, price and location for each commodity traded. In the United States, the integrity of these standardized contract terms is overseen by the relevant commodity exchange organization, which is in turn overseen by a federal government regulatory agency. Only through standardization of contract terms and the underlying assurance of performance by buyers and sellers is a futures exchange able to perform its functions.

Most hedging operations do not themselves result in physical exchange of the commodity between buyers and sellers. Most futures contracts acquired for hedging purposes are liquidated by offsetting futures contracts prior to their respective call dates. Futures are not intended to act as cash markets, but rather to provide financial instruments to reduce forward price risk in cash markets. In the majority of hedging operations the specifications of the contract are thus decided with respect to the physical exchange of the commodity.

In instances where the purchase or sale of the futures contract results in physical acquisition or delivery of the commodity, the terms of the contract may be unattractive for traders in a distant developing country because of grade, quality or location. These matters need to be weighed when considering the acquisition of futures contracts. In any case, the purpose of hedging should be distinguished carefully from that of speculation and physical commodity trading.

Futures contract periods may be shorter than the developing country hedging horizon. The longest futures contracts currently traded in grains and oilseeds at CBOT are 18 months (for maize). In fact, few futures contracts are liquid for more than nine months. For developing country importers wishing to hedge against commodity price risk over several years, futures markets offer limited opportunity. Technically, it would be possible for the developing country importer to use a succession of overlapping short-dated contracts to fix a price at some future date beyond a single crop year – a procedure known as "rolling over" futures contracts. This procedure has two limitations – the accumulated transaction costs and the longer-term exposure to adverse margin change, which suggest that developing countries will find hedging in futures best-suited to addressing short-term (intraseasonal) price risk or as an adjunct to longer-term (interseasonal) price stabilization programmes.

There are credit and hard currency limitations in several developing countries. While hedging with futures contracts provides a means of reducing price risk, the buyer or seller of such contracts assumes margin risks, which in volatile agricultural commodity markets can be substantial.

In hedging, the basis (i.e. the difference between the spot or cash price of the commodity to be hedged and the futures price of the contract used) is of primary importance. Although cash and futures prices move in a roughly parallel pattern because they react to the same underlying market supply and demand factors, they are by no means perfectly correlated. The basis may at times deviate substantially, depending on buyer and seller expectations, availability and quality of market information on the part of buyers and sellers, activities of speculators and other factors. Generally, however, the basis tends to be more stable and predictable than the actual cash and futures price levels and is therefore the key to placing and lifting effective hedges.

Buyers and sellers of futures contracts are required to post a performance bond margin, which is a financial guarantee to ensure that the obligations of the futures contract will be fulfilled. The minimum margin requirements generally range from 5 to 18 percent of the contract's face value, depending on the volatility of the underlying market. Brokerage firms may require a larger margin. Margin requirements for agricultural commodities tend to be at the upper level of the range because of their high price volatility.

The initial margin account of each buyer and seller of a futures contract is adjusted daily by changes in the contract's basis – a practice known as "marking to the market". Negative changes in basis that reduce the margin account to a previously specified maintenance level result in a "margin call" to restore the account to its initial level. Because each futures contract is highly leveraged (by a factor of between ten and 20 depending on the commodity and the margin requirement) and is available only in incremental units specified by the commodity exchange (5 000 bushels for grains and oilseeds, for example), a modest change in basis can generate a much larger change in cash requirements for margin calls. The capital required over the life of the hedge can therefore be substantially greater than the initial margin requirement. For traders with insufficient liquidity, margin calls can pose a major problem.

As much of the trading in futures markets is denominated in dollars or other hard currency, the developing country trader is also subject to exchange rate risk. To reduce this type of risk, such a trader may decide to hedge in financial market futures or options, thereby assuming margin call risks for both commodities and currencies.

More sophisticated strategies could, however, mean prohibitively high costs. In developing countries that do not have an adequate and readily accessible supply of hard currency, hedging may be inadvisable or infeasible. In fact, credit limitations and inadequate foreign currency reserves in many developing countries appear to be the main constraints on such countries' more extensive use of futures for commodity hedging.

Of course, not all changes in basis (commodity or financial contracts) necessarily have a negative effect on the financial interest of the developing country trader. For example, in an empirical analysis of commodity and currency cross-hedging opportunities in Egypt and the Republic of Korea, when both were net grain importers, in has been demonstrated that substantial net gains are possible for each country, although primarily from currency rather than commodity hedging.[29]

Lack of financial and management expertise. Effective hedging requires an intimate knowledge of futures markets procedures and operations and the ability to respond promptly to market changes. Although brokerage or commission services can be obtained, few traders will be prepared to delegate fully all major decision-making responsibilities. Thus the development of appropriate expertise in the developing countries is a prerequisite for effective hedging.

Lack of access to reliable, timely information. Although electronic communication makes market information far more accessible and transferable than was possible even a few years ago, the developing country trader must be prepared to invest substantial resources to develop and maintain the timely and relevant data systems necessary for effective trading.

Perceptions of futures markets trading. Futures market trading is sometimes perceived as being inherently speculative or excessively transparent and subject to public scrutiny and misunderstanding. Alternatively, in some countries there may be an unwillingness to transfer authority to a foreign agent. The financial risk associated with margin calls and losses from hedging operations may be considered to be too politically risky for public traders in developing countries.

---

[29] K.M. Gordon. 1982. *Food security: a mean-variance approach.* Department of Agricultural and Resource Economics, University of California, Berkeley, CA, USA. (Ph.D. thesis)

Public- and private-sector problems.
The public institutions in developing
countries are often very rigid and
bureaucratic practices are so time-
consuming that efficient operation in
futures markets is practically
impossible with public organizations.
The private sector may be very
underdeveloped, particularly where
there has been until recently, or still is,
monopoly and monopsony power in
the hands of a state trading
organization. Furthermore, access for
private-sector traders to hard currency
on a sufficiently reliable basis may be
problematic.

This brief analysis indicates that
there are many good reasons to
explain why developing countries
have made relatively little use of
futures markets. The conclusion to be
drawn is that hedging in futures
markets (contracts and options) has a
very limited but potentially useful
function in the international trading of
agricultural commodities for some
developing countries. Conceptually,
hedging offers a means of reducing
short-term, intraseasonal price risk for
developing country importers as well
as for exporters of grains and oilseeds.
However, it is not a means of avoiding
or eliminating the price instability
inherent in many agricultural markets,
nor should it be promoted
indiscriminately in circumstances
where it is manifestly unsuitable as
this would be tantamount to
encouraging countries to incur
additional debt burdens where the
outcome is likely to be economically
disappointing. Hedging does not
necessarily improve the overall
financial outcome of trading but, in
appropriate circumstances and when
effectively executed, it can reduce risk

in trading by making the outcome
more certain.

Where the availability of credit and
hard currency are limiting factors,
governments could assess the
feasibility of making additional lines of
credit available to private traders or,
alternatively, underwriting loans by
private credit institutions in instances
where it can be demonstrated that
hedging is appropriate and likely to be
conducted in an effective manner. The
security for such loans could be the
underlying commodity or other assets
of the borrower. The World Bank and
the International Monetary Fund (IMF)
might be approached for additional
lines of hard currency credit to
facilitate hedging, where suitable, as
part of their development assistance
programmes.

BALANCE OF PAYMENTS SUPPORT

As part of its statutory purposes, IMF has funds and programmes under which it can make resources available to member countries to help solve certain balance of payments problems such as difficulties resulting from a rise in international cereal prices. IMF can provide financial assistance either under a special facility or by adjustments in regular funding arrangements.

The Compensatory and Contingency Financing Facility (CCFF). This is a special facility designed to help countries in the case of shortfalls in their export receipts or where there are excess cereal import costs. It is one of the financing tools provided as an option for use in the search for an appropriate blend of additional financing and adjustments to assist countries facing adverse external shocks in maintaining the momentum of their adjustment programmes.

Compensatory financing was first established in 1963 to provide assistance with balance of payments problems resulting from temporary declines in export earnings. The facility was broadened in 1981 to include coverage for balance of payments difficulties caused by excesses in cereal import costs. In 1988, a contingency financing element was introduced and combined with the compensatory financing and cereal import financing elements to create CCFF. The basic elements of the facility continue, although there have been some amendments affecting certain details since then. The conditions, which are rather complex, are given in Box 18.

For the period 1981 to 1989, the total cereal import drawings of the five low-income developing countries taking advantage of the facility amounted to only special drawing rights (SDR) 179.1 million, of which SDR 21.7 million was accounted for by immediate repurchases owing to overcompensation. Thus the actual amount was SDR 157.4 million. Five middle-income countries drew a total of SDR 563.2 million for cereal imports. More recently, purchases under the cereal element of CCFF have been made by Algeria, Moldova and South Africa. No cereal purchases have been made under the facility in the last several months, however, and, as the figures above indicate, the scheme was used to only a limited extent during the 1980s.

A brief inspection of the conditions outlined in Box 18 shows that the scheme has several features that limit access for cereal-importing countries: the calculation of the excess costs of the cereal imports; constraints on total drawings; repurchases of drawings; conditionalities attached to drawings; and the integration of excess import costs and excess export earnings. The current underuse of CCFF probably has two main causes. One is that in several country cases the prices of export commodities have also risen, reducing the balance of payments problem and also the eligibility of the member country to use CCFF. This feature of CCFF – the integration of excess costs of cereal imports with excesses in export earnings – has been criticized on a number of grounds, perhaps the most compelling being that of linking two components of the balance of payments where no real link in fact exists, as it would do if a particular imported item was used to produce a specific export item. "There is no justification for assuming that an excess of one specific item on the receipts side of the balance of payments will always be available to finance an excess of another specific but unrelated item on the payments side."[30] For example, high cereal prices could coincide with high prices of non-cereal imports. The food security argument for giving priority to financing cereal imports would arguably be better answered by decoupling the balance of payments support, but empirical studies indicate that this would substantially increase the volume of drawings under CCFF, putting IMF's limited resources under severe strain. One way of dealing with this problem could be to tighten the quota restrictions, another would be to restrict the assistance to a proportion of excess cereal import costs. Alternatively, other sources of balance of payments support or foreign exchange assistance could be instituted.

The second reason for underusage of CCFF is that most potential users have access to another IMF facility with more favourable terms, i.e. the Enhanced Structural Adjustment Facility (ESAF).

Low-income member countries with excess cereal import costs who need balance of payments support have apparently preferred to apply for

---

[30] H. Ezekiel. 1993. Integration between export compensation and cereal financing under the IMF Cereal Financing Scheme. *In* P. Berck and D. Bigman, eds. 1993. *Food security and food inventories in developing countries.* Wallingford, UK, Commonwealth Agricultural Bureaux International.

assistance under ESAF, for which IMF has concessional loans. Recently ESAF has been used for cases of excess import costs arising from higher than usual cereal prices. ESAF financing is through concessional loans that carry an annual interest rate of 0.5 percent with repayments semi-annually beginning five and a half years and ending ten years after each disbursement. Recently, 81 low-income countries were eligible to use ESAF. Of these, 27 had ESAF arrangements as of the end of February 1996, with a total amount approved of SDR 3.25 billion and undrawn balances of SDR 1.43 billion.

Financing under the programme can be obtained through inclusion of a contingency mechanism and/or through augmentation of access under an existing arrangement. A contingency mechanism may be used where the programme, as established under an ESAF arrangement, could allow for automatic adjustment in programme targets to accommodate some or all of the increased cereal import costs. This approach could be helpful in keeping the structural adjustment programme going in the case of an external shock such as higher cereal prices.

The other possibility, an augmentation of an arrangement to help meet additional financing needs caused by the adverse shock, can be considered either at the time of a regularly scheduled review or at the request of the member. Such reviews allow for an up-to-date assessment of changed conditions, including higher cereal import costs and the availability of donor assistance and food aid in determining the need for adjustment of existing arrangements.

BOX 18
IMF'S COMPENSATORY AND CONTINGENCY FINANCING FACILITY (CCFF)

The compensatory element for cereal imports is designed to provide financing quickly, within stated limits, to member countries experiencing temporary excess costs of cereal imports. An excess in cereal import costs is calculated as the amount by which the cost of cereal imports in a given year exceeds the arithmetic average of the cost of cereal imports for the five years centred on that year.

A request for compensatory financing must be submitted by the member country no later than six months after the end of the excess cost year. The specified excess cost year may be the latest for which data are available or it may be more recent to include the current period where some or all of the year's data must be estimated, as long as complete data for the previous two years are available. If estimated data are used for nine months or more of the excess cost year, however, access will be phased over two purchases. The first purchase may use up to 65 percent of the amount of financing available and the second purchase may be made as soon as at least six months of actual data are available for the excess year.

To qualify for compensatory financing, the excess in cereal import costs must be temporary, largely beyond the control of the member country and must result in a need for balance of payments financing. In addition, excess cereal import costs can be covered under the facility only in conjunction with calculation of the member country's export

Short-term balance of payments support is suitable for dealing with a short-term price fluctuation problem but is quite unsustainable if the underlying problem is one of long-term adverse price trends unless, as in the ESAF case, the support is used to enable the process of adjustment to long-term changes to continue.

The World Bank's role in direct assistance to low-income countries in financing food imports is usually a subsidiary, but complementary, one to that of IMF. Actions that assist a country to overcome food shortages or related problems can, however, clearly be considered to be within the Bank's mandate. This is particularly true in earnings position and deduction of any export earnings excess from the excess cereal import costs. The amount of funds that can be made available under the facility to a member country is the smaller of the calculated excess cereal import costs, after adjustment where appropriate for higher than normal export earnings, or the member country's access limit under the facility.

Access limits under the facility vary according to whether the member country's balance of payments problems are limited to the specific shock and whether the member country has a satisfactory record of cooperation with the fund. If the balance of payments position is otherwise satisfactory, basic access under the cereal element can be up to 65 percent of the quota. Where there are more general balance of payments difficulties, access is limited to a lower percentage of the quota, usually between 15 and 35 percent, depending on the member country's record of cooperation with the fund and the degree to which the country's economic policies are evaluated as favourable.

IMF generally provides financial assistance to member countries by selling Special Drawing Rights (SDRs) or the currencies of other member countries in exchange for a member country's own currency. Under most programmes, therefore, the member country makes a "purchase" from IMF, rather than receiving a loan. At the end of a specified period or an agreed schedule the account is settled by an opposite transaction in which the member country "repurchases" its own currency.

Financial resources obtained through CCFF have the same terms and costs as those under regular IMF credit tranches. Repurchase/payback is due between three and a quarter and five years after receipt of the funds. The cost is equal to that of the fund's general resources, somewhat on the low side of commercial rates and recently about 5 percent per annum. Financing resources obtained through CCFF are in addition to resources available under regular fund arrangements.

cases where a country needs to import food because of an unusual combination of events and where failure to provide the assistance would be likely to have an adverse effect on progress in macroeconomic management and sectoral policies. An important part of the World Bank's contribution is to provide relatively broad balance of payments support while the affected country is in the process of overcoming the temporary food problem.

Adjustment of World Bank project plans and resource use in connection with food problems caused by drought or international food price increases appears to be relatively common. The types of action taken may include modification of planned project expenditures in order to increase a country's financial flexibility in dealing with the problem; the provision of new loans designed to help with economic recovery from drought or other production problems; and an increased focus on rural development to strengthen food production and rural incomes in order to mitigate the impacts of future shocks.

For modification of planned project expenditures, the World Bank and national government may agree on how funds in existing projects are to be reallocated in order to help with the increased food import costs. The reallocated funds are likely to be used to finance activities related to food imports, such as transport and storage, rather than for direct financing of imports. However, since the funds are in foreign exchange, which is fungible, the country may be able to use the redirected funds indirectly for food imports, as well as to provide general support to the import activity.

Economic recovery loans. These are generally designed to assist in restoring farmers' capacity to increase output following such events as droughts or other natural disasters that seriously affect domestic food supplies. Such loans are not likely to be appropriate for dealing with temporary price spikes in the world market, but could provide an indirect form of balance of payments assistance by reducing the medium-term demand for supplementary imports.

Apart from the limitations and restrictions of the balance of payments support programmes themselves,

countries making use of such facilities face the problem of increasing their debt burdens. As the following section shows, some of the countries most in need of balance of payments support are low-income countries that are already severely indebted. Balance of payments support in such cases therefore raises important policy questions for both borrowers and lenders.

DEBT REDUCTION

The debt crisis of the 1980s, mostly in middle-income countries, was initially largely concerned with commercial debt and, as such, was perceived as posing a threat to the stability of the global financial system. The Brady Plan, among other initiatives, was a response to this crisis, which now appears to have receded. The 1990s have seen a different type of debt problem, which also has its roots in the 1980s – that of low-income countries' debts mainly to developed country governments and multilateral creditors. Much of this lending took place to help poor countries to cope with falling export commodity prices, rising world interest rates and escalating repayment schedules to commercial banks. Figure 15 shows the change in total external debt as a percentage of GDP by region since 1970. Of particular concern is the continuing sharp increase for sub-Saharan Africa, the region least able to sustain such a debt burden; the improving overall situation for Latin America and the Caribbean and Asia masks the serious difficulties faced by a small number of countries.

In fact, 32 countries are classified by the World Bank as "severely indebted low-income countries" (SILICs), defined as having, for 1991-93, either debt-service-to-GNP ratios of more than 80 percent or debt-service-to-export ratios of more than 220 percent (each measured at net present value). Some 25 SILICs are in sub-Saharan Africa, three in Latin America and the Caribbean, three in Asia and one in the Near East.[31] Debt service repayments for sub-Saharan Africa were almost 20 percent of export earnings in 1995, up from

17.3 percent in 1994. Yet this understates the long-term and growing seriousness of the situation: in many countries, the stock of debt has been rising because actual repayments have been lower than scheduled repayments; and arrears have doubled since 1991 and now total three-quarters of annual export earnings. In 1994, for example, scheduled debt service payments for sub-Saharan Africa were over US$20 billion, while actual repayments amounted to $13 billion. The total debt stock of the SILICs was just under US$210 billion in 1994, four times as much as in 1980. Furthermore, whereas in 1980 the total debt as a proportion of national income was about one-third, in 1994 it was about 110 percent; the region's debt-to-total-export proportion increased to 389 percent (and was over 800 percent for three of the SILICs), compared with 150 percent for all developing countries. "The surge in interest arrears (US$11 billion

_____

[31] The 32 SILICs form the majority of the 41 countries classified by the World Bank in *World Debt Tables 1994-95* as heavily indebted poor countries (HIPCs). The remainder of the HIPCs consist of seven countries that have received concessional treatment from the Paris Club and two lower-middle-income countries that have recently become IDA-only countries. See S. Claessens, E. Detragiache, R. Kanbur and P. Wickham. 1996. *Analytical aspects of the debt problems of heavily indebted poor countries.* Policy Research Working Paper No. 1618. The World Bank Africa Regional Office, Office of the Chief Economist, and East Asia and Pacific Regional Office, Office of the Regional Vice President, and International Monetary Fund Research Department.

Figure 15

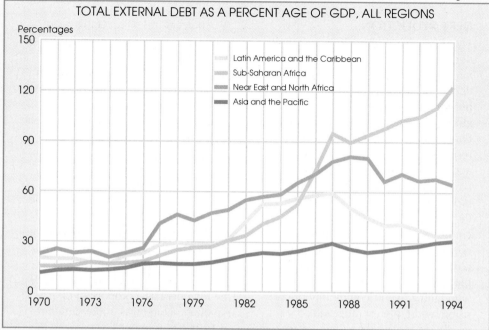

TOTAL EXTERNAL DEBT AS A PERCENT AGE OF GDP, ALL REGIONS

Source: World Bank, World Tables, various issues

since 1990) and capital repayment arrears ($23.5 billion) highlights just how unsustainable the situation has become."[32]

The Paris Club, the coordinating body for negotiating the rescheduling and restructuring of the credits of western governments, has taken a series of steps to reduce the outstanding debt of some of the poorest countries, but the conditions for reduction have severely limited the potential impact. However, one-quarter of the debt stock and one-half of the debt service payments for 1991-93 are accounted for by multilateral creditors.[33] The World Bank, together with its soft-loan affiliate the International Development Association (IDA), accounts for just

over half of the multilateral total of debt stock, IMF and the African Development Bank each accounting for 14 percent. Negotiations have started between the World Bank and IMF to find ways of reducing the debt burden of the SILICs. The support of the G-7 governments will also be of vital importance for finding a solution to this problem. Whatever solution is reached should ensure that the qualifications for debt relief, including

_____

[32] *Financial Times,* **20 May 1996.**

_____

[33] **The discrepancy between debt stock and debt service payments arises because the multilateral creditors are the first to be paid because of the severe penalties incurred if a country falls into arrears with IMF or the World Bank. For a detailed analysis of the issue, see Oxfam. 1996.** *Multilateral debt: the human costs.* **Oxfam International Position Paper. Oxford, UK.**

the definition of what constitutes an unsustainable debt burden, are not so tough that very few countries can ever hope to meet them.

The debt burden has many negative implications for food security, not the least of which is the constrained ability to import food and non-food items that could increase domestic food production. It is rather ironic that 14 of the SILICs have ESAF arrangements that could assist in supporting their balance of payments in the face of rising cereal prices, thereby increasing their longer-term debt burden. However, the problems caused by high levels of external debt go far beyond the balance of payments issue and seem likely to have had a negative impact on long-term economic growth, including agricultural sector growth.

In the first place, the use of hard currency earnings for debt servicing has led to import compression and this has affected industry because, as essential imported inputs have been cut, the effect has been underused industrial capacity. It has also affected agriculture through a reduction in the supply of agricultural inputs that cannot be produced domestically. The multiplier effects of slow-downs in sectoral growth rates, or even on occasion negative growth rates, must have been substantial. Among these should be numbered a thinner and perhaps narrower tax base, with all that implies for government revenue collection. In addition, the ability to import capital goods for investment has been reduced. Then, there is the impact of external debt servicing obligations on domestic budgets if governments have to resort to domestic sources at high interest rates

for financing public expenditure; this can of itself push up interest rates and "crowd out" investment.

Cuts in public expenditure or attempts at cost recovery often hit the poorest hardest, particularly those in rural areas, since it may be politically more feasible to cut rural health workers than city hospitals, for example, or village schoolteachers rather than university lecturers. This amounts to a disinvestment in human capital with very long-term repercussions. To put the problem into perspective, according to the United Nations Children's Fund (UNICEF), an additional US$9 billion per annum would provide the resources necessary for sub-Saharan Africa to meet the main human welfare objectives agreed at the 1990 World Summit for Children, among which were universal access to safe drinking-water, sanitation and primary education.[34] As noted above, the actual (as opposed to scheduled) debt repayments were US$13 billion in 1994.

Furthermore, the development of agriculture and domestic food supply is hindered by the lack of finance available for development purposes. A substantial proportion of official development assistance (one estimate puts it at about one-quarter)[35] is transferred to multilateral creditors for multilateral debt financing; this is in addition to the attempts by the World Bank and IMF to refinance debt through softer loans which has meant, for example, that in 1994, total IDA disbursements amounted to US$2.9 billion, of which just under

---

[34] **Ibid.**
[35] **Ibid.**

$2 billion were used to repay World Bank debt and part of the rest was used to finance payments to IMF! Not only is the quantity of the effective aid reduced, but also its quality as increasing amounts of aid money are diverted to balance of payments support rather than efforts to alleviate poverty. The ability to achieve food security is obviously compromised.

The existence of heavy external debt burdens has also tended to force the pace of structural adjustment programmes; the costs of adjustment are a rising function of the speed of adjustment and growth usually suffers more with shock-treatment adjustment.[36] The corollary is that more gradual adjustment requires more external financial support, and hence more debt, to bridge the gap until the macroeconomy is balanced.

Reducing the debt burden of the SILICs is not a panacea for the ills of poverty and food insecurity but, when the long-term impacts on the balance of payments and growth are considered, it is difficult to see a single positive factor that could have a potential effect of comparable magnitude, as long as the resources released are in fact used for the purposes intended. Any discussion of debt reduction invariably raises the perceived problem of moral hazard. In this context, it needs to be recognized that, as well as borrowers, bilateral, multilateral and private-sector lenders also have responsibilities, and to lend for the wrong reasons – whether

because of political or institutional pressure on the lenders' side, to governments that lacked popular legitimacy and have since been removed, for projects that were not really appropriate for the country concerned, for consumption or for investments where the return flow could not cover debt service costs – argues for a more flexible approach to the whole question of indebtedness. Mistakes have been made by all parties and lessons can be learned. If the overriding concern is to assist the poorest countries to reduce poverty and achieve food security then this concern should guide attitudes to and support the provision of resources for reduction of the debt stock and not merely for partial subsidization of debt servicing. Perhaps the idea would be more acceptable to the creditors if any debt reduction were made conditional on an agreed proportion of the accrued benefits being used in approved ways to alleviate poverty and food insecurity in the long term.

---

[36] T. Killick. 1993. *The adaptive economy: adjustment policies in small, low-income countries.* EDI Development Studies. Washington, DC, World Bank.

Language choices
• The initial default language for FAOSTAT TS is English. To change the default language to French or Spanish:
- go to the FILE menu
- select LANGUAGE using the arrow key (↓) and pressing ENTER
- select your choice of language from those displayed and press ENTER

The language selected will remain the default language until another is selected.

Navigating the menus
The main menu bar consists of FILE, DATA, GRAPH, TABLE and HELP menus. Most menu options are disabled until you open a data file.
• Navigate the menus by using the arrow keys (↑↓↔) and make a selection by highlighting an item and pressing ENTER. To back out of a selection, press the ESC key.
• If you have a mouse, menu items can be selected with the mouse cursor. The left mouse button selects an item and the right mouse button acts as the ESC key.

After you have made a menu selection, the menu will redraw and highlight a possible next choice.
• Several short-cut keys are available throughout the program:

Key	Action
F1	- HELP: displays context-sensitive help text.
ESC	- ESCAPE: backs out of the current menu choice or exits the current graph or table.
ALT+N	- NOTES: displays text notes associated with the current data file, if the text file is available. This text may be edited. Notes will not appear while a graph is displayed.
ALT+X, ALT+Q	- EXIT: exits FAOSTAT TS immediately, without prompting.

Help
• You will see context-sensitive help displayed at the bottom of each screen. Press F1 for more extensive help on a highlighted option.
• Select HELP from the main menu to access the help information. Introductory information on the software, help topics and an "About" summary screen are available from the HELP menu.
• The HELP menu options call up the same Help windows obtained by pressing the F1 key at any of the menu screens:
- The FAOSTAT TS option displays the top-level help page.
- The TOPICS option lists the help contents.
- The ABOUT option shows summary program information.

Opening a data file
• To display a list of FAOSTAT TS data files:
- go to the FILE menu
- select OPEN.

All of the FAOSTAT TS data files in the current directory are displayed. Initially, only SOFA96 will be present. Other FAOSTAT PC data files, version 3.0, can be used with FAOSTAT TS.
• Use the arrow keys to highlight the file you wish to view and press ENTER to select it. Files are shown with the date of their last revision. You can also highlight your choice by typing the first letters of the file's name. The current search string will appear in the lower left corner of the list.
• You can change the default data drive and directory from the file list by selecting the directory or drive of your choice.

If a current data file is open, loading in a new file will return FAOSTAT TS to its defaults (time trend, no trend line, no user-specified units or scalar). Only one file can be loaded at a time.

Once you have made a file selection, all the menu selections are activated.

Selecting a data series
• Use the DATA menu to select or modify a data series or to fit a statistical trend.
• Select a data series by choosing the name of a

country and a data element from the scrolling menus. The first entry displays a list of country names, the second entry displays a list of data item names and the third displays a list of data element names.

If you type the first letters of a name in a list, the menu selection bar will jump to the matching name. For example:
- type *NEW* to skip to New Zealand
- press ENTER to select the highlighted name

Displaying graphs and graph options

The GRAPH menu allows you to view the data in chart form. You can display time trends and table or column profiles. Options under the GRAPH menu change the data series shown as well as its display.

For example, to show a plot of the data selected:
- go to the GRAPH menu
- select DISPLAY

Many options to modify, save or print a graph are available only while a graph is on screen. Remember to use the F1 help key for a reminder of the options.

Graph action keys. You have several options when a graph is displayed:
• Press ESC to exit the graph and return to the main menu.
• Press F1 for help on the graph action keys. The help box lists the choices available while a graph is on the screen. You must exit the help box before making a selection.
• Press the arrow (↑↓) and PAGEUP PAGEDOWN keys to change the series displayed.
• The plus key (+) allows you to add up to three other series to the one displayed. Press the minus key (-) to remove a series. This is the way multiline charts are created:
- display an initial series
- press the + key to add subsequent series to the chart
• Press A to display a table of the axis data with statistics. Press T to show a table of the fitted trend data, the residuals and fit statistics (if a

trend line is selected, see below).
• The INS key permits you to insert text directly on the graph. While inserting text, press F1 for help on your text options. You can type small or large, horizontal or vertical text.
• To print a graph, press P and select your choice of printer from the menu. The print output is only a screen dump of the display, so the quality is limited.
• To save a graph for printing or viewing later, press S. The graph image will be saved in the common PCX bitmap format. You can use the PRINTPCX program or other software to view or print multiple images later. PRINTPCX also permits you to convert colour PCX images into black and white images suitable for inclusion in a word processing document.

Fitting trend lines
• To fit a statistical function to a data series, select FIT from the DATA menu. The options under FIT allow you to select the type of function, data year limits to include in the fit and a final projection year for a statistical forecast.
• By fitting a trend line (selecting the option under FIT) with a projection (selecting PROJECTION under FIT), a statistical forecast can be plotted. Use the + key to add a new data series to the graph, which can be made with only a few key strokes.

Charting profiles
• The options under the GRAPH menu allow you to change the year span or style of the graph display (options LIMITS and STYLE, respectively), or to switch from a time trend to a table or column data profile (VIEWPOINT). The VIEWPOINT option is an easy means to compare data for a particular year.

Viewpoint
• If you want to change from a time series display to a country or item profile display for a given year, select VIEWPOINT from the GRAPH menu. Select DISPLAY from the GRAPH menu, and the profile will be drawn. The initial profile display is

for the last year of historical data. To change the year, use the arrow (↑↓) keys. Press F1 for help.The initial profile display is for the last year of historical data. To change the year, use the Arrow keys. Press F1 for help.

• For a tables profile (profile of data across countries), you can either choose the tables to be displayed or let FAOSTAT TS select the top members and array them in order. A limit of 50 items can appear in one profile.

By selecting TOP MEMBERS instead of SELECTED MEMBERS, FAOSTAT TS will sort the values in the file and display a ranking of table or column values.

Viewing tables

• The TABLE menu allows you to look at data in a tabular format and to define subset tables that may be saved and imported into other software packages:
- go to the TABLE menu
- select BROWSE DATA to view individual data tables from the current file.

• When viewing tables, a help bar appears at the bottom of the screen. Press PAGEUP or PAGEDOWN to change the table displayed or press ALT+1 or ALT+2 to choose from a list of tables. Use the arrow keys (↑↓↔) to scroll the columns and rows.

Series data

• The I SERIES DATA option under the TABLE menu displays the last data series selected, including summary statistics. This is the series used to plot a graph. To change the series, you must make a new choice from the DATA menu.

• The SERIES DATA screen can also be displayed while you are in a graph by pressing the letter A. If more than one series has been plotted, only the last series is shown. The range of years used for the series and statistics can be adjusted through the LIMITS option under the GRAPH menu.

• To view country or item profile lists and statistics, select VIEWPOINT from the GRAPH. You can quickly see a list of the tables with the greatest values (for example, countries with the highest commodity consumption) by choosing a table profile from VIEWPOINT and selecting the TOP MEMBERS option. Then select SERIES DATA from the TABLE menu to view the list, or select DISPLAY from the GRAPH menu to plot a chart.

Trend data

• If the FIT option has been selected (from the DATA menu) for a time trend, then the values composing the trend can be displayed with the TREND DATA option. Summary statistics for the original series and for the trend as well as residual values are included. The list scrolls with the arrow keys, and you can toggle between the axis and trend data with the A and T keys.

Exporting data

• The EXPORT option under the FILE menu allows you to export FAOSTAT TS data into other file formats or to create custom tables for viewing or printing. By selecting EXPORT, you will jump into another set of menus.

• To select the tables and columns you want to view or save, go to the DATA menu. You must mark your choice of options with the + key. To undo all your selections quickly, select RESET MARKS.

• To arrange, view, save or print data, go to the options under EXPORT (in the FILE menu):
- FAO TABLE: creates a table with data from the last four available years.
- VIEW: displays a temporary text file of the data selected. It is a convenient way to view a subset of the tables and columns in a FAOSTAT TS file and can also be used to see the effects of the ORIENTATION or LAYOUT selections before using the SAVE or PRINT options.
- SAVE: displays a list of file formats to let you save your data choices in a file. You will be prompted for a file name. If you need to export FAOSTAT TS data for use with other software, use this menu item. The WK1 and DBF file format selections are not affected by the LAYOUT options (see below).
- PRINT: prints your current table and column

selections. Many printers cannot print more than five columns of FAOSTAT TS data. Select VIEW to check the table width before printing.

- LAYOUT: allows you to display years across rows or down columns. The default is down columns.

• To get back to the main FAOSTAT TS menu or to clear your selections and create more tables, go to the RETURN option.

Making notes

• To read or edit textual information on the current data file, select NOTES from the FILE menu. You also can call up the notes box by pressing ALT+N at any of the menus. The option NOTES allows you to read or edit text associated with the data file.

DOS shell and exit

The DOS SHELL option under the FILE menu returns you to the DOS prompt temporarily but keeps FAOSTAT TS in memory. This is not the normal way to exit the program. It is useful if you need to execute a DOS command and would like to return to the same data file. The data file itself is dropped from memory and reloaded on return, so default values will be in effect.

Exiting FAOSTAT TS

• To exit FAOSTAT TS:
  - go to the FILE menu
  - select EXIT.

The ALT+X or ALT+Q key combinations are short cuts to exit the program from almost any screen.

WHERE TO PURCHASE FAO PUBLICATIONS LOCALLY
POINTS DE VENTE DES PUBLICATIONS DE LA FAO
PUNTOS DE VENTA DE PUBLICACIONES DE LA FAO

• ANGOLA
Empresa Nacional do Disco e de
Publicações, ENDIPU-U.E.E.
Rua Cirilo da Conceição Silva, N° 7
C.P. N° 1314-C
Luanda

• ARGENTINA
Librería Agropecuaria
Pasteur 743
1028 Buenos Aires
Oficina del Libro Internacional
Alberti 40
1082 Buenos Aires

• AUSTRALIA
Hunter Publications
P.O. Box 404
Abbotsford, Vic. 3067

• AUSTRIA
Gerold Buch & Co.
Weihburggasse 26
1010 Vienna

• BANGLADESH
Association of Development
Agencies in Bangladesh
House No. 1/3, Block F, Lalmatia
Dhaka 1207

• BELGIQUE
M.J. De Lannoy
202, avenue du Roi
1060 Bruxelles
CCP 000-0808993-13

• BOLIVIA
Los Amigos del Libro
Perú 3712, Casilla 450
Cochabamba;
Mercado 1315, La Paz

• BOTSWANA
Botsalo Books (Pty) Ltd
P.O. Box 1532
Gaborone

• BRAZIL
Fundação Getúlio Vargas
Praia do Botafogo 190, C.P. 9052
Rio de Janeiro
Núcleo Editora da
Universidade Federal Fluminense
Rua Miguel de Frias 9
Icaraí-Niterói
24 220-000 Rio de Janeiro
Editora da Universidade Federal
do Rio Grande do Sul
Av. João Pessoa 415
Bairro Cidade Baixa
90 040-000 Porto Alegre/RS
Book Master Livraria
Rua do Catete 311 lj. 118/119
20031-001 Catete
Rio de Janeiro

• CANADA
Le Diffuseur Gilles Vermette Inc.
C.P. 85, 151, av. de Mortagne
Boucherville, Québec J4B 5E6
UNIPUB
4611/F Assembly Drive
Lanham MD 20706-4391 (USA)
Toll-free 800 233-0504 (Canada)

• CHILE
Librería - Oficina Regional FAO
Calle Bandera 150, 8° Piso
Casilla 10095, Santiago-Centro
Tel. 699 1005
Fax 696 1121/696 1124
Universitaria Textolibros Ltda.
Avda. L. Bernardo O'Higgins 1050
Santiago

• COLOMBIA
Banco Ganadero
Revista Carta Ganadera
Carrera 9ª N° 72-21, Piso 5
Bogotá D.E.
Tel. 217 0100

• CONGO
Office national des librairies populaires
B.P. 577
Brazzaville

• COSTA RICA
Librería Lehmann S.A.
Av. Central
Apartado 10011
San José

• CÔTE D'IVOIRE
CEDA
04 B.P. 541
Abidjan 04

• CUBA
Ediciones Cubanas, Empresa de
Comercio Exterior de Publicaciones
Obispo 461, Apartado 605
La Habana

• CZECH REPUBLIC
Artia Pegas Press Ltd
Import of Periodicals
Palác Metro, P.O. Box 825
Národní 25, 111 21 Praha 1

• DENMARK
Munksgaard, Book and
Subscription Service
P.O. Box 2148
DK 1016 Copenhagen K.
Tel. 4533128570
Fax 4533129387

• DOMINICAN REPUBLIC
CUESTA - Centro del libro
Av. 27 de Febrero, esq. A. Lincoln
Centro Comercial Nacional
Apartado 1241
Santo Domingo

• ECUADOR
Libri Mundi, Librería Internacional
Juan León Mera 851
Apartado Postal 3029
Quito

• EGYPT
The Middle East Observer
41 Sherif Street
Cairo

• ESPAÑA
Mundi Prensa Libros S.A.
Castelló 37
28001 Madrid
Tel. 431 3399
Fax 575 3998
Librería Agrícola
Fernando VI 2
28004 Madrid
Librería Internacional AEDOS
Consejo de Ciento 391
08009 Barcelona
Tel. 301 8615
Fax 317 0141
Llibreria de la Generalitat
de Catalunya
Rambla dels Estudis 118
(Palau Moja)
08002 Barcelona
Tel. (93) 302 6462
Fax (93) 302 1299

• FINLAND
Akateeminen Kirjakauppa
P.O. Box 218
SF-00381 Helsinki

• FRANCE
Lavoisier
14, rue de Provigny
94236 Cachan Cedex
Editions A. Pedone
13, rue Soufflot
75005 Paris
Librairie du Commerce International
24, boulevard de l'Hôpital
75005 Paris

• GERMANY
Alexander Horn Internationale
Buchhandlung
Kirchgasse 22, Postfach 3340
D-65185 Wiesbaden
Uno Verlag
Poppelsdorfer Allee 55
D-53115 Bonn 1
S. Toeche-Mittler GmbH
Versandbuchhandlung
Hindenburgstrasse 33
D-64295 Darmstadt

• GHANA
SEDCO Publishing Ltd
Sedco House, Tabon Street
Off Ring Road Central, North Ridge
P.O. Box 2051
Accra

• GUYANA
Guyana National Trading
Corporation Ltd
45-47 Water Street, P.O. Box 308
Georgetown

• HAÏTI
Librairie «A la Caravelle»
26, rue Bonne Foi, B.P. 111
Port-au-Prince

• HONDURAS
Escuela Agrícola Panamericana,
Librería RTAC
El Zamorano, Apartado 93
Tegucigalpa
Oficina de la Escuela Agrícola
Panamericana en Tegucigalpa
Blvd. Morazán, Apts. Glapson
Apartado 93
Tegucigalpa

• HUNGARY
Librotrade Kft.
P.O. Box 126
H-1656 Budapest

• INDIA
EWP Affiliated East-West Press
PVT, Ltd
G-I/16, Ansari Road, Darya Gany
New Delhi 110 002
Oxford Book and Stationery Co.
Scindia House, New Delhi 110 001;
17 Park Street, Calcutta 700 016
Oxford Subscription Agency
Institute for Development
Education
1 Anasuya Ave., Kilpauk
Madras 600 010
Periodical Expert Book Agency
D-42, Vivek Vihar, Delhi 110095

• IRAN
The FAO Bureau, International and
Regional Specialized
Organizations Affairs
Ministry of Agriculture of the Islamic
Republic of Iran
Keshavarz Bld, M.O.A., 17th floor
Teheran

• IRELAND
Publications Section
Government Stationery Office
4-5 Harcourt Road
Dublin 2

• ISRAEL
R.O.Y. International
P.O. Box 13056
Tel Aviv 61130

• ITALY
Libreria Scientifica Dott. Lucio de
Biasio "Aeiou"
Via Coronelli 6
20146 Milano
Libreria Concessionaria Sansoni
S.p.A. "Licosa"
Via Duca di Calabria 1/1
50125 Firenze

WHERE TO PURCHASE FAO PUBLICATIONS LOCALLY
POINTS DE VENTE DES PUBLICATIONS DE LA FAO
PUNTOS DE VENTA DE PUBLICACIONES DE LA FAO

FAO Bookshop
Viale delle Terme di Caracalla
00100 Roma
Tel. 52255688
Fax 52255155
E-mail: publications-sales@fao.org
• **JAPAN**
Far Eastern Booksellers
(Kyokuto Shoten Ltd)
12 Kanda-Jimbocho 2 chome
Chiyoda-ku - P.O. Box 72
Tokyo 101-91
Maruzen Company Ltd
P.O. Box 5050
Tokyo International 100-31
• **KENYA**
Text Book Centre Ltd
Kijabe Street, P.O. Box 47540
Nairobi
• **LUXEMBOURG**
M.J. De Lannoy
202, avenue du Roi
1060 Bruxelles (Belgique)
• **MALAYSIA**
Electronic products only:
Southbound
Sendirian Berhad Publishers
9 College Square
01250 Penang
• **MALI**
Librairie Traore
Rue Soundiata Keita X 115
B.P. 3243
Bamako
• **MAROC**
La Librairie Internationale
70 Rue T'ssoule
B.P. 302 (RP)
Rabat
Tel. (07) 75-86-61
• **MEXICO**
Libreria, Universidad Autónoma
de Chapingo
56230 Chapingo
Libros y Editoriales S.A.
Av. Progreso N° 202-1° Piso A
Apdo. Postal 18922, Col. Escandón
11800 México D.F.
• **NETHERLANDS**
Roodveldt Import b.v.
Brouwersgracht 288
1013 HG Amsterdam
• **NEW ZEALAND**
Legislation Services
P.O. Box 12418
Thorndon, Wellington
• **NICARAGUA**
Libreria HISPAMER
Costado Este Univ. Centroamericana
Apdo. Postal A-221
Managua
• **NIGERIA**
University Bookshop (Nigeria) Ltd
University of Ibadan
Ibadan
• **NORWAY**
Narvesen Info Center
Bertrand Narvesens vei 2
P.O. Box 6125, Etterstad
0602 Oslo 6
Tel. (+47) 22-57-33-00
Fax (+47) 22-68-19-01
• **PAKISTAN**
Mirza Book Agency
65 Shahrah-e-Quaid-e-Azam
P.O. Box 729, Lahore 3
• **PARAGUAY**
Libreria INTERCONTINENTAL
Editora e Impresora S.R.L.
Caballero 270 c/Mcal Estigarribia
Asunción

• **PERU**
INDEAR
Jirón Apurimac 375, Casilla 4937
Lima 1
• **PHILIPPINES**
International Booksource Center (Phils)
Room 1703, Cityland 10
Condominium Cor. Ayala Avenue &
H.V. de la Costa Extension
Makati, Metro Manila
• **POLAND**
Ars Polona
Krakowskie Przedmiescie 7
00-950 Warsaw
• **PORTUGAL**
Livraria Portugal,
Dias e Andrade Ltda.
Rua do Carmo 70-74, Apartado 2681
1117 Lisboa Codex
• **SINGAPORE**
Select Books Pte Ltd
03-15 Tanglin Shopping Centre
19 Tanglin Road
Singapore 1024
• **SOMALIA**
"Samater's"
P.O. Box 936
Mogadishu
• **SOUTH AFRICA**
David Philip Publishers (Pty) Ltd
P.O. Box 23408
Claremont 7735
South Africa
Tel. Cape Town (021) 64-4136
Fax Cape Town (021) 64-3358
• **SRI LANKA**
M.D. Gunasena & Co. Ltd
217 Olcott Mawatha, P.O. Box 246
Colombo 11
• **SUISSE**
Buchhandlung und Antiquariat
Heinimann & Co.
Kirchgasse 17
8001 Zurich
UN Bookshop
Palais des Nations
CH-1211 Genève 1
Van Diermen Editions Techniques
ADECO
Case Postale 465
CH-1211 Genève 19
• **SURINAME**
Vaco n.v. in Suriname
Domineestraat 26, P.O. Box 1841
Paramaribo
• **SWEDEN**
Books and documents:
C.E. Fritzes
P.O. Box 16356
103 27 Stockholm
Subscriptions:
Vennergren-Williams AB
P.O. Box 30004
104 25 Stockholm
• **THAILAND**
Suksapan Panit
Mansion 9, Rajdamnern Avenue
Bangkok
• **TOGO**
Librairie du Bon Pasteur
B.P. 1164
Lomé
• **TUNISIE**
Société tunisienne de diffusion
5, avenue de Carthage
Tunis
• **TURKEY**
Kultur Yayiniari is - Turk Ltd Sti.
Ataturk Bulvari N° 191, Kat. 21
Ankara
Bookshops in Istanbul and Izmir

• **UNITED KINGDOM**
HMSO Publications Centre
51 Nine Elms Lane
London SW8 5DR
Tel. (071) 873 9090 (orders)
(071) 873 0011 (inquiries)
Fax (071) 873 8463
and through HMSO Bookshops
Electronic products only:
Microinfo Ltd
P.O. Box 3, Omega Road, Alton
Hampshire GU34 2PG
Tel. (0420) 86848
Fax (0420) 89889
• **URUGUAY**
Libreria Agropecuaria S.R.L.
Buenos Aires 335
Casilla 1755
Montevideo C.P. 11000
• **USA**
Publications:
UNIPUB
4611/F Assembly Drive
Lanham MD 20706-4391
Toll-free 800 274-4888
Fax 301-459-0056
Periodicals:
Ebsco Subscription Services
P.O. Box 1431
Birmingham AL 35201-1431
Tel. (205)991-6600
Telex 78-2661
Fax (205)991-1449
The Faxon Company Inc.
15 Southwest Park
Westwood MA 02090
Tel. 6117-329-3350
Telex 95-1980
Cable FW Faxon Wood
• **VENEZUELA**
Tecni-Ciencia Libros S.A.
Torre Phelps-Mezzanina
Plaza Venezuela
Caracas
Tel. 782 8697/781 9945/781 9954
Tamanaco Libros Técnicos S.R.L.
Centro Comercial Ciudad Tamanaco
Nivel C-2
Caracas
Tel. 261 3344/261 3335/959 0016
Tecni-Ciencia Libros, S.A.
Centro Comercial, Shopping Center
Av. Andrés Eloy, Urb. El Prebo
Valencia, Ed. Carabobo
Tel. 222 724
Fudeco, Libreria
Avenida Libertador-Este
Ed. Fudeco, Apartado 254
Barquisimeto C.P. 3002, Ed. Lara
Tel. (051) 538 022
Fax (051) 544 394
Télex (051) 513 14 FUDEC VC
Fundación La Era Agricola
Calle 31 Junin Qta
Coromoto 5-49, Apartado 456
Mérida
Libreria FAGRO
Universidad Central de Venezuela (UCV)
Maracay
• **ZIMBABWE**
Grassroots Books
100 Jason Moyo Avenue
P.O. Box A 267, Avondale
Harare;
61a Fort Street
Bulawayo

Other countries / Autres pays / Otros países
Distribution and Sales Section
Publications Division, FAO
Viale delle Terme di Caracalla
00100 Rome, Italy
Tel. (39-6) 52251
Fax (39-6) 52253152
Telex 625852/625853/610181 FAO I
E-mail: publications-sales@fao.org